EDITING AND DESIGN 3

News Headlines

Harold Evans

Editor, *The Sunday Times*, London

EDITING AND DESIGN
A Five-volume Manual of English, Typography and Layout

Book Three
News Headlines

Published under the auspices of the
National Council for the Training of Journalists

HEINEMANN : LONDON

William Heinemann Ltd
15 Queen St, Mayfair, London W1X 8BE

LONDON   MELBOURNE   TORONTO
JOHANNESBURG   AUCKLAND

DESIGNER: VICTOR SHREEVE

To Michael

Preface

Headlines excite emotion. It was the language of headlines that broke—no, instantly melted—the ice at the first working seminar for journalists from all over India in Delhi in 1960. I was then an assistant editor on the *Manchester Evening News* and I had been invited to India by the International Press Institute to teach sub-editing. 'Use a verb in the active voice and present tense in the headline,' I said. I had been struck by the deadness of the headlines in many of the English-language Indian papers. The headlines seemed mostly to be collections of abstract nouns. 'That is a shocking idea. You cannot do that violence to our language,' said a senior man from a Hindi language paper. 'That is all right in English or a big city newspaper. It would never do for us.' Against such a rebuff there seemed no argument, certainly not from someone like me who had not two Hindi words he could rub together. But there was argument, fierce and furious. It came from the other Indian-language journalists. The first objector was denounced as a reactionary: then the denouncer was condemned as 'radical.' We soared off into Hindi grammar, then Gujerati and Tamil. Everybody wanted the chalk to make his point on the blackboard.

I would not pretend to be an authority on the scholarship of the argument, which went on for some time, but it was clear (*a*) we 'active voice' campaigners were not mindless pillagers of a national heritage, and (*b*) there was a lot to argue about in headline writing.

This book, the third of the series of five, is an attempt to fine down the argument about headline wording to conclusions of general validity and to relate the headline to developments of newspaper typography and display. I cannot expect it, and would not want it, to be received as definitive, but my hope is that without hindering the geniuses or convulsing the conservatives it will help journalists writing headlines.

If it fails it is not in any way due to the people whose assistance I have had, either in the general series or with this volume. Specifically for Book Three I would like to thank the Ludlow Corporation; Linotype & Machinery Ltd; The Monotype Corporation Ltd; Intertype Ltd; and Stephenson Blake for their specimen settings. A book like this would not be possible at its cost without their generous provision of settings. The text was read and many helpful suggestions made by Walter Tracy of Linotype, Leslie T Owens of the London College of Printing, Walter Partridge of Westminster Press, Richard Vickers, former chief sub-editor of *The Sunday Times*, and of course the series editor, Oscar Turnill. He is also part-author of the glossary of newspaper and print terms which is relevant to all five volumes but is included here for convenience.

HAROLD EVANS
Highgate

Contents

1 Looking at Headlines

Reporters write the paper; sub-editors make it.
—NORTHCLIFFE

Big headlines came late to newspapers. The front page of the first daily newspaper, the *Daily Courant* in 1702, did not have any at all. This is curious because the sensational pamphlets which preceded newspapers went in for large and active headings. A 1613 pamphlet had the bold heading:

THREE BLOODIE MURDERS

As Robert E Garst and Theodore Bernstein suggest in their intriguing discussion[1], perhaps the first real modern headline was the *Boston Gazette* which in 1781 printed a special sheet leaflet extra:

CORNWALLIS TAKEN!

What was distinctively modern about that was the spread of the type across the whole of the leaflet; the size of the type; and the introduction of the verb. These are three of the elements of the modern headline. The London *Times* had some hint of them as early as 1789 in a headline which the official history rightly calls sensational and unprecedented (**below**).

There was no finite verb in the headline, but eight lines of type for a heading was extraordinary. *The Times* did not

F R A N C E.

C O N F I N E M E N T

OF THE

KING, QUEEN,

AND

ROYAL FAMILY,

AND

The Attempt to Murder the QUEEN.

develop its early innovation, nor was it copied in England. Some English newspapers did let the verb into the headline. One of the headings in the first issue of *The Sunday Times* of London in February, 1823, had this modern phrasing:

FIVE GENTLEMEN CONVICTED OF STEALING DEAD BODIES

But this was small capitals, only one size up on the 7pt body type and the other headings were the customary labels:

> Accidents
> Offences
> Sporting
> Law Report
> Latest Intelligence

Fifty years later there were more active headlines, and though the proprieties of civilised society were still observed—A GENTLEMAN CHARGED WITH ASSAULTING HIS WIFE—there had been little development in display. The headline remained in single column in one or two lines of capitals. It was left to the Americans to develop the headline as display. The invention of the headline deck was pushed hard, in response to the news, especially to the urgent impulses of the Civil War and the transmission of news by telegraph which first occurred on a large scale during the fighting.

Let us not confuse deck and line. A deck is a distinct headline on its own and as such it may consist of one or more lines. A headline of six lines is a single deck if the lines are in the same type and read one on to the other. If the six lines of type are divided into two units, each of three lines, each making some kind of sense self-contained, then you have a double-deck headline. A multi-deck headline is any with more than one deck.

Sometimes the American decks extended to the foot of the column, an absurdity, but by varying the number of decks in proportion to the story's importance and detail, the Americans had introduced the important concept that display should be proportionate to the worth of the story. Newspapers were still limited by the lack of colour

THE OCEAN TELEGRAPH.

VICTORY AT LAST!

THE FIRST MESSAGE.

ENGLAND GREETS AMERICA

QUEEN VICTORIA

TO

PRESIDENT BUCHANAN.

THE PRESIDENT'S REPLY.

TRIUMPHANT COMPLETION

OF THE

GREAT WORK OF THE CENTURY.

The Old World and the New United.

GLORIA IN EXCELSIS.

1

AWFUL EVENT.

President Lincoln Shot by an Assassin.

The Deed Done at Ford's Theatre Last Night.

THE ACT OF A DESPERATE REBEL

The President Still Alive at Last Accounts.

No Hopes Entertained of His Recovery.

Attempted Assassination of Secretary Seward.

DETAILS OF THE DREADFUL TRAGEDY.

2

in heading type, a deficiency the American papers began to meet, crudely, by raiding the jobbing cases. The main heading was still a label; still restrained within a single column; and all the headings were still in caps. But the verb and active news were creeping in as in this nine-decker head:

The Civil War added to the extravaganzas. There were twelve decks on the *New York Times* announcement of the fall of Atlanta (compared with four on the December, 1851, French revolution). But, more significantly, the heading which really told the news was becoming more prominent; the all-capitals style was disappearing; and the decks were descending in size (**1, 2**).

The second deck of the Lincoln heading is as good a headline as one could wish and all the language is vigorous. In all the London daily papers, by contrast, the heading

ASSASSINATION OF PRESIDENT LINCOLN.
SURRENDER OF LEE.
THE ROAD MURDER CONFESSION.

Opening of Chapel-School at Diss Heywood
THE REJOICINGS AT REDGRAVE.
UNITED FREE METHODIST MISSIONARY MEETING.
DISS PETTY SESSIONS.

Titled COCK FIGHTERS; DREADFUL DEATH; SHOCKING BARBARITY; The EDMUNDS SCANDAL; Gardening for the week; Dr. Hunter's Letters, Continued; Mysterious Death; BLONDIN'S £10,000 CREDITOR; IMPERIAL PARLIAMENT; and all the News of the week, in the

DISS EXPRESS,
FRIDAY, APRIL 28, 1865.
ONE PENNY.

PUBLISHED BY EDWARD ABBOTT, ME.   ⁓SS.

on this event was in three decks, a gesture to display, but the first line was a label (America or Latest from America) and the passive was used for the main news:

ASSASSINATION OF PRESIDENT LINCOLN

In vigorous display, newspapers were behind pamphlets and publicity. For instance (3), this striking contents bill was put out by the *Diss Express*, a small paper in Norfolk.

The superior vigour of the American wording is reflected in the *New York Daily Tribune's* three headings:

HIGHLY IMPORTANT!
THE PRESIDENT SHOT!
SECRETARY SEWARD ATTACKED!

The first deck is still without a verb but by contrast with the English practice it is alive with the excitement of the news. While the London newspapers tended still to label the main news inactively, the first deck in American newspapers developed more subtle moods (and in this was a forerunner to some of the popular tabloid treatments today when the main news is already familiar from television and the paper instead tries to express the sense of popular feeling). In 1882 the *Kansas City Daily Journal* caught the popular mood in its first deck while delaying the news to the second:

GOOD BYE, JESSE!

The Notorious Outlaw and Bandit, Jesse James, Killed at St. Joseph

The *Kansas City Daily*, however, and other papers, had also developed a bad habit which still plagues papers retaining multi-deck headings, especially in the United States. This is the practice of writing decks as partial sentences which read on one to another instead of being self-contained telegrams as they should be:

The Notorious Outlaw and Bandit, Jesse James, Killed at St. Joseph

BY R. FORD, OF RAY COUNTY,

A Young Man but Twenty-one Years of Age.

THE DEADLY WEAPON USED

Presented to His Slayer by His Victim but a Short Time Since.

A ROBBERY CONTEMPLATED

Of a Bank at Platte City—To Have Taken Place Last Night.

JESSE IN KANSAS CITY

During the Past Year and Residing on One of the Principal Streets.

KANSAS CITY EXCITED

Over the Receipt of the News—Talks with People—Life of the Dead Man.

The next breakthrough in display was the multi-column rather than the multi-deck headline. The *Philadelphia Inquirer* cut through the column rules for the Battle of Antietam in 1862, but it was not a practice till the 1870s and 80s. William Randolph Hearst's celebrated headline on a San Francisco fire was a departure by being two whole columns wide, almost overcoming the sensation of the wording itself:

HUNGRY, FRANTIC FLAMES
'LEAPING HIGHER, HIGHER, HIGHER
WITH DESPERATE DESIRE'
RUNNING MADLY RIOTOUS THROUGH
   CORNICE,
ARCHWAY AND FACADE,
RUSHING IN UPON THE TREMBLING
GUESTS WITH SAVAGE FURY

The banner, full eight columns wide, was really developed in the great circulation war between Hearst's *New York Journal* and Pulitzer's *New York World*, and was taken up in London by the new (1900) *Daily Express*, and the *Daily Chronicle*. But the types were thin, and it was another war before the real bold banners could be said to have arrived with new display faces (**opposite**).

There is no need for me to detail all the developments. Some are described by Stanley Morison[2] and Allen Hutt[3]; there are two fascinating books of plates of newspaper pages[4]; and I have dealt with the development of newspaper design separately in Book Five in this series.

I hope I have presented enough evidence, however, for the view that the headline is a developing form, conditioned by the ideas it has to express, by its technology, and by its audience. The Americans went to multi-deck single column headlines to achieve impact and also proportion between display and story. But there is no need to keep multi-deck headlines when it is possible to print column-breaking horizontal headlines and to print them in display types which are bold, economical and readable. Yet the multi-decks survive. Today we can achieve variety, if and where we want it, by changing the weight of the same type family or by setting headlines across different measures in different styles. Yet type-mixing survives. And even modernists need to pause and question their responses. The banner headline, considered the hallmark of twentieth century display, is less appropriate than it was in the generation after 1890. Then it retailed hot news in telegraphic wording before radio, still less TV, could tell the customers. But what is the role of the banner head-

line when the newspaper must develop more and more as an interpreter and explainer of events we already know about? And is the urgent telegraphic style of heading still right for signalling all the contents, and still right when street sales are less significant?

The history of the headline should show us that newspapers, specialists in the up-to-the-minute, may be years behind changing their style to new needs and opportunities. At our back, as we write, we should always hear Time's winged chariot hurrying near.

The News Headline

Simplicity, informality and impact are the essence of the modern headline. We consider first the appearance of the headline (rather than content), which means the look of the headline in setting style and choice of type.

Every paper has its own personality to express, its own attitude to the news, from staid to sensational. But every newspaper must choose a headline which meets as many as possible of a number of requirements. It must be a clear signal; swiftly readable; economical in editorial, production, and reading time, and in newsprint space; proportionate to the news; and flexible. These requirements are met, in appearance, by the way the newspaper deploys the visual constituents of the headline:

Headline pattern
Multi-deck or multi-line
Letter form—capitals, lower-case, italic
Spread—single- or multi-column
Arrangement—centred or indented lines

Headline typography
Fount
Size of type
Character of type—condensed or expanded
Weight of type
Spacing

Clearly, individual requirements can conflict. The most economical headline style would be the capitals of the body type, but that would neither be a sufficient signal nor swiftly legible. Again, there would be little point in achieving a clear signal by large type for every headline, for this would not be economical, and would impose more limitations on varying the headline size to indicate the varying worth of the news.

Headline patterns

DECKS: Perhaps the most important single freedom of the modern deskman is that he does not have to achieve degrees of emphasis by building deck on deck of headline, each deck consisting of several lines. Yet such is the influence of tradition that sheets as different as Indian-language newspapers and the *New York Times* still cling to the wasteful multi-deck; and it is only recently that the English *Daily Telegraph* has moved quietly away from rigorous multi-decking. The *New York Times* still produces five-decker headlines with as many as twelve lines of head altogether. Multi-deck headlines like this consume editorial time in writing; production time in setting; and space. These wastes are further aggravated by the practice of separating each of the headlines by a dash or fancy rule. All this is to little purpose. People do not seem to bother to read more than the main heading. The modern reader scans the headlines and expects to be able to take in their message almost at a glance. He wants a signpost, not a gazetteer.

The single-deck headline provides this. For basic single-column items, two or three lines are usually needed to write an effective headline. When the measure goes beyond three columns, two lines of headline are plenty for ordinary news display, and one is often right. There is really no need for multi-deck headlines anywhere. The single deck will meet any situation. Its weight and style can be varied enormously. The most that can be conceded to the declining tradition is that one or two main top stories on a page may carry two or three decks —never more. Multi-decks down page as well are a grotesque waste; Greek and Indian newspapers are the most profligate, 5 inches on a headline down page, two decks of two lines each and the story itself only 7 in. long.

Let us not confuse a deck with a *strapline*—the subordinate line above the headline, usually one line in smaller type (say 14 or 18pt). The American expression indicates its relationship to the headline: on many US papers it's an *eyebrow* (on others a *kicker*).

The strapline, though abused, is more useful than the traditional deck. It is a highly flexible device and being small it is economical in space. The commonest use is as a departmental label—Business News; Rugby; Moors Trial: 4th day; and so on. It can be set left on a set left or centred head; or it can be centred on a centred head. There are two other uses for the strapline—it can give a point of detail from the main story; or it can set the scene.

In terms of the headline pattern, the essential point to remember now is that the strapline should not be written full out. It should not take light (i.e. white space) from the main heading; or compete with it in any way, typographically or verbally.

Here are some examples:

Easy Humphrey Victory

Two More House Veterans Toppled In Primaries; Boston Jesuit Wins

This is correct. The strapline need not have been underscored, but there is sufficient white and the kicker adds information.

Vol. XXIV No. 348   BANGKOK WEDNESDAY DECEMBER 16, 1970

JAPAN PROPOSAL NOT FULLY SUPPORTED BY INDUSTRY

TEXTILE PACT 'VITAL TO SATO SURVIVAL'

Wrong. Even if the underscoring were taken away, to give the main deck more light, the overline is too full.

THE NORTHERN ECHO.   Thursday, July 28, 1966

NEWSPROBE

After amalgamation of the police, is it now the fire brigades' turn? North-East fire chiefs are to discuss the prickly question, which will take on added importance following the recruit shortage admitted by Newcastle yesterday.

— Firemen in distress —

To merge, or stay? It's an incendiary hint

A case for regionalism

ONE RULE FOR THE RICH . . . ONE FOR THE POOR

FIREMEN'S already hot tempers are expected to ignite as the incendiary hint of regional amalgamation is dropped into a meeting of the Northern Fire Chiefs' Committee at Durham next Monday.

The dozen members, each either jealously guarding his own record or hoping to improve efficiency, are expected to be split. Other items are on the closed meeting's agenda—but the idea of putting the brigades under an unknown supremo is likely to bring out the firemen's hatchets.

The self - contained brigades with fixed perimeters of operation — such as Darlington and South Shields — are adamantly against surrendering their fire-fighting authority to a regional command.

The larger units, Northumberland, Durham County, North Riding and Cumberland, are most likely to be sold the idea of regionalisation.

Others with a voice at the No. 1 Region meeting will be fire chiefs from Newcastle and Gateshead, Carlisle, West Hartlepool, Sunderland, Tynemouth and

Around the North-East brigades

Who they are, what they feel

County Durham
Strength: Whole-time, 427; retained, 281.

way of recompense for the job—in other words more pay."

He said a bigger unit could perhaps help in recruitment.

A STRONG champion of the regional fire services scheme is Mr. Terry Parry, general secretary of the Fire Brigades Union.

His point is that with one fire service there would be "one standard of fire cover."

Mr. Parry remarks: " At present we have the "wealthy" brigade, which is considering closed circuit television for lecture periods.

"And then we have the paradoxical example of another brigade temporarily suspending breathing apparatus drill because until the next financial year there was an economy drive on the use

Enough, enough. The deskman apparently could not make up his mind which was the main heading and which the subsidiary. The strapline on the two-column 'Who they are' head is well matched in size and style to the main head, in contrast to the strapline 'A case for regionalism', which should have been one line only. But even with perfect straplines there would still have been too much confusion.

Stamp-your-card TV

'HP' PLAN TO HELP PAY THE £5 FEE

Express Staff Reporter

TELEVISION

—TALKING OF TV, THE DALEKS RETURN—FACING RIVAL MONSTERS

Me? I'm a Mechanoid

INTRODUCING the newest horror from space: Mechanoids.

Above are headlines on two unrelated stories (despite the absence of cut-off rules). The italic caps strapline to the second might just have got by, despite its wide measure and lack of white space, but here it just adds to the jumble.

LETTER FORM: The early headlines were in capitals of the body type. Later the ransacking of display founts produced capitals, too. Today the range of distinctive head-line faces gives us freedom to put headlines in lower-case and we should do it for several reasons.

The first is readability. The superiority of lower-case letters for easy reading is discussed fully in the volume on text typography (Book Two) but **(left)** we read by recognising the shapes of words and groups of words, rather than individual letters, and there is a greater variety of word silhouette in lower-case. Words in caps have distinctive lengths but not shapes. Lower-case words are distinguished by their ascenders and descenders.

The superior readability of headlines in lower-case is evident and it has been demonstrated that they retain this superiority when embedded in a page of a newspaper. An experiment with *The Times* showed that about ten per cent more lower-case headlines could be located in a limited time than headlines printed in capitals.

The preference for lower-case is reinforced by custom: we have grown used to reading lower-case because it is the commonest style in all reading material. Compare the styles **below,** in the *New York Times*.

Headlines in roman capitals are harder to read than headlines in roman lower-case. But roman caps are easier than italic caps, and especially italic caps multi-column. All headings in caps need extra spacing between the lines, which means there is a second argument against caps headings: economy. The liberal rule is that for read-ability lines of caps should be leaded to the depth of the

Compare the Linotype

Compare the Linotype

Compare the Linotype

HERE ARE CAPS

VOL. CXVII..No. 40,184   © 1968 The New York Times Company.   **NEW YORK, WEDNESDAY, JANUARY 31, 1968**   *10 CENTS*

NATION IS WARNED UNREST IN CITIES IMPERILS SYSTEM

Advisory Unit Calls Failure

State Senate Votes to End Ban on Church-School Aid

Repeal Backed 35 to 17 | Aid to All Colleges Urged

By **THOMAS P. RONAN** | By **M. A. FARBER**
Special to The New York Times | A special committee appoint-
ALBANY, Jan. 30—After a | ed by Governor Rockefeller has

PRESIDENT URGES WIDER PROGRAM TO AID VETERANS

Congress Asked to Provide

FOE INVADES U.S. SAIGON EMBASSY; RAIDERS WIPED OUT AFTER 6 HOURS; VIETCONG WIDEN ATTACK ON CITIES

face appearing (i.e. nearly as much as 24pt on a 24pt Century Bold which has a large x-height and rather less on a Bodoni).

Failure to approximate to this rule is one of the reasons why the *New York Times* headings are so hard to read. Lower-case headings by comparison are more economical in space since the ascenders and descenders create their own white space within the appearing face of the type. This gives a third reason for preferring lower-case headlines, which is that the ascenders and descenders give an impression of life and movement, ideal for conveying the urgency of news, whereas caps are static and formal (though the correct spacing needs care—*see* pp. 85–9).

There is one final reason which is not a matter of appearance but which is vital to editorial time and the ease of writing meaningful headings: you can say more in a given space with lower-case headlines:

Watson merger
wins approval
WATSON MERGER
WINS APPROVAL

By lower-case headlines I mean that all letters are lower-case except the initial letter of the first word and any proper names. Some newspapers, especially in the United States and Canada, follow a style which is a pointless half-way house—the headline is formally in lower-case but every word has an initial capital letter:

Britain Will Resume
Bargaining On Price
Of North Sea gas

Others inconsistently drop the capitals for the short words like prepositions and conjunctions, which is some improvement:

Britain will Resume
Bargaining on Price
of North Sea gas

The *New York Times* mixes it, capping prepositions if they begin a line but not otherwise and creating some very odd effects.

Britain Will Resume Bargaining on Price Of North Sea Gas

But this is superior:

Britain will resume
bargaining on price
of North Sea gas

This style has become commonplace in English papers, both serious and popular, without provoking any demonstrations in the streets. The ultra-serious *Le Monde* follows it. The *Sydney Morning Herald* and the London *Daily Telegraph* have changed. Some Who Argue For Initial Capitalisation In Lower-Case Heads Say That The Initial Capital Enables Space To Be Saved Because Since The Capital Letter Indicates A New Word All WordSpacingCanBeEliminatedOnATightLine. This is rubbish. The space gained is still less than that lost by the extra space taken by capitals, and the result is illegible and ugly. The line **below** is from the *Washington Post*.

The late John E Allen who has had a great influence on American newspapers argued for capitalising the initial letter of each line on the grounds that the all-lower-case style created a 'ragged' effect. The aesthetics of this are arguable. For 'ragged' one could say 'dynamic'. But the other considerations are decisive. The lower-case style is superior to all caps, and to initial capping, on two of our relevant requirements of legibility and economy.

The argument for lower-case headlines has sufficient force to persuade an increasing number of newspapers to move to lower-case throughout for news—in Britain *The Sunday Times*, *The Northern Echo*, *The Observer*, *The Guardian*. But this trend is not inevitable. Though I believe the staple headline should be in lower-case, there

18 Sunday, Dec. 17, 1967 THE WASHINGTON POST

Moss, Reid Again Demand That Saigon Be Forced to Effect Promised Land Reforms

By Richard Harwood
Washington Post Staff Writer

For the second time in five months, ranking members of the House Foreign Operations Subcommittee have demanded that the United States force the government of South Vietnam to carry out land redistribution to landless peas-

Moss (D-Calif.), subcommittee chairman, and Rep. Ogden R. Reid of New York, ranking Republican member.

Since 1954, the two Congressmen said, the Saigon government has acquired about 2.5 million acres of land for distribution to landless peas-

ing to Moss and Reid, the Vietcong have carried out a far more effective land distribution of their own and "have eliminated landlord domination."

Reid is so exercised about the problem that he has privately recommended that

the State Department yesterday but it is known that the Administration attaches less urgency to the land reform problem than do the two Congressmen.

The Administration does not even accept the Reid-Moss definition of what the problem is.

tween 150,000 and 200,000 peasant families in tracts of 7 to 10 acres.

But the Agency for International Development says the size of the undistributed government holdings is a mirage. About a million acres of the government land is abandoned

government's control, by AID's reckoning.

Reid and Moss nevertheless insist that land reform is a basic need in South Vietnam. They have visited the country twice and their subcommittee has prepared a highly critical report on Saigon's land poli-

Operations, headed by Rep. Charles Dawson (D-Ill.).

There have been unconfirmed rumors that Dawson has pigeonholed the document to avoid embarrassment to the Administration. Dawson denies the rumors. In any case the failure of the committee

the problem was "being studied." Since then Reid has received a letter from the former Ambassador to Saigon, Henry Cabot Lodge, who blamed the Saigon bureaucracy for land reform failures.

Reid blames the American bureaucracy for failing to give ultimatums to Saigon. Either

can be an effective mixture of capitals and lower-case headings (as, for instance, in the early 1967 redesign of the London *Times*). These styles can be mixed between stories and also between decks—the lead deck in caps and the subsidiary deck in lower-case.

SPREAD: The first headlines were confined to a single column. Now they can range over as many columns as the newspaper. Few newspapers today miss the opportunities for display in mixing single-column and multi-column headlines. A headline style all single-column limits the capacity of the headline to match the infinitely varying importance of the news item. The way they mix is discussed in Book Five on newspaper design, but there is one factor which should be mentioned here since it is a limitation on the lower-case style.

A newspaper which standardises on lower-case but also retains a banner headline across a full text page will have to retain a capital letter headline here. Across such a wide measure lower-case letters look straggly. Moreover, headlines should be crisp in their wording and lower-case at practical sizes across eight columns means being unduly wordy. (The answer is either to abandon the banner or deliberately to choose, say, an expanded typeface that is ungenerous in the number of words it affords.)

ARRANGEMENT: There is a rich range of possibilities here. A paper can standardise on one form, such as the centred head, or it can mix them between headlines. Some North American newspapers mix four or five patterns even between the decks of the same multi-deck headline, which is variety gone to seed. One form is certainly best on the serious newspapers which wish to present a calm face for the same reason that one display family is preferred: a single consistent style emphasises the journalistic effort of the newspaper to produce some semblance of comprehensible order from the disordered world. But this should not be a rigorous rule. Much depends on the skill of the page planners, and the ideas they are trying to communicate.

Basic typography

The basic arrangements are: flush left; centred; stepped; flush right; and hanging indention. Let us look at them in turn.

FLUSH LEFT: The flush left heading is a heading of one or more lines in which all the lines are set flush to the left. This should not be hard up against the column rule. The flush left head looks better when each line is indented on the column rule, say 6 points or half an em on an 11-em

is such a supply/demand imbalance prices are high.

One explanation to account for the unusual situation at present is that the shortfall in production is believed now to be much smaller than the 5,000-10,000 tons estimate a few months ago. — Reuter

NEW MARK FOR U.S. ECONOMY

WASHINGTON, Tues — The US economy will officially reach a million-million dollar rate of output today.

President Nixon will mark the occasion by unveiling a gross national product (GNP) clock, a timekeeper that will also show the estimated GNP minute by minute.

It will be similar to the

'GUNNY MARKET IMPROVES'

THE situation in the gunny bag industry has been improved after a slowdown in business caused by the cut-throat competition among local manufacturers according to Mr Phinich Leenawat, a director of the Siam Gunny Co. Ltd, the country's gunny bag manufacturing pool.

Intervention by the Government's National Economic Development Board and the Board of Export Promotion has saved the pool from collapse, Mr Phinich said.

Members of the pool were now working in closer cooperation, he added.

Mr Phinich also revealed

column. **Above** are the two styles uncomfortably in adjacent columns.

The flush left heading has become more popular, being recommended by Allen Hutt[5] as easier to write and by Ed Arnold[6] as optically better (in the latest edition of his book Arnold does not, however, repeat his 1956 assertion that it is easier to write). Arnold's argument, following John E Allen, is that when the eye has finished the end of the first line of a head it sweeps back to the start of the first line, which he calls the axis of orientation. If the second line of head is indented, as it is in a centred head, then the eye must not only drop to the second line but search momentarily for where it begins. Conversely, it can be argued that the eye does not always return to the axis of orientation and, habituated to centred headlines, might benefit by the shorter return sweep to the second line of a centred headline. My own view is that the balance of that argument here goes to flush left; but it is very doubtful whether the effective flush left heading is significantly, indeed at all, easier to write. Walter Tracy, Linotype's Typographic Manager in London, has argued[7] that many of the flush left headlines in newspapers need a second glance to take in meaning:

'Many headings, though continuous, have three parts: (1) who did it; (2) what he did and (3) to whom. This means there are two natural breaks in the heading. Where the two or three lines of the heading are all centred, it does not seem to matter whether the turnovers occur at the natural breaks. But in flush left headings it really does matter that the lines should end at the correct part of the sentence. I think the reason for this is that the eye scans the heading.'

Consider these examples. Conceivably, if the second line here were centred the second thought would be nearer to the first and more immediately grasped.

Middle East

Confident King Husain/claims
a big victory|over
invading Syrian tank forces

King Husain told correspondents last night that his forces had stopped the Syrian invasion and wrecked building, hit yesterday, was still smouldering 100 yards from the bullet-pocked Intercontinental in contacts with the guerrillas, who were reported to have increased somewhat the number of hostages

Confusion over |who does
what in NHS

By Our Medical Reporter In the National Health Service tal but it could mean that managerial roles are thrust upon the

Home news

Owners criticized |after oil
tank disaster :|new
safety rules to be enforced

New safety rules for demolition "like a bull in a china shop". It On the day of the explosion

I do not think this proves the superiority of centred heads since these are 'windy' flush left headings. But if we are to avoid weak flush left headings there must be rather more care than there is in the spacing of the wording. It is not perhaps so vital to vary the line lengths to a pattern as in centred heads, but some proportion should be kept. Shapes like these should certainly be avoided:

United Nations
agrees to
veto all
arms

President Johnson
fit

Jones
escapes
recapture

The preferred patterns are shown in this diagram:

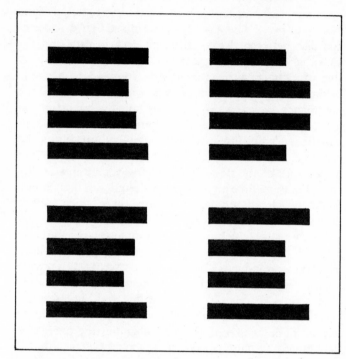

CENTRED: Each line of headline type is centred on the white of the column. The well-constructed centred heading, whether of a multi-line or a multi-deck, has its own symmetry; it is neatly framed in white. The patterns created by centring need slightly more attention than the patterns the flush left heading creates; but neither needs as much worry as some other headline patterns. If one is writing headlines for a multi-deck newspaper they will invariably be centred. Multi-deck headline look best centred. Decking is a severe formal style of headling and centring is a matching formal device. When writing multi-line headings the most important single injunction is to write a full top line. Then the headline cannot go wrong. There can be three or four or more lines of roughly the same measure of these patterns.

China refuses
access to
Briton

(Longest, short, shortest)

Callaghan
under
fire
from
his own
followers

(Long, short, shortest, short, short, long)

Fault found in Gnat jets

Express Staff Reporter

A DEFECT has been found in Gnat jet aircraft used for the advanced training of R.A.F. fighter pilots.

The Ministry of Defence said last night that it was a minor **I**

Petition duplicationsat Tynemouth?

H OLDING a copy of a petition, alleged to have been signed by 297 residents, protesting against the recent increases in rent for pre-war council houses, Coun. T. W. Crawshaw, chairman of the **2**

Plane rushes SOS baby to England

Express Staff Reporter

ON BOARD THE PENDENNIS CASTLE

LAS PALMAS, Monday

THE baby picked III **3**

The longest–short–shortest points like an arrow at the text. The forms of centred head to avoid are the short–short–long or the short–long, which look ugly and which confuse the eye on the return to the left to begin reading the second line. Above are some bad centred heads in lower-case (**1, 2, 3**).

These suggestions are fairly easy to follow with lower-case headlines. For caps it is harder because caps take more space across the column and there are fewer letters for the headline wording. For caps headings one can write a short–long–short heading provided the two short lines are roughly the same length and each only indented about two units on the long centre line. The preferred pattern is on the left, the inferior on the right:

BID TO SALVAGE GOLD SHIP

from BRIAN BLACKWELL:
Hongkong

THE HIT PARADE'S ANGRY YOUNG MAN

By CHARLES WESTBERG

A MID screams, sweet throw-ing and smashing, of instruments. The Who pop group ended the first house

The commonest double-column headline is a single deck of two lines. With centred headings always write the second line here shorter than the first by at least two units. Never try to write tight caps heads. Caps heads need more white around themselves for legibility.

STEPPED: This has been popular in America (where it is called a drop line) but it has little to recommend it as a regular style. The shape is:

SYRIANS SHELL   Paris Cycle Track
  ISRAEL BORDER   Will be Renovated
                     For Other Sports

The first line is set flush left, the last flush right, and the middle line(s) centred. Each line has to be about the same length, which is, of course, somewhat under the full width of the column. To achieve a smooth step requires great care in the headline writing—and to what purpose?

What some regard as a pretty pattern strikes others as contrived fussiness; and it is a contrivance which is less legible. Compared with the flush left style, the eye has to do rather more work in transferring from the end of one line to pick up the indeterminate beginning of the second. But the more important failing is that stepped styles depend too much on a precise count, and failure produces ugly results:

WILSON RESCINDS
HIS OFFERS
    TO RHODESIANS   AMERICAN FACES
                                  JAIL TERM

FLUSH RIGHT: Each line is pushed against the right-hand margin to create a stepped effect on the left. The flush right has even more limited application than the stepped headline. It is all right as an occasional variant but not as a regular style. The ragged left gives the eye no fixed point in its traverse; the flush right is slower to set.

THE PROBLEM OF FINDING VOTERS IN 'BED-SIT' WORLD

We should distinguish between individual lines set right line by line and acceptable arrangements which off-set decks of head, one deck set left and the other deck pushed to the right (but with all the individual lines set left or centred).

HANGING INDENTION: The first line is set full out and the others indented, usually to the left:

Tension rises on
    frontier following
    week of sabotage
    by Syrians

There is no virtue in this as a regular headline style. It appears most frequently as a variant in the decks of American multi-deck headlines.

Quotes and dashes

There is one final refinement affecting the pattern of the headline—the placing of quotation marks and dashes. Single quotes are essential. Anyone who finds himself writing a headline which needs both single and double quotes should start again. The ugly habit of regarding the quote or dash as a full letter must be broken, too. Headline spacing should disregard these. With flush left headings, the flush line should be the initial letter of each line—not the quote. The quote should be left to hang in the white. Compare the awkwardness of the pedantic alignment on the quote (**below left**) and the realistic arrangement lining up on the initial letters (**below right**).

'Patience is
needed on
Rhodesia'

do not matter if we can achieve this
result peacefully and quietly."
    The speech, reported by the Press
Association and by Reuters news agency,
in its overseas service, caused immediate
discussion among diplomats in London.
    A Buckingham Palace spokesman was
asked last night whether the Duke's

'Like the Cold War' says bitter Smith

2 What the News Headline Says

If I choose to head an article 'An Inquiry into the Conditions of Mycenaean Civilisation in the Heroic Epoch, with Special Reference to the Economic and Domestic Functions of Women Before and After the Conjectural Date of the Argive Expedition against Troy',—if I say, I choose for my article some snappy little title like that, I really have no right to complain if (when I send it to the Chicago Daily Scoop), *they alter it to 'How Helen Did the Housekeeping'.*

—G K CHESTERTON

They might nowadays have changed Chesterton's manuscript to the even pithier 'How Helen Kept House'. But Chesterton would clearly have made a brilliant features sub-editor. The difficulty in writing headlines is precisely in conveying in a few attractive words the essence of a complicated set of facts. I would say that writing good headlines is fifty per cent of a deskman's skill. He has to catch the reader on the wing. In half a dozen words he has to inform him tersely and accurately of a shattering or confused event, or arouse his curiosity in a subtle manifestation of human behaviour. This skill can be developed because there are certain principles for good headline writing; the man of genuine flair may occasionally break all the rules, but no more often than the composer who deliberately introduces discord into his harmonies. Every bit of available time spent on chiselling out the right words in the right sequence is time well spent.

The headline gives emphasis to a few words in bold type and every word must be weighed. There is a double responsibility on the headline writer. He has to attract as many readers as he can into the text of the story; or condemn it to unread obscurity; but even where he fails he has an effect, for many who do not read the story none the less retain an impression from scanning the headline.

Accuracy, intelligibility, and vigour are the requirements, and any newspaper which is careless with its headline writing is careless with its own purpose and vitality. Where headlines are wordy, vague, or confused, the newspaper seems to be in its dotage. Where every headline goes unerringly to the point with precision or wit, the whole newspaper comes alive. The art of the head-

line lies in imagination and vocabulary; the craft lies in accuracy of content, attractiveness of appearance, and practicality. For a start the headline must fit the space available to it.

Counting the Units

It is not long before any news headline writer, engaged on this fascinating business, is confronted with the oldest newspaper joke. 'Do you think,' the printer will say, 'this bloody type is made of rubber?' The headline writer will have written a 'bouncer', a headline with too many letters to be accommodated in the width and type required. Bouncers are a poor joke. They waste everybody's time. You must write headlines which will fit. When you have produced a superb headline which will not fit, you should confide in the chief sub-editor or managing editor and ask for a different headings scheme. (And if they are wise they will agree, if they can, because type exists to serve the news, not the other way round.)

You count the units in the wording you write. These units must not exceed the number of units allowed by the size of the type; its style; and the number of columns the headline is being allowed to run. A fat type across a single column will yield a few units; a condensed type across two columns will yield many more. The units in the wording and in the type are counted the same way. The unit count system begins by giving a unit value to every letter and figure in the alphabet. It is based on a count of one for most letters, with adjustments for thinner and fatter letters, and for capitals when they are mixed with lower-case letters. In the lines of letters below there are twenty letters in each line and it is easy to see why some letters, taking more space, should have a higher unit count.

Count as 1 unit:

aaaaaaaaaaaaaaaaaaaaa
bbbbbbbbbbbbbbbbbbbbb
ccccccccccccccccccccc
ddddddddddddddddddddd
eeeeeeeeeeeeeeeeeeeee

and so on through the alphabet.

Count as $1\frac{1}{2}$ units:

mmmmmmmmmmmmmmmmmmmmm
wwwwwwwwwwwwwwwwwww

Count as $\frac{1}{2}$ unit:

iiiiiiiiiiiiiiiiiiiii
lllllllllllllllllllll
fffffffffffffffffffff
ttttttttttttttttttttt

Punctuation marks

The logic is clear. The two fat letters, m and w, are wider; the thin letters are narrower. The relative width of the letter varies little from type to type: an m is big in every type.

But, of course, you do not write headlines entirely in lower-case. The first word has a capital letter, and so do proper names. Where capitals or numerals occur in a headline which is otherwise in lower-case, you must make allowance for the extra space the capital letter or numerals will take compared with the lower-case letter. Therefore in a headline set u/lc (upper- and lower-case), you count any ordinary capital letter or numeral as an extra $\frac{1}{2}$ unit, i.e. $1\frac{1}{2}$ units. Thus:

Ape = $3\frac{1}{2}$ units ($1\frac{1}{2}$ units for the capital A, one unit each for the lower-case p and e)

However, there are four capital letters and one numeral which need adjustment:

Count as 2 units in upper- and lower-case headings

M, W

Count as 1 unit in upper- and lower-case headings

I, J

Numeral 1

The other kind of headline you will write is one composed entirely of capital letters. Here the basic unit count becomes the ordinary capital letter. It is counted as 1, just as the ordinary lower-case letter in a lower-case heading is counted as 1 unit. But again, we have to adjust the count for the exceptional letters.

Count as $1\frac{1}{2}$ in capital headings:

M, W

Count as $\frac{1}{2}$ unit in capital headings:

I

Numeral 1

In many faces numerals are actually slightly narrower than capital letters. Make no adjustments for this when counting an ordinary caps headline which is mainly capital letters with only a few numerals. But remember it when there may be a choice between a word and a numeral heading:

£5,000

may fit where

GRANT

would bounce

Finally, spaces between words. Here the figure is somewhat arbitrary—some experienced sub-editors count a half unit, some a full. My suggestion is to count spaces as a full unit, which they often need to be; if it is in excess it is on the right side and it simplifies the count.

This is how the system works:

ATOMIC FALLOUT
'POISONING US'

Count:

A	T	O	M	I	C		F	A	L	L	O	U	T	
1	1	1	2	$\frac{1}{2}$	1	1	1	1	1	1	1	1	1	= $14\frac{1}{2}$

Add as you go:

1   2   3   5 $5\frac{1}{2}$ $6\frac{1}{2}$ $7\frac{1}{2}$ $8\frac{1}{2}$ $9\frac{1}{2}$ $10\frac{1}{2}$ $11\frac{1}{2}$ $12\frac{1}{2}$ $13\frac{1}{2}$ $14\frac{1}{2}$

'POISONING US'

$\frac{1}{2}$ 1 1 $\frac{1}{2}$ 1 1 1 1 $\frac{1}{2}$ 1 1 1 1 1 $\frac{1}{2}$ = 12

Say the headline in type, size and column width would take only a unit count of 12. The headline writer would then have to lose $2\frac{1}{2}$ units in the top line, changing the wording to, say, ATOMIC DUST. In upper- and lower-case headlines the system works like this:

England wins
World Cup 3–1

Say the unit count you have is 12. The count is:

England wins

Count: 1 1 1 $\frac{1}{2}$ 1 1 1 1 1 $1\frac{1}{2}$ $\frac{1}{2}$ 1 1 = $11\frac{1}{2}$

World Cup 3–1

2 1 1 $\frac{1}{2}$ 1 1 1 $1\frac{1}{2}$ 1 1 1 $1\frac{1}{2}$ $\frac{1}{2}$ 1 = 14

The second line of this head is two units over the top:

it is a bouncer. The headline writer would have to omit the result figures 3–1, thereby reducing the unit count of the headline to 10.

So much for counting the words. You use the same system to arrive at the number of units the headline type, size, and spread will provide. This is the other side of the equation. Obviously before beginning to write the headline you should know the number of units you have to play with. You discover this by counting the units in specimens of type as set in the office style book: and if one is not available ask an experienced man to mark the newspaper for you with the size and type in the headings. A type schedule looks like this, with the typeface set in different sizes and the em-count marked:

If the instruction to you is to write a headline in 24pt Century Bold italic upper- and lower-case across two columns you find the Century Bold italic section in the type schedule, find the specimen of 24pt and then count how many units it allows to the measure requested.

There are two ways in which this whole transaction can be superseded. For the common headline specifications, offices set up number or letter codes, so that, say, an 'A' headline is a 24pt Century Bold italic single column. This saves the executive repeatedly writing off on the copy for the sub '24 CB ital u/lc × 1'; and it saves the sub-editor or deskman writing the same words on the headline copy sheet for the printer. The second device enables you to avoid consulting the type schedule each time and counting off. Instead of doing that, you should prepare a unit count card which will give the various counts at a glance.

It is sometimes said a unit count card means the deskman will lose the 'feel' of the type. I doubt it. To commune each time with the type chart for a type being used every day for news headings is not dedication but a time-wasting affectation.

The unit count card should be compiled from the type chart but checked with experience. For instance, check whether the numerals do in practice merit the same width rating as the capital letters. In many types the figures are fractionally more condensed, so that a four-unit figure would just fit where a four-unit word would bounce.

UNIT COUNT TABLE

Century Bold	1 col (11 ems)	2 col (22½ ems)	3 col (34 ems)	4 col (45½ ems)
18pt caps	11	23	34½	46½
18pt u/lc	14	28½	43	58½
24pt caps	8	16	24½	33
24pt u/lc	11	23	34½	47
30pt caps	6½	13	20	27
30pt u/lc	9	18	27½	37

and so on up the sizes

Century Bold Italics				
18pt caps	10½	21½	32	43½
18pt u/lc	12	25	38	51½

and so on up the sizes

Century Bold Extended				
18pt caps	8½	17	26	35
18pt u/lc	10½	22	32½	44½

and so on up the sizes

The unit count card can be prepared from the type schedule, or, better, by counting headlines as published in your newspaper for each style, size and spread. Count half a dozen representatives of each headline and average the unit count obtained. Working in this way from published examples gives a proper 'feel' for the head that will fit first time, and gradually enables the deskman to write heads that fit *without counting*. With experience he resorts to a unit count only in cases of doubt. It is a useful skill—but the real art in headline writing is using language so that a unit count of 12 or 20 fitly sums up a unique fragment of life.

The Headline's Purpose

A prize young bullock escaped one day in 1965 from the cattle market at Darlington. The bullock was chased by nine men along several shopping streets in town until it was recaptured. The bullock did no damage but provided a lot of temporary excitement. The reporter duly described all this with quotes included, and the copy came to a deskman for a headline. On it, after deliberation, he inscribed the following headline, which passed into print.

NO DAMAGE AND
NO ONE HURT

The reporter the next day complained that his story had not been used. Clearly if he had been extraordinarily assiduous he would have found it, but only the more dedicated readers of the text type that day would have been drawn to the story of the bullock.

The headline was not merely negative. It could have been written about the bulk of the proceedings in Darlington that day. It was undistinctive to the point of extinction: but it will survive in the pages as one of the finest examples of a headline that wasn't. The headline must tell the news; and the man who writes it must have a sense of what news is, just as much as the reporter. What is it that has happened to arrest attention? What is it that is new and interesting? What is it that is different? Clearly the *result* of the activity is none of these things. 'No damage and no one hurt' could be news—if it happened after an explosion or if it recorded, say, a day without traffic accidents.

But here the result of the activity is not surprising; it is the *cause* of the activity which is different. A bullock in its normal way will be expected to do no damage and hurt nobody. But a bullock does not run through the shopping streets every day. The headline writer, then, must at least begin by using the word bullock. Should the headline then be: 'Bullock does no damage'? That headline is certainly accurate. But has it told the reader what the news really is? Is it the bullock's failure to decimate the population which is surprising—or is it simply the diversion of the bullock's chase through the streets?

The trouble with 'Bullock does no damage' is not that there is anything in it which is wrong but that there is not enough in it which is right. It is not related enough to the events of the day. It does not tell the news. Clearly the headline will have to be built on the simple news fact of a bullock running loose through shopping streets. We could write 'Men chase loose bullock'. But that, too, is too unspecific, too unrelated to the story. It would be much better to write 'Nine men chase bullock'; or, if there is room 'Nine chase bullock in town'. Better still, we could change the tone of the headline to emphasise that the

news lies in the antics of the bullock rather than in any heavy drama: 'Prize bullock goes shopping'.

I have explored the case of the galloping bullock because I want to emphasise that the headline must sum up the news in the story it serves—and no other. It must distil the news. It must be specific. The first task, then, in writing a good headline, is to read the copy carefully and decide on the basic news point. This may not be in the first paragraph. With most news stories it should be there, and if it is not, you may have to reorganise the story to bring the news to the top. But sometimes the news point is legitimately delayed and often the news is a complex of various facts in the story, so that enjoining the deskman to write a headline based on the first paragraph is not enough.

The headline writer must think hard on what single element in the story it is which makes it new, different, and worth its space in the paper. To make this judgment he needs to know the background to the news item he is editing: if it is a developing story he must be fully aware of the previous developments and how other newspapers assessed the news point at their publication time. Unimportant details and subsidiary information are put aside, to focus on the real significance of the story. As he reads the copy, the deskman sums up the news in his mind, and scribbles on notepaper at his side the sentence, words, phrases or ideas which are at the heart of the story. These notes will serve as the basis for constructing the headline; just when he should stop to write it is more debatable. When production is not pressing there is a great deal to be said for writing the headline first and editing the copy afterwards. There may be a temptation to make the copy fit the headline, but so long as this is constantly recognised, there is no doubt that the difficult process of trying to write a headline does concentrate the mind wonderfully.

If, before editing the copy, the headline has accurately expressed the essence of the news, it will at once be evident whether the existing intro on the story is right and how it may need to be rewritten. So far as writing the headline first does force attention to an underlying news point, and with it critical attention to the intro, it is the better method. But on busy newspapers it is not possible to leave the copy unsubbed while wrestling with the headline, especially if the copy is long.

Here production will take priority, and it is preferable for the deskman to supply quickly some copy for setting even if it is less than perfect in its prose. On a busy evening newspaper, going quickly to press with a series of editions, it will generally be preferred if he sends, say, three or four folios of copy, then writes the headline and then continues with the text. In this way in emergency the paper could go to press with the first few folios.

Each of us develops his own preferences here, depending largely on the production requirements of his paper, but at whatever stage the headline is written the first essential remains: to jot down the basic news sentence.

We will try this technique with a simple hard news story.

> Groups of Royal Marine Commandos came under heavy mortar and small arms fire in Steamer Point, Aden, today. One Marine was wounded as NLF guerillas fired on six posts simultaneously.

We have now, say, to write a headline for this with a unit count of 27. Strip away the secondary details and the articles and we can write down a sentence which sums up the news: 'Royal Marine Commandos under heavy mortar and small arms fire in Aden today'. This is our headline sentence capturing the news. It is, of course, much too long for a headline of 27 units. What can we cut out? Royal Marine Commandos can become 'Marines'. The location in Aden can be dropped since stories on troops in Aden have been running through the news for weeks. We can omit 'today' because in a news context the reader takes it for granted the item is about current events.

So now we have: 'Marines under heavy mortar and small arms fire'. That is 16 units too long for a headline. If we eliminate the description of the attack as 'mortar and small arms' we have a headline:

Marines under heavy fire

At 23 units this fits and is readily understood. But as 27 is allowed, can we use the other 4 units to effect? We can, if we take out the word 'heavy' and put back the more specific word 'mortar'. Mortar fire is, in any event, more significant than small arms fire:

Marines under mortar fire

This headline meets all the requirements: it fits; it makes immediate sense; it attracts the reader; it tells the news.

How Many Ideas?

What we have just done is to write a headline by editing a sentence. That was a simple story and a simple one-line

headline, but the same technique of sentence-editing serves for more elaborate stories and more elaborate headline structures. Let us write a headline now of three lines with 12 units to a line on the following story:

> Teams of rescuers brought an injured girl of 25 to the surface at the Giant's Pothole near Castleton in the Peak District of Derbyshire yesterday, after a perilous 14-hour struggle through icy water and narrow rocky passageways 450ft underground.
>
> Caked in mud and swathed in a special insulation suit, Miss Donna Carr was carried from the hole at 5 a.m. by grimy-faced rescuers. She is believed to have a fractured skull and leg injuries after falling 30ft soon after entering the 1,317ft hole at 4 p.m. on Saturday. Last night, as she was reported fully conscious and fairly comfortable at Sheffield Royal Infirmary, some of the 50 rescue workers told of what they had done and of two heroes, Dr G Kidd, and a nurse, Mrs Margaret Aldred.

We cannot cope with all these details in the headline. The girl's age and the pothole's location are secondary. Shorn of such secondary information, what is the core of the news? In a sentence it is: 'A girl down a pothole has been rescued after 14 hours.' Leave out '14 hours', 'has been' and the indefinite articles and we have a truncated sentence which becomes the headline, 'Girl down pothole rescued.'

This splits into three lines as:

Girl down
pothole
rescued

This fits easily, but is rather drab. It is also slow. We want to relay the news as quickly as possible. This structure delays until the third line the news that the girl has been saved. We should hasten to an earlier line the introduction of this news point. So for the first line let us write:

Girl saved

That truncated sentence leaves a lot of questions. In what circumstances? Where? This time when we answer these questions let us try to flesh the skeleton with something specific: 'She has been saved after 14 hours down a pothole'. Delete the repetition and the indefinite articles and we have 'after 14 hours down pothole'. This could split as:

after 14 hours
down pothole

The trouble now is that the second line bounces. Clearly rearranging the same wording on different lines does not help:

after 14
hours in pothole

We have, therefore, to change the wording. Is there any other way we can express the same idea of 14 hours? Yes, there is. The girl spent *the night* in the pothole, so we can write:

Girl saved
after night
in pothole

This is an adequate headline, but it would be improved if we could inject one detail of the drama, something, say, about the icy water down there. We cannot do this with the existing line structure since the phrase 'after icy night' would bounce as a second line. If we are prepared to delay the core news point to the second line we can try:

Girl in pothole
saved after
icy night

Fine, but the first line 'Girl in pothole' bounces. There is a device which will make it fit—a device which should be used sparingly, but which is legitimate and is accepted by the reader when it makes sense within the headline sentence. This is the device of the compound noun. 'Girl in pothole' becomes 'pothole girl':

Pothole girl
saved after
icy night

Grammatical Traps

In each of these instances we have taken the core news point, expressed it in a sentence, shortened the sentence, and then simply transcribed the sentence, in the same order, into lines of headline. Where the words fell on the lines was determined simply by whether in that sequence they fitted the space available. If a newsy sentence has been edited comprehensibly there is no need to worry very much where the words fall. There is one caution, which I will give in a moment, but there is certainly no need for the fuss made by some newspapers in the United States. They insist on each line having its own grammatical integrity, and therefore ban headlines where, say, a preposition is on one line and the object is on another.

Rules like this are a pedantry which has developed from one soundly based restriction on the word pattern in the multi-line headline. This simple real difficulty is one of meaning. There are a few occasions when you must watch the way the words fall between lines because this can change the meaning of a clear basic headline sentence. For instance, compare the one-line headline and the two-line headline of the same wording:

Judge Gets Drunk Driving Case

Judge Gets Drunk
Driving Case

That sort of split stands out as objectionable. Equally so if not as potentially costly are headlines where the writer splits hyphenated words:

'More time' call
for help-
jobless scheme

Never split a hyphenated word; look for another way of saying the same thing without using a hyphen at all. There usually is one:

'More time' call
for scheme to
help jobless

Splitting a compound verb produces the effect of marching the reader in two different directions:

GUNMEN HOLD
UP BANK

HEAVY TAXES WILL GO
ON BEER, WINE

WILSON: SMITH RIGHT
OFF COURSE

As a general caution, then, never split compound verbs or compound nouns between lines. But the simplest test is to read the headline to oneself, pausing slightly at the end of each line. If there is awkwardness or doubt, rewrite. For instance, the deskman who wrote this one would have detected the trap if he had *said* it:

VIETNAM VOTE: U.S. MIGHT WILL WIN

Decks

The purpose of a deck is to cope with a more complicated or important story where several news points have to be made in presentation. If there are not several news points, the deck has no function other than decoration. If there are separate news points, they should be given expression. It is a waste to use the space provided by headline decks for repeating the same information in several decks. Each deck, then, will have its own information, and each one will be based on a separate headline sentence. Only the first deck, however, needs to be completely self-contained. Once it has declared the subject area, the other decks can take that for granted and use the space to supplement and elaborate.

This being so, the most important task in writing decks is to decide the order of priority of news points and detail in the story. The first deck will carry the most important news point, simple and unadorned; the second deck may elaborate this with a significant detail, without repeating a single word; or it may add a further news point.

Occasionally you may be forced to repeat a word from a previous deck, but it is to be avoided as wasteful and irksome. It is better to repeat a word than descend to elegant variation; and it is altogether better to restructure the headline so that the space is used to effect. For instance:

ARSON PROBE AFTER £¾m TIMBER INFERNO 'Biggest London blaze since the war'

Whole streets in an area of North London were evacuated during the night as firemen fought the biggest blaze in the capital since the war. Today detectives started an arson probe into the £750,000 inferno. The blaze was in the timber yard of Bambergers (Timber and Plywood) Ltd, Tottenham. And today the chairman, Mr Cecil Bamberger, revealed: 'I have been told that about 9.30 last night an anonymous caller telephoned the yard and said there would be a fire.'

'Inferno' is an overworked headline word. The elegant variation 'blaze' adds further irritation. Of course, in

this second deck it would have been all right to have said: 'Biggest in London since the war', because the reader would carry from the first deck the knowledge that the subject was 'the inferno'. There is no need to repeat the information that the subject is a fire. But the best course here is to write a second deck elaborating the main deck: 'Mystery phone call to owners'.

Here are two good instances of properly constructed headlines in decks:

BIG DRUG HAUL BY YARD SQUAD LSD SEIZED IN LONDON HOUSE RAIDS WOMAN AND SIX MEN CHARGED

BOMB CLUE TO COMET CRASH DAMAGED CUSHION FIND SUGGESTS EXPLOSION 'OTHER EVIDENCE' OF SABOTAGE

Both the main decks would be meaningful if the subsidiary decks were lost. Both signal the main news. Both headlines, in the second deck, elaborate a missing point of interest. The drug headline goes on, in the third deck, to add an entirely different news point. The second deck of the plane headline continues to elaborate the main news point in the first deck—but still without repeating a single word. The second and third decks in the plane story would not make much sense without the main deck, though with it they elaborate effectively.

The reader understands quite well that each deck is a separate thought; that is the way decks function best and that is the way he reads them. What is quite wrong is to go against this functional and conventional pattern and write a headline which means reading on between separated deck:

DAMAGED CUSHION FIND IN Crashed Comet gives clue to disaster

But it is not enough to avoid such absurdities. The news must be digestible in a gulp from the main deck and it is confusing and irritating to have to read subsidiary decks before one can appreciate the significance of the main deck:

THE WAR IN VIETNAM New US Proposal

Opinion Headings

The worst form of confusion occurs in opinion headings.

'WE WILL NOT
DEVALUE'

The news is who is saying it—the Prime Minister of Britain or Chile? In this instance it was the Leader of the Opposition in Britain, a fact which should have been in the main deck because there it puts the statement in perspective. To withhold that vital information to the second deck or overline is careless and potentially misleading. Occasionally one set of quotes in one deck may pass if they are arresting, but this is exceptional. More typical is:

'INFLUENCE UPON
WEAK MIND'
'Censorship unless . . .
MP warns TV

The story here was that the BBC and ITV companies in Britain were being warned by an MP that unless they showed 'a little more moral responsibility' the state would be called on to intervene to protect public morals. He went on to say that television was a bad influence on weak minds. Nobody wanted censorship if it could be avoided, but liberty was not the same as licence.
These thoughts should be split like this:

MP WARNS BBC
AND ITV
'They are risking
censorship'

Overlines

These strictures on what the decks should say apply with equal stringency to overlines (the kickers, snappers, or eyebrows of America). Where there is a large headline preceded by a small overline it is the large headline which will be read first. The overline should be regarded, in its wording, as a second deck. For instance:

IF TALKS WITH
CHINA FAIL

This headline is not rescued by the presence of a small overline saying:

India tells what it will do. . . .

The overline should elaborate or supplement the main deck. Failure to do this really muddles the reader:

LATE CALL TO
SHIP, NOW HE'S
MISSING

Who, for heaven's sake? You had to read the small overline:

Young Wirral engineer overboard

Such overlines in fact are more trouble than they are worth. But let us try now to write a headline in two decks, the unit count of the top deck being 16, 16, and the second deck being one line of 20 units. Begin the headline task by noting down, in terse sentences, the two key points for the headlines:

> At the request of the Home Secretary (Mr James Callaghan), the Lord Chief Justice will issue fresh instructions to judges following the one-minute murder trial on Thursday. The instructions are expected to follow the lines of Home Office recommendations issued to the Director of Public Prosecutions and Chief Constables last year.
>
> In the Leeds case a man was sentenced to life imprisonment for murder without any of the evidence against him having been published at any stage. The case was not reported in the committal proceedings under the ban imposed by the controversial new Criminal Justice Act, which came into force on January 16.
>
> At the trial, after the man had pleaded guilty, the prosecution asked for permission to outline the facts, but the judge indicated that this would not be necessary.
>
> The Home Office instructions specifically meet the case of documentary committals where evidence is not given orally in the magistrates' court and the defendant then pleads Guilty in the higher court. In these circumstances the Home Secretary said it would be 'in the public interest that the prosecution should give a fairly full account of the facts after the defendant has pleaded guilty'.
>
> Mr John Boyd-Carpenter, Conservative MP for Kingston-upon-Thames, has put down a question to Sir Elwyn Jones, Attorney-

General, seeking amending legislation in view of the case at Leeds.

The Home Office attitude to the case is expected to be that if these instructions are followed then the Act will prove satisfactory in this respect. Certainly it seems at present that there is no intention of interceding any amending legislation.

If we wrote a headline sentence based on the first paragraph we would have something like 'Fresh instructions for judges after one-minute murder trial'. There are two troubles with this as the basis for the headline. Firstly, it does not tell us what is the intent of the 'fresh instructions'. Secondly, it presumes that the phrase 'one-minute murder trial' is sufficient in itself to remind everyone that the essence of it was that no outline of the case was given. What we want to tell the reader is that the Home Secretary is telling the judges through the Lord Chief Justice, that there should be no further instances where a man is sentenced without the facts being made public. This is what the story as a whole means; this is the news significance of it; it is around these ideas that we must build our headline. But though the headline thought is now specific enough to be meaningful it conveys too much for a single deck. Let us therefore split the headline thought into two sections:

1 The Home Secretary is stopping the possibility of convictions without publicity.
2 He is doing this by asking the Lord Chief Justice to give new guidance to judges.

We can abbreviate the first point to the sentence:

'Home Secretary to end trials without publicity'; but it is ambiguous and too long. We need to use the name 'Callaghan' for 'Home Secretary' and devise a crisper more accurate way of summing up 'trials without publicity'. That is a negative way of saying the details remain 'private': So we now want to say:

CALLAGHAN WILL END PRIVATE TRIALS

This meets the count requirements, being 16 and 14. We can improve the wording. 'Secret trials' is more colourful but perhaps takes the story too far. 'Silent trial' would be accurate and telling. Not until the first deck is written must you begin even to consider the second deck (or the third deck until the second is written, and so on).

The second deck must now deal with the secondary news point which was squeezed out of the first—how Callaghan proposed to act, which was by directions to the judges rather than an amendment of the Act.

The sentence is 'He gives directions to judges', which can be shortened to fit as:

Direction to Judges

If we had a second line to that deck (or a third deck) it would be as well to elaborate the main deck with the reminder that the fuss is based on a one-minute trial:

CALLAGHAN TO STOP SILENT TRIALS
Direction to Judges
after one-minute case

What we would not do is to write a split deck:

HOME SECRETARY WILL STOP
Private Trials

Impartiality

So much for the basic news structure of headlines. But before we turn to some of the detailed points which help to make headlines live, I must emphasise accuracy and impartiality as the most important basic constituents.

First, look at impartiality and ways of maintaining it. A news headline expresses the news, not the deskman's views. Curiously, in five years of provincial editorship, when I trained scores of sub-editors, this simple point was the one I never seemed able to put across.

There were moments, it was true, when there was a certain arresting quality about the result:

TEACH SEX TO NORTH-EAST BOYS' BRIGADES

Headlines which seem to put the newspaper solidly behind some outsiders' expressed opinion, however enticing, have no place in the news columns. The worst tendentious headlines seem to commit the newspaper to a particular political policy when in fact it may be merely reporting someone else's views:

STEEL BILL APPALLS WORLD

ELECTIONS NOW A CLEAR DUTY

This kind of editorialising must be avoided by using

quotes or naming an authority in the main deck of the headline. It is a simple mistake. More reprehensible still are the headlines where the writer lets either his cleverness or his prejudice run away with him:

'I'm not threatening',
Brown threatens

It is a step from this twisted headline writing to the odious practice of using loaded words in heads:

Smith gloats   Strikers whine
over racial   for more time
policy

The headline writer must put his personal opinions aside. He is there to reflect as accurately as possible the content of the story. The headline writer is neither for nor against. He is neutral—and when he is headlining a controversial debate in Parliament or Senate in a dispute of any kind, he should be balanced in his choice of points for the headlines. Some of the trouble arises because the headline writer is hypnotised by a good headline phrase. The Conservatives at one local council attacked a Labour airfield project as a 'white elephant' so when the decision was reached the sub-editor wrote:

Thornaby Labour men
back white elephant

This headline seemed to accept the 'white elephant' tag without question. Even with quotes around 'white elephant' it would hardly have been a fair headline because the words are so strongly biased (despite their merit of suggesting controversy).

Placing the Quotes

Quotes are, of course, one of the devices for dealing with strong opinions in headlining speeches. How you give the authority for the opinion—and authority you must give—depends in part on the news value.

When you have a famous speaker, it is right to put his name in the first line or main deck. There are several ways of doing this:

Wilson says victory in sight
Wilson: Victory in sight
End in sight – Wilson
'We'll win', says Wilson
'Rhodesia weaker' – Wilson

Headlines entirely in quotes are weak and should always be avoided when the people involved are important. But all-quotes headlines are weak even for good speeches by unknowns, because it is rare that three or four words of quotes are so sparkling that they deserve such prominence. A better way is to reserve the quotes—single quotes always—for that part of the headline which needs them:

Benn attacks US 'bait' for scientists

The authority for the quotes can be implied:

Judge 'astounds'
car-park chief

It is clear here that the car-park chief has said the judge 'astounds' him. The alternative way of conveying this information is much weaker in an all-quotes headline, or in a headline where a longer version of the quotation squeezes relevant information out of the headline:

'I am astounded by   'I am astounded',
judge's remarks'   says car-park chief

There is one other device for indicating authority, which is to make it clear that an audience is involved and someone is speaking:

RHODESIA
GUILTY,
UN TOLD

Where the headline is in decks, the attribution is often given in the second deck, which is bad practice. An opinionated headline, unquoted, cannot be made acceptable by putting an attribution in a second deck. Attributions must be contained in the same deck as assertions, otherwise the statement in the first deck seems to have the authority of the newspaper for it:

DISTORTION OVER
EEC POLICY
Lord Chalfont's charge

The correct way of writing this headline would be one of the following:

CHALFONT SAYS EEC
POLICY DISTORTED
'DISTORTION' OVER
EEC POLICY
Lord Chalfont's charge

I should add there is no need for quotes or attribution of any kind when the opinion is obviously the opinion of the newspaper (i.e. in its leading articles) or the individual writer whether critic or columnist. It is unnecessary to quote the opinionated headline of a critic's review of a performance of the Barber of Seville, thus:

Youthful
tenor sang
'delightfully'

This merely sounds as if the critic has relayed some gossip in the gallery or intends some subtle innuendo.

Taste and Tact

Another source of deplorable partiality in headlines is in refining the subject, the 'who' of the story. The headline writer naturally wants to say something more precise than 'man' or 'woman', but this sometimes leads him into persecuting a minority on grounds of race, colour, religion or national origin. These identifications may sometimes be strictly relevant to the story. This is rare. The test is simple: They should only be used when the *story would be meaningless without them*. They should not be used indiscriminately and especially they should not be used on court reports.

In discussions with fellow editors who take a different view I have never had a satisfactory answer for the question why only one minority, one race or religion, is identified in the headline. Why, for instance, a newspaper which headlines a court story 'Pakistani jailed six months' should fail to head its other court stories 'Irishman jailed six months', 'Jew jailed six months', 'White Catholic jailed six months', and so on. Headlines like this are unfair and they are also an encouragement to selective perception, and thereby to prejudice. The *New York Times* style book has this to say:

'People in the news should not be identified by race, colour, religion or national origin unless such identifications are pertinent in the news context. Although "Negro" in a segregation story and "Hungarian" in a refugee story are perfectly proper, in contexts where such designations are not relevant they tend to be invidious. We should not write of an American, "O'Rourke, a lean, white-haired, red-faced, blue-eyed, Irishman of 57...." "Irishman" may seem to slip through the typewriter innocuously, but you wouldn't dream of writing "Carmine de Sapio, a tall, gray at the temples, dark-spectacled Italian". Identifications of that kind are irrelevant and conceivably offensive.'

Headlines must be compassionate as well as fair. There is no need to be mealy-mouthed. 'Passed away' is a euphemism that has rightly passed away, though the *New York Times* still announces that so-and-so has 'succumbed'. But 'dies in fire' is enough without the appearance of gloating produced by 'roasted alive'. The headline wording must not only be accurate; it must also have a sense of appropriateness for the story. Funny headlines do not sit happily on sombre events: it is wrong to indulge in puns when the subject is death, injury, physical affliction or religion. When the new superintendent of an Arkansas jail discovered a mysterious graveyard in the grounds, it was reported by *The Times* of London: 'The most appalling aspect of this ghoulish affair is that three graves identified by a long-term convict have produced three bodies. As things stand at the moment it is almost impossible to exaggerate the prospect of further horrors'. The language was well chosen, and the jokey headings produced by *The Times* (the first two heads below) and *Mirror* were self-consciously and tastelessly bright:

Burialsville
Grim search for the bodies of
200 murdered prisoners

Grisly secrets of 'Bodiesburg'

When a ship capsized in harbour in New Zealand, with forty-nine deaths, the *Daily Mirror* rather gaily headlined its picture 'The ship that died so gracefully'. And there is inaptness about the way the Darlington evening headlined the news that lung cancer is killing more people in County Durham every year:

Durham smashes record for lung cancer deaths

Accuracy

The headline must be accurate in its details and true to the meaning of the whole report. It is easy to escalate the meaning of the story by choosing the wrong heading: 'Worst unemployment rate in country', said the headline. The story said: 'One of the highest unemployment rates...' which is not the same thing. 'Boots take over Timothy Whites' said the headline when the bid had been made, but before the deal had gone through. On a story about a court delaying a pay rise by three months it was inaccurate to write 'Court cancels pay rise'.

The Press Council in Britain has given some useful judgments on standards in headlines and a good reference source is *The Press Council*, by H Phillip Levy (London: Macmillan, 1967). The Council, for instance, rightly upheld complaints where mild criticism has been headlined 'slammed' or 'lashed'. It has insisted that a headline should be wholly true to the purport of the text and not merely to part of it. When Viscount Amory, for instance, made a speech reviewing the advantages and disadvantages of Britain entering the Common Market, and coming down in favour of entry, the *Daily Express* was reported to the Press Council for headlining the speech: 'Amory lets it out—Common Market will bring painful changes'. The Press Council ruled that it was misleading to focus on one part of his speech which did not, in the end, represent his considered conclusion. In another case, the *Eastern Evening News* reported an inquest on AB, a professional footballer who died from injuries received in a road collision under the headline: 'AB had been drinking, inquest told'. The report, however, said that the medical evidence was given that the alcohol content of his blood was not unduly high, and the Press Council ruled that the headline was grossly careless.

Striving for effect in a headline has led other newspapers into censure. The report of the death of a baby was headlined in the *Scottish Daily Express* 'Baby killed by "bottle of orange"'. The story clearly stated that the child died after he had been seen to play with an orange-juice bottle which had been used to hold liquid weedkiller. Manufacturers complained that the headline was misleading. The Editor submitted that as the words 'bottle of orange'

were in quotes it should have been clear to the reader that the expression was not what it appeared to be. But the Press Council agreed that the headline was undoubtedly misleading, that the child had been poisoned by weedkiller and 'orange' had nothing to do with the tragedy.

The *Daily Herald* was censured for saying 'Non-union men built union club' when, in fact, only one or two of the builders were non-union men and they had been persuaded to join the union while the work went on. Care should be taken with nouns used as adjectives. Relatives complained when *The Northern Echo* used the headline phrase 'Drug woman' for an inquest on a woman found dead from narcotic poisoning'. The implication, they said, was that she was a drug addict and she was not. As Editor, I thought that complaint justified.

As they tread their way through these undoubted perils the more experienced deskmen will also watch for the ribald gremlin who lurks in every sub-editors' room, introducing double meaning into the chastest subject:

Builders scan virgin far north

There is little I can do to protect you except to caution you always to read the headline to yourself and to add perhaps that some of the choicest do seem genuine Freudian slips. As the Texas paper said:

Woman hurt while cooking her husband's breakfast in a horrible manner

3 How the News Headline Says It

Good headlines are written in vigorous, conversational idiomatic language. Good headlines should be capable of being read aloud—which the mind does subconsciously.
—ARTHUR CHRISTIANSEN

Having discussed the general principles of news and accuracy which are the foundations of the headline, we now examine some of the detailed techniques for making the headline effective. Let us, first, however, dispense with Helen of Troy, whom we left with G K Chesterton at the beginning of the last chapter. 'How Helen did the House-keeping' is an acceptable headline on the feature text in mind there, but it is not the kind of headline we shall spend most of the time discussing. It does not tell us how Helen did the housekeeping. It only holds out the promise that the text will. It does not inform. It tempts. The distinction of the hard news headline is that it always gives information. How to give the crucial information quickly and intelligibly within the confines of a column is the major skill of news headline writing.

The Helen type of headline is more appropriate for the longer feature or news-in-depth piece, where the aim is not to give immediate information but to explore, discuss or relate a rich narrative whose ideas are too complex and diffuse to be done justice by a hard news headline focused on a single key point. There are a few other occasions when you will want to write a Helen type headline in the news columns, to use temptation rather than information. It will never happen with a real news story where the emphasis is on quick communication of information—where the information is a real attraction to the reader.

But on lighter stories in the news columns it may be better for a change of pace to write 'Why the General saw red' rather than 'painted flagpole angers General'. That might be enough for many readers without their reading further; and the hard news heading might also seem to give such newspaper trivia an undue ring of importance.

A better guide for news headlines than Helen of Troy is the old newspaper adage 'Man bites dog'. It is not merely a good story. It is also a good headline, in its own right, for reasons I will adduce.

It may seem odd to be writing about 'the headline' when you consider the rich and often comic differences in the headlines of different newspapers. The headline writer stands in the middle between the newspaper's sense of its identity with its attitudes to life and news, and the newspaper's audience with its levels of education and knowledge.

It is not surprising that newspapers sometimes disagree about what is the most important feature of a news report, still less that they find themselves expressing this in different tones. 'Mr Charles Chaplin returns', says one in the manner of a butler at a banquet. Another shouts 'Charlie's back!' But the differences in news selection and even in tone do not mean there are two sets of opposing principles for headline writing. All good news headlines follow certain rules, in what they say and how they say it. What they say is the single most urgent news point (as the newspaper sees it), accurately, intelligibly, and impartially. How they say it varies much less than appears.

Verbs

For instance, here are some headlines which say the same news point in different ways—but there is something common in the construction of all these headlines and you should see if you can spot what it is. There are three pairs of headlines for three separate stories, and in each case the 'serious' headline is on the left and the 'popular' headline on the right.

Radio relay satellite put in orbit by US	Up goes 'flying post office'
Students challenge de Gaulle's rule	Danny the Red humbles de Gaulle
Benn accuses US firm	US atom brain poachers warned

The popular papers were trying to emphasise the personal, dramatic or romantic elements. But every headline had a single common characteristic—a verb. News is activity and a verb represents action. It could be an excellent rule always to have a verb in the headline: but there are occasions when it is better to include the verb by implication, rather than by statement, and others when a rich phrase without a verb may be preferred (*see* pp. 44–5).

But these are the exceptions. Headlines must live. Most headlines without a verb are only half alive. They tell the reader nothing and produce an effect of dullness and monotony: no news today. The deadest kind of news headline is the simple generalised label:

FRANCE AND
THE
CONCORDE
AMERICAN VIEWS
ON CHINA

Well, thinks the reader, get on with it, what about France and the Concorde? What are America's views on China? There always have been American views on China; what the headline should be telling is what is new or significant about them.

This kind of no-news label turns up most frequently in newspapers setting headlines in decks (though it need not):

BRITISH
DEFENCE
POLICY
Navy League's
proposals

Again we learn nothing, but if we force a verb into this headline we force in news. This fits the same shape available:

NAVY LEAGUE
SEEKS SWITCH
IN DEFENCE

The second deck is now free for a detailed point of news. By introducing the verb we have gained in urgency—and in economy. Look at these from a leading provincial daily and an American paper:

ALTERNATIVE TO   VIETNAM PEACE
STATE OWNED   MISSION
STEEL   China's refusal
Support from
Mr Strauss

By reading both decks here we do eventually get to the news, but what a tedious route. Both could be made active headlines.

STRAUSS
BACKS   CHINA REFUSES
PRIVATE   VIETNAM TALKS
STEEL PLAN

Again notice how we have said actively in one deck what the previous wording took two decks to say inactively. Sometimes the two-deck headline can be revived simply by transposing an active second deck into the first deck:

RUSSIA'S   KOSYGIN
DESIRE FOR   WARNS
PEACE   CHINESE
Kosygin warns   'Russia is firm
Chinese   for peace'

It is odd the way the label has persisted. It does not follow naturally from regarding a headline as a truncated sentence. It is an artificial form, a legacy from a more pompous age. Who would ever dream of transmitting news verbally in the way these headlines do in print:

CLIMBER'S   GREEK PURGE
400 Ft   OF CIVIL
DEATH FALL   SERVICE

It is much more natural and fresh to write as you would say:

CLIMBER   GREEKS PURGE
DIES IN   CIVIL
400ft FALL   SERVICE

Active verbs

It follows that if the verb is the secret of the active headline, it should be the most active verb which fits the facts. If the verb is weak, the headline is weak. The normal headline has no room for adjectives. Its colour and spice must come from a rich verb. If a wife goes to court to make an emotional appeal for her husband, who has not stopped after a road crash, it is too pallid when you say in the headline 'Wife asks judge for leniency'. A livelier and more informative headline might be: 'Wife pleads for hit-and-run driver'. The verb 'pleads' gives an immediate and arresting impression of what happened; and the construction of the headline then allows room for the added information that he is a hit-and-run driver.

A verb is better than no verb, but vague portmanteau

verbs will not do. Avoid, for instance, saying: 'Archbishop gives views on racial policy' when what the Archbishop has done is *condemn* the policy in vigorous terms. Do not say 'Lorry damages shop' when in fact the lorry has *wrecked* the shop completely. (And vice versa.) Avoid when you can, using parts of the weak verb 'to be' and 'to have' as the main verbs in headlines. A headline gains in strength when a stronger verb is used:

Istanbul has earthquake   Earthquake rocks Istanbul

Tory is out   Tory beaten

Nor are parts of the verb 'to be' and 'to have' needed as auxiliaries. An intelligible headline is often much more emphatic without them. For instance, 'Jones arrested' is more urgent than 'Jones is arrested', and 'Miners told to quit' is better than 'Miners are told to quit'.

There will be occasions, too, when the verb 'to be' should be omitted even though this seems to leave the headline without a verb. In headlines like this the verb 'to be' is clearly implied:

> TOWN HALL (is)
> IN DANGER
>
> POLICE (are) IN
> GUN DRAMA
>
> (There is) TWO-STAGE PLAN FOR SAIGON
> PEACE
>
> (There is) BITTER MOOD IN PANAMA
> ELECTION
>
> (There are) SHADOWS OVER PARIS TALKS

Present and future tense

A further point about the verb in the headline may already be apparent. The headlines have used the present tense to describe events that have already happened. There are good reasons for this. First, the present tense is active. It puts the reader into the middle of the action. It gives him a feeling of participation. Secondly, the event may be past, but it is recent past, and the reader is learning of it for the first time. He perfectly well understands the convention and will imply from a present-tense headline that the event occurred within the publishing time of the newspaper: that a headline in the present tense in his morning newspaper is presenting the news of yesterday. Similarly a weekly newspaper is understood to be presenting the news of the week and may use present tense for the events of the week. There is a point at which it will no longer do. It cannot be used in a report of a court case based on earlier events where it would suggest that the offence was being committed again: 'Baker sold loaves underweight', not 'Baker sells loaves underweight'. And clearly any heading with a past time element built into it must carry past tense in agreement: 'Attlee backed Truman in 1946 dispute'. (Further, there is one headline construction, of which more later, which reports even contemporaneous events in the past tense: 'The girl who hid under the bed'.)

The way the tenses are used may be illustrated by an imaginary example. A speaker who on Thursday denounces a current dock dispute may properly on Friday be headlined: 'Dockers strike for selfish reasons, says union leader'.

His remarks were made the day before, but they earn the present tense. Imagine now that the dockers' dispute had ended a few days before. The union leader's remarks would then be headlined: 'Dockers struck for selfish reasons, says union leader'. To have retained the form 'dockers strike' would have suggested the strike was still continuing, or that the union leader was referring to a more general attitude of dockers. Past time is rarely specified. 'Yesterday', for instance, is a word almost never justified in a morning paper headline because almost every item could be headed 'yesterday' and the reader, anyway, takes it for granted it was yesterday.

But since a newspaper's future is infinite, it is generally best to specify future time: 'Dockers will strike tomorrow/next week/next month'. Note here how the omission of 'will' could still imply future tense, thanks to the specific future date.

Most headlines are in the present or future tense. Deaths happen in the present: 'Mayor dies' is better than 'Mayor has died', or, of course, 'Death of Mayor'. But there is one caution; it would be macabre to add a time reference to such a headline: 'Mayor dies today'.

After a death, headline references to the person naturally carry past tense—except that a headline on a will may be present tense, since the legacy when declared is a contemporary act: 'Johnson bequeaths park to town'.

There is, by the way, a bonus in using the present tense: it is shorter. To say 'lorry rammed shop' needs $2\frac{1}{2}$ more units than 'lorry rams shop'.

The active voice

But above all prefer the active voice to the passive. In other words, write headlines with somebody saying something or doing something, rather than having it told to them or done to them. 'Boy falls into well' is what people say and what deskmen should write as a headline, rather than this published but unnatural back-to-front headline:

FALL INTO WELL
INJURES BOY

Compare the active voice with the wordier passive version:

U S DEMANDS RELEASE OF SEIZED SHIP
RELEASE OF SEIZED SHIP DEMANDED BY U S

WILSON AUTHORISES FRESH TALKS WITH RHODESIA

FRESH TALKS WITH RHODESIA AUTHORISED BY WILSON

Notice how the passive voice breeds extra words, excess weight which exhausts the headline. Given the same headline constituents, the active voice can say more. Rejecting a passive construction can lead to a more vivid construction altogether, because it may offer a chance to exploit a gain in headline units.

For instance:

WOMAN FOUND DEAD BY HUSBAND

'Husband finds woman dead' is the active voice. This more direct approach immediately opens up other possibilities. 'Wife' is a shorter word than 'woman' and also shows that she is married. There may be room for a better headline altogether:

CITY BANKER FINDS WIFE DEAD

or

MAN FINDS WIFE DEAD IN CAR

Sometimes, on a tight unit count, the gain in units from using the active voice is not enough to retain all the headline constituents or give more, and it is necessary to write a passive head giving less information.

VIOLENCE FEARED BY WASHINGTON AS POOR MARCH

(Passive and too many units)

WASHINGTON FEARS VIOLENCE AS POOR MARCH

(Active and shorter but still just too long)

VIOLENCE FEARED AS POOR MARCH

(Passive but fits by omission of Washington)

News is paramount

In seeking to use the active voice, there is one important qualification. As I indicated earlier (p. 17) the deskman should strive to bring the news point as near to the beginning of the headline as possible. For instance, 'U.S. Survey finds Red Aid to Hanoi totals 3 billion' is a badly delayed headline with attribution of secondary importance coming first—an attribution not worth the emphasis it gains from leading a headline in the active voice (an altogether better head which indicates the news by concentrating on a specific point in this story, is 'Russians send 10,000 heavy guns to North Vietnam'). There are occasions when the injunction to bring in the news point early overrides the injunction to use the active voice. These are the times when rigorous insistence on using the active voice would mean distorting the news emphasis. They are not frequent. They usually occur when the subject is much less significant than the predicate—when what has been done to this individual or nation or company is more important than who has been doing it. In these instances, there should be no hesitation in starting the headline with the predicate and using the passive voice:

MAYOR KILLED BY FALLING STONE

FALLING STONE KILLS MAYOR

The first is passive and wordy, but it is quicker with news than the second. It has the verb and the whole of the news in the first line. For the same reason 'Banker fined' is preferable to 'Court fines Banker' or 'Luther King shot at motel' is better than 'Unknown gunman shoots Luther King'.

Lack of information in the text can also reinforce the claims of the passive construction. No one would write 'Strangler strangles schoolgirl'; and 'Killer strangles schoolgirl', though active, is also tautological. 'Schoolgirl strangled at riverside' has better news emphasis.

Subject omitted

So far I have argued that we want a verb; a verb in the present tense; and, as a rule, a verb in the active voice.

Considering the headline as an edited sentence leads us now to another important element: the subject of the sentence, the 'who' of the headline. Failure to appreciate that the headline is really a truncated, but still meaningful, sentence, and that the reader understands it as such, is the reason for the appalling habit, spread from North America, of writing headlines where the subject is casually omitted and the headline begins on a verb. This has grown not from any urgent theory about bringing in the verb first, but because it is easier to make a heading fit if you can drop the subject. It is indeed easier—easier on the deskman but harder on the reader. A headline is not a choice number of words arbitrarily bolted together. It has its own integrity. It is a crisper version of the way we communicate by speech and prose. In prose we omit the subject (though it is understood) only for injunctions or commands. To do the same thing for a narrative headline in the present tense is to do violence to the language:

Hunt H-bombs
in Greenland

What does that convey? It is a command. The reader is to go off and hunt H-bombs in Greenland. But what the headline was trying to say was that American air force search parties were already looking for H-bombs in Greenland. 'Airmen seek lost H-bombs' would have made sense and it would have fitted. Even Robert Garst and Theodore Bernstein in their excellent little book *Headlines and Deadlines* (New York: Columbia University Press, 1961) argue that the subject-less headline is valid. The contention is that only the subject-less headline can cope with a story like this:

STEALS PISTOL TO END LIFE
Jobless stenographer arrested for
taking policeman's revolver

It would not be possible, they say, to write a main deck which would include the subject without sacrificing the news. I have three comments on this. First, headlines exist to serve the news and not the other way round. If a story is so difficult—with a word like 'stenographer', say—then a good managing editor or layout man will change the page so that a meaningful headline can be written. Secondly, if one is going to write a headline without a subject it should not be done merely by writing the full headline ('Stenographer steals pistol to end life' and then deleting the excess word 'Stenographer'). Indeed,

'End Life' in the subject-less headline does not make it clear whose life it is. And, thirdly, it is possible in this instance to write an acceptable headline, admittedly with a compound noun, but none the less a headline which is intelligible and tells more of the story than the subject-less heading:

GIRL STOLE GUN FOR SUICIDE

More often the subject-less heading has not even the superficial validity of that example. For instance:

DOUBTS JERSEY READY
FOR HEART TRANSPLANT

Who has the doubts is surely part of the news. It happens to be a heart surgeon, an associate professor of surgery at the New Jersey College of Medicine. Surely it would be better to write a headline with a subject:

SURGEON CAUTIONS STATE
ON HEART TRANSPLANTS

On one point I will agree with Garst and Bernstein. If you are engaged on a newspaper which accepts subject-less headlines, you must immediately bring in the subject as the first word of the second deck if you are to avoid the ambiguity shown here (top example), which at first glance suggests an infant prodigy:

KNOCKS OUT BIG THIEF
New Born Baby Inspired Him
Says Ambitious Policeman

KNOCKS OUT BIG THIEF
Policeman Seeking Promotion
says Baby Inspired Him

Who's Who

The subject should be there. How you describe the 'who' of the story is a matter for further discussion. There are all sorts of ways. John Jones, say, is at once a Welshman, a baker, a Unitarian, a driver, a father, a golfer, a man, an objector to a road proposal, a rescuer in a river accident, or simply 'he'. Which of the words you use to describe him in the headline must in part depend on the nature of the news. I have already criticised the practice (fairly common in Britain, rare in the United States) of identifying racial and religious minorities in pejorative headlines. A man's name will also rarely be used in the headline: it has to mean something to readers. Thus 'Mr Jones protests at shop closing hours' says less than 'Baker protests at shop closing hours'. If Mr Jones the baker is chased by a bull while playing golf he would become 'Golfer chased', rather than 'Baker chased' since the latter headline would give the impression the bull was in his bakery. A man's name should, of course, be used in the headline when it gives authority to the news. The headline in a national daily:

MP says it is time for Mr Brown to go.

read oddly with the story because the MP was a celebrated Mr Duncan Sandys, a former Minister.

If the name is known, use the name and not other titles —retaining the definite article for *the* Queen, *the* Pope. If there is doubt about whether a man is well enough known, the good deskman will use a title, since his doubt will become a certainty for the average reader. But there is one exception to this: to err generously on the side of headlining the name in an obituary. The most important piece of information is who has died, and it is contortion that produces a headline such as:

HE LED JUNGLE
GUERILLAS

when the news is

CHE GUEVERA
SHOT DEAD

There is a middle course, which is to give both the name and the achievement:

FLEMING
(he gave world
penicillin)
DIES AT 73

The 'he did this or the other' headline is justified only when it concerns the death of a person who has become obscure but who once did something outstanding or bizarre: 'He rode Niagara Falls in a barrel'. Otherwise, stick to names in obituaries. Almost as fatuous as the 'he did' variety are the formulae:

Famous Manchester-born   Death of well-known
comedian dies   Cheshire peer

These confuse the purpose of a headline with the pur-

pose of a sale bill (*see* pp. 96–8). The concealment of the name on the bill may induce people to buy the paper. In the page it does not invite them to read it.

The weakest form of subject in a headline is 'he' or 'she'. It is not an identification.

He forecasts a
30 hour work
week soon

That story, in a big daily, turned out to be about a Labour MP and former Cabinet Minister. 'MP' would have been more specific and would have given the headline more authority. The simple subject pronoun 'he' is more acceptable over a picture: 'He will run car factory'. There is no doubt who the 'he' is. The convention is that the overline refers to the content of the picture. Here the picture helps to identify the subject. How absurd, then, for the overline to begin with a possessive noun:

His post with car firm

The writer failed to appreciate the connection between a headline and a grammatical sentence. And, of course, the picture did not show 'his post'; it showed the man.

There is a rule for identification. 'Man' or 'woman', for instance, are weak, though sometimes inevitable. 'Wife, father, mother, husband', are better because they narrow the field—always provided the story is something to do with the individuals as wives, fathers, and so on. It is not good practice, for instance, to use the word 'husband' as another word for 'man' or 'driver' when the fact that he is married has nothing to do with the story.

HUSBAND
BANNED
AT RACES

This suggests his wife can go in and he has been barred —it could even be for some matrimonial reason. But, given that the specific description does not introduce a distortion into our understanding of the story, always prefer the specific. Do not say 'child' in a headline if the child is not yet two. Say 'baby'. For instance:

Terrorists kill young Israeli

'Young' is too vague. The story is that terrorists killed a three-and-a-half-year-old boy. 'Israeli boy' would have been better here, and altogether better:

Raiders kill Israeli boy of 3

There is one final device affecting the subject in the headline. This is the construction of headlines beginning 'the man . . . who'. This formula is acceptable when identification is important:

> The man with bright ideas
> does it again for £1,000

It is more appealing to say 'the man with bright ideas' than 'factory worker', or the man's name which is not widely known. It suggests that he is interesting beyond his windfall. 'The man who' formula can also be used on headlines over pictures of the subject or on lighter stories where the headline relaxes:

> The boy who pulled out a tooth
> with an E-type Jaguar

The odd circumstance can itself be enough to justify this, but not always. The implication of this style of headline is that the reader is going to be given extra details about the subject, and so it will not do on a news report which merely states a fact without elaborating any personal details. For instance, the heading 'The one in ten who fails at university' will not do on a story reporting that one in ten fails at university when it tells us nothing else about these people.

Be Specific

The vaguer the description the duller the head. What, for instance, is there in this to make the skimmer of the headlines stop and read the story:

> DEVELOPMENT PLAN
> HELD UP

Every rebuilding story could be headed 'Development', just as the architect's model of a redevelopment scheme could be headed, as I once saw it, 'Development in miniature'. Nobody is interested in 'development', but they are interested in new schools, roads, shops, banks, parking garages, swimming pools. They are interested in specifics, in short, and not the abstract and the general. The head 'Development Plan held up' was on a story which really said:

> NEW SCHOOL
> DELAYED

'Plan' itself, of course, is another headline killer. It is so general, so vague, so meaningless:

> £500,000 plan
> inquiry

Figures rarely sing in heads. This head seems quite remote from the real world of the reader. In fact the story announced that there was to be a public inquiry into a proposal to build an hotel costing £500,000 near York Minster—an hotel, with a shopping precinct and a bank. Any one of those specifics—hotel, shops, Minster— would have sent a signal to the reader. Always look for the specific which will illuminate a head, which will give you an instant picture of the activity: not that someone has a 'big new appointment', but what it involves; not 'river accident' or 'road tragedy' or 'daring raid', but what happened. For instance:

> CITY
> GANG
> MAKE
> BIG HAUL

might be anything from stealing the Crown Jewels to robbing the Bank of England. Contrast the interest of the head based on the real specific activity in that story:

> GANG ROBS
> 400
> PARKING
> METERS

These injunctions apply especially strongly to headlining speeches. It is never enough to say 'Opposition attacks Government'. That is what we expect. Only by pinpointing the detail can the headline writer hope to provoke interest. Abstracts fail:

> Incentive and reward must
> be order of day,
> says Sir Alec

One way of seeing this is a washout as a head is by applying the test of reversing the meaning. If the reversed meaning surprises and alerts, the original head fails. And, of course, it does. It would be news if a Conservative leader attacked incentives and rewards: indeed if anybody did in so many words. Yet in the speech which carried this empty head there were specific promises which were the news and which in the head would make most people stop and read the story:

> Tories will cut 'crippling'
> income tax,
> says Sir Alec

Another source of the wan, generalised head is the

conference report, or the report putting together a number of different stories:

MANY TOPICS   MPs' WEEK OF
AT TEACHERS'   CONTENTION
CONFERENCE

But there is rarely any justification for the deskman reaching for the blunderbuss. This kind of head is really cowardice in the face of generality: if the reporter has failed to make the judgment on what is the most important topic the deskman must do it for him:

Teachers will debate school meals

MPs to press on Rhodesia

The reader perfectly well understands that this may not be the only thing teachers or MPs will debate. It is not the total truth of the gatherings, but it is accurate and it means something. Almost always in the undergrowth of waffle there is a specific head fact waiting to be brought down. Here are two more blunderbuss heads:

SPATE OF   RESCUERS'
RESCUES AND   BRAVERY
FLOODS   AWARDS

The deskman who takes aim on one piece of action can always write a more fetching head:

GIRL DIVES
TO RESCUE
IN RIVER

Saying where

The injunction to be specific means specific about genuine news and not about irrelevancies. Of these the most intrusive in the headline is the location of the news; the 'where' of the story. It should only be included when the location is an integral, rather than incidental, part of the news, and this should be the rule for local as well as national newspapers. Where something happened is usually less newsy than what happened. Including in the last headline the fact that the river is at Newcastle would crowd out part of the news already there—and to what purpose? (I will go a little further into the considerations for local newspapers in a moment.)

It is normally said that foreign stories should carry locations and home stories should not. This is some help, but it needs refining: How specific a foreign location? And when does a domestic place name warrant inclusion in the head? The real test must be whether including the

place name adds significance. It is normally enough to say 'Czechs investigate Masaryk's death' without adding that the inquiry is going on in Prague. There is clearly no need to say 'De Gaulle condemns rioters in Paris speech'. It will do just to say 'De Gaulle condemns rioters'. Normally where someone makes a speech does not matter. What matters is the content of the speech, and a foreign name in the head is sufficient clue that the riots referred to are not English. Yet again the rule of significance does from time to time necessitate inclusion of a precise foreign place name. When de Gaulle made his speech in Quebec advocating French nationalism it was essential to the headline to say that he made it in Quebec. The fact that he addressed French Canadians in this way in a French-speaking city while a guest of the Canadian Government was not incidental to the news: it was an integral part of it. Again, the headline 'Vietcong raid city' is unsatisfactory when the news is that the Vietcong have raided the capital city of Saigon.

Some locations qualify for headline status at once; others emerge into it as they come into the news because the essence of the news is territorial. For instance, the valley known as Khe Sanh in Vietnam: it was right to headline the news 'Air Cavalry relieve Khe Sanh' because it had become a focal point. 'Air Cavalry relieve hill post' would have failed to tell the news.

The test of significance should be carried over into home and local news. It is right for a national paper to headline a story 'Epidemic moves into Cheshire' because *where* foot-and-mouth disease spreads is itself the news. A local paper would be right to refine that further, since doing so would add significance for local readers: 'Foot-and-mouth spreads to Tarporley farm'. But I would suggest that local papers should pause before automatically thrusting locations into headlines irrespective of significance. The theory is that local readers will be drawn to the story because it has a local place name. For sports stories there are special considerations (see p. 52), but the practice of place names in every news head needs rather more than custom to justify it.

Broadly, there are two types of local paper: those circulating in a limited local area, usually evening and weekly newspapers in Britain; and those circulating in a wide area, over two or three counties for an English provincial morning or part of a state, say, in the United States or India.

If the paper with a concentrated circulation area is doing its job properly and cramming the inside pages with local news, its readers should safely be able to assume that headlines there automatically refer to local news. There is no need to labour the fact by putting in the town every time. Moreover by encouraging the reader in this assumption, by proper grouping of the news, the headlines can be made to work harder. Without monotonous repetition of place names, heads are at once livelier and there is more space to say something meaningful.

Now consider the paper circulating over a wider area. When I joined *The Northern Echo*—which sells rather more than 110,000 copies over three Northern counties— it was a rule that local place names should be in the headings. I had two thoughts about this. First, the local name was only local to a limited number of people in each wide edition area: in other words by including the local name we were as likely to repel as many readers as we attracted, or even more. I believe this consideration applies to regional papers, circulating over a large area, anywhere in the world. Secondly, it is undoubtedly true that local names in heads give an inhibiting and parochial air when the stories themselves are in fact good enough to survive on their genuine news merits.

Elwick man on murder charge: Remanded again at Hartlepool

This was a story which might have been headlined:

Farm worker of 21 denies murdering teacher

Again, 'Two-car crash at Middlesbrough' might have been headed: 'Baby escapes unhurt in two-car crash'. And when a good headline also has a place name, does the place name really ignite more interest? 'PC bitten by howling Alsatian' is enough for most people wherever they live; the addition of 'at Gateshead' can be something of an anti-climax. Of course, none of these considerations applies where the place name is part of the news—where something is to happen to an area. For instance, it is clearly essential to say 'State aid for Teesside airport' or 'Start soon on Tyne Tunnel'. But these again are place names which meet the general test of adding significance: they would be included in the heads of a national paper, too. For these reasons I believe that local and regional newspapers everywhere should consider most carefully the policy of location headlines. I can say that at *The Northern Echo* the omission of place-names was not followed by cancellations; on the contrary, circulation continued its gratifying rise.

Be Positive

Be specific, then: but also be positive. Some stories must carry a negative statement in the headline ('Dockers refuse pay offer'), but there is nothing more deadening than a series of abominable 'No' headlines, which merely say 'No news today'.

NO CLUES REPORTED ON MISSING BANKER

New York City Police yesterday reported 'no luck' in their hunt for a missing Lockport banker and attorney who disappeared from his home on August 26. 'We've got no clues', said a Missing Persons Bureau spokesman in the search for 44-year-old Joseph Thomas Symes, married and the father of three. 'The mystery just gets deeper', etc.

NO RECORD IN DUBLIN

Alan Simpson, the United Kingdom mile record holder, produced another blistering finish to win the international mile event in three minutes 56·9 seconds at the John F Kennedy Stadium last night. But any hopes of the Yorkshireman breaking Michel Jazy's recently set world record of three minutes 53·6 seconds faded on a slow second lap.

These are different types of 'No' stories. That on the top would clearly be news if there were a clue. The other depends for its justification on the degree of expectation of Simpson breaking the record. But both could convey their information more positively, the Simpson headline by highlighting the 3 seconds from a record:

MYSTERY OF MISSING BANKER GROWS

SIMPSON 3·3 OFF RECORD

If the line about the mystery had not been in the banker story the head could still have been expressed without the direct negative: 'Police draw blank on missing banker'. In the sports story, the 3·3 will be understood in its context—but it would be necessary in editing the text to write in that Simpson missed the record by 3·3 seconds. The text should immediately support the head without the reader having to do a calculation. The most frequent source of a 'no' head is the denial story:

Jackpots 'not down'

Mr William Testo, the Bingo King, yesterday denied housewives' complaints that he had lowered his jackpots since thieves robbed him of the biggest jackpot of all—£4,000.

Epidemic 'is not threat to meat'

A report that the foot-and-mouth epidemic was threatening the domestic meat supply was described by the Minister of Agriculture yesterday as premature.

Both those stories could carry the news more actively and positively:

'BINGO KING'   MEAT SUPPLY IS
ANSWERS WIVES   STILL SAFE

Most heads containing the off-putting 'no' or 'not' can, on inspection, have their news expressed more positively.

ROCKEFELLER NOT IN RACE
ROCKEFELLER OUT OF RACE

NO PRICE RISES TO BE ALLOWED
PRICES WILL BE PEGGED

NO STATEMENT ON TAKE-OVER BID
DIRECTORS SILENT ON TAKE-OVER BID

It is a good rule for newspapers to ban 'no' heads except by permission of an executive. The rare occasion when 'no' or 'not' is justified is when the precise form of the words a speaker uses needs to be reflected in the head, to convey either a subtle meaning or emphasis: 'No, no, a thousand times no' is hard to beat for emphasis, and the speaker's careful double-negative 'not unscathed' is probably preferable in the following story:

Sheppard: Book left me 'not unscathed'

The Rev David Sheppard, aged 38, former England cricketer and East End social worker, gave the all-male jury at the Central Criminal Court yesterday his opinion of the controversial American novel *Last Exit to Brooklyn* written by Hubert Selby, Jun, and published in Britain in January, 1966.

'I am afraid it left the impression that it is pandering to all that is worst in me', he said. 'I feel I am not unscathed by reading a book like this.'

It is harder to avoid hesitant headlines, but do ration the insipid 'may'. Obviously neither deskman nor reporter must press the facts for a headline, but some stories which invite a 'may' headline could often carry more positive emphasis. 'Pocock likely to earn place in first Test' is better and may even be more accurate, too, than 'Pocock may. . . .' 'Forecast', 'expects', 'fears', 'considers' are equally useful variants.

A succession of polysyllabic words slows the reading and comprehension of a headline. Consider the opposite:

GIRL LOST TEN DAYS
FOUND DEAD
IN LOVERS' LANE

That is nine words and ten syllables. It gives all the information quickly and coherently. It does no violence to the language. It is true that some short words have been abused. 'Probe' is now a nicely sinister word for any sort of tedious inquiry: 'Vice' covers a multitude of sins. But without maiming the language or twisting the facts it is possible to insist on short, simple words. English is rich in them. *Banned* is acceptable for *prohibited; neutral* for *uncommitted; talks* does express the meaning of *negotiations; goods* are *commodities* (except perhaps in the business pages). Consider the way the long (and often abstract) words obscure the facts; and the way short simple words charge the heads with meaning:

IMPLEMENTATION OF SCIENCE
EDUCATION PROGRAMME

MORE SCIENCE TEACHING
IN SCHOOLS SOON

STRONG AGRICULTURAL BASE
'NECESSARY FOR PROGRESS'

BETTER DEAL FOR FARMERS
'WILL ENRICH US ALL'

HOUSE RENT RECOMMENDATION
NOT TO BE IMPLEMENTED

COUNCIL REJECTS BID
TO PEG HOUSE RENTS

389 SUSPECT BEEF TINS
UNRECOVERED

389 SUSPECT BEEF
TINS STILL LOST

JOHNSON ATTACKS HANOI'S
TERGIVERSATION IN PARIS

JOHNSON SAYS HANOI IS
HEDGING IN PEACE TALKS

UNPRECEDENTED EXODUS
FROM NORTH

MIGRATION FROM NORTH
REACHES NEW PEAK

A good test with these, and other, headlines is to say them aloud. Does the wording trip lightly off the tongue? If instead it trips up, try writing another.

Single Thoughts

Simplicity in headlines does not merely mean simple words: it equally means the simple expression of a single thought. Effectively to convey one single idea in the limited space of a headline, requires skill; to convey two ideas in the same space, with the same intelligibility, requires a rare genius. Just as a sentence becomes difficult to follow when it is overloaded with separate ideas (*see* pp. 17–18) so does a headline. Two breaths are needed for 'Gambling ice-cream man's brain operation called off as he seeks group help'. The 'as he' construction generally means that the writer is wandering too far from a vivid single news point.

In the next instance, the headline writer tries to encompass a debate in six words. The head does not really convey anything until you have read the story:

QUALITY STABILISATION
PRICE FIXING, SAY FOES

Washington—The House Commerce Committee has wrapped up an old conflict in a new package for sale to Congress and to the public.

Sponsors call it 'quality stabilisation'. Critics say it is nothing more than 'fair trade' and 'price fixing' in a slight disguise.

Advocates of the 'quality stabilisation bill' argue that it is essential to the survival of the small retailer and vital to the protection of brand names and trade-marked products.

Opponents contend it would cost the consumers billions in higher prices and would not accomplish the purposes intended.

In essence, the law would permit a manufacturer or brand-name owner to fix the price at which his goods could be sold by wholesalers and retailers.

It would be better to concentrate the limited resources of this head on a limited objective. This means making a decision—there is no way round it—about what the news really is. It then means expressing that idea without resorting to long words like 'stabilisation'. The news here is that there is a proposal from the House Commerce Committee to permit manufacturers of branded goods to fix prices. The fact that this proposal is being opposed is secondary to that: the reaction follows the action. But either way the headline writer has to choose one of these points for the headline, and one only:

MOVE TO BAN PRICE CUTTING IN BRANDED
GOODS

In a different way the next head suffers from the same defects of trying to say too much in one breath and the separated form of attribution here—increases the confusion.

Critical six months, but, despite
pressure, no reflation—Chancellor

It is best to omit one of the thoughts in the headline and simply say:

CHANCELLOR RESISTS PRESSURE FOR
QUICK REFLATION

The attempt to combine two thoughts may not always be quite so confusing, but often it obscures the impact of the news:

Men with 'gate fever' refuse jail parole

This extraordinary story was that 500 prisoners in British jails specifically asked to be excluded from the new parole system—they did not want to leave prison to re-join the outside world. 'Gate fever' was a piece of prison slang for this symptom, and though it is colourful, it was not the main news point and certainly not worth its prominence in the first line, thereby delaying the real news to the second line. The head should have been:

500 prisoners want to stay in jail

The deskman handling a complicated story which creates difficulties for headline writing should mentally stand back from its intricacies and ask himself: what is the simple effect of all these words? Without retreating into meaningless generality it may then be possible to write the head on the broad intent of the story. For instance, during the British pre-Budget discussions it was reported that the Chancellor, Mr Roy Jenkins, was urging the need for permanent legislation to enforce a statutory twelve months' pause in trade-union claims for increased pay, unless justified by increased productivity. This naturally led the headline writer to try out headlines using the words 'Jenkins argues for permanent 12-month pay pauses except for productivity'. Of course, that was a non-starter as a headline and it is indeed very difficult to write an intelligible and fair headline including the main points of the proposal. Here was a case where it was better to write a headline in bold strokes:

Jenkins plans pay shock for unions

We have now analysed all the basic constituents of a good headline sentence, which can be edited into the actual headline. To recapitulate, they are:

An uncluttered single thought
which is positive
and specific
expressed with a strong verb
in the active voice
in short simple words.

These ground rules are summed up in the old newspaper adage:

MAN BITES DOG

That is a good news story—but also a first-class headline. It expresses a specific and single item of news positively, with an active verb and in simple words. Some of the headline deficiencies I have discussed would produce this version:

Inflicts wound on canine, aver police

The Key Word

We know what the constituents of the news headline should be; and the general rules. These are a guide for livelier, clearer headlines, not a prescription for monotony. The rules are not meant to restrict your native genius or torture the news. A rule can be broken—if you know why you are breaking it. I have given instances where the rules collide: but there are also criteria for making a choice. Before moving on to specialised headlines and variations, I would like briefly to discuss the label headline and suggest another technique which may help towards the right headline.

I advised earlier that the first thing to do as you read the text is to note separately the sentence summing up the news and then edit it for the headline; a headline sculpted from a sentence should have a better chance of retaining some grammatical integrity and intelligibility. There is another technique for headline construction, which is to note down the individual words that make the story unique, that make it news. Sometimes a single word is the key to the headline and however the headline sentence is constructed, the head will be weaker without the key word, whether it be noun, verb, or adjective. Flaubert put the matter more elegantly to Maupassant:

> 'Whatever one wishes to say, there is only one noun to express it, only one verb to give it life, only one adjective to qualify it. Search, then, till that noun, that verb, that adjective are discovered; never be content with 'very nearly'; never have recourse to tricks, however happy; or to buffooneries of language to avoid a difficulty.'

This is too idealistic a doctrine for headline writers, and too extreme as well: a headline writer denied all synonyms might occasionally create prose but he and his colleagues would risk their sanity in the process. What we should do, in approximation, is seek out the single word or words which at least make this headline different from any other.

Two cinemas in New York were told to take off 'strip' or 'nude' films; yet the key words were crowded out with a head about unspecified films being 'rescheduled'. A policewoman chased a boy who was brandishing a bayonet and was rewarded with the head 'Policewoman stuck to duty'; a label heading without the inappropriate verb would have been better—'Policewoman and bayonet boy'.

Labels that work

There are times when we have to take this middle course, retaining the key words and relinquishing the verb. This produces a label headline, but there are labels and labels. Having exhibited some traditional label headings as warnings-off, I can now safely add that there are times—perhaps one news story in a hundred—when one may with a clear conscience use a label. There may be a mixture of reasons: to avoid a weak verb while retaining key words; to meet a difficult unit count; to suit the text when there is no active news point; or to create a change of pace. But the words of the verb-less label must be potent. If they do not actually tell the news they should indicate it. A few varying examples will emphasise the essential points.

When the first British heart transplant patient was recovering on the day after the operation, the doctors reported that he was well and added that he had given them a thumbs-up signal. Now a headline merely saying that the heart transplant patient was well would have been accurate but it would also have fitted several other operations. The key phrase for every headline was 'thumbs up'. The headline had to be built round it in a unit count of 21.

HEART MAN GIVES THUMBS UP
(Active but too long)

HEART MAN DOING WELL
(Active and fits but too weak
with omission of key words)

HEART MAN'S THUMBS UP
(A label, but it fits and with the
key words it is quite strong)

HEART MAN: THUMBS UP
(An awkward split but newsy.
Compare the traditional uninformative
label: 'Heart man's condition')

The label using the possessive to carry the key words is a useful economy device. Another story, in the middle of a period of Labour party disaffection, says MPs face a crucial test of their loyalty in a vote on the Government's incomes policy. The active head with verb would be:

LABOUR MPs FACE LOYALTY TEST

But if the active head is too long you can get by with the label bearing the key words:

LABOUR'S LOYALTY TEST

A light story on what a champion jockey was dreaming of doing on retirement might have carried the active head 'Champion jockey dreams of . . .' but that was already taking the full unit count. The possessive label 'The champion jockey's dream' did not tell the news but it indicated its area in a fairly tempting way by retaining the key words.

In another story the news is that the French have performed a third heart transplant operation; there is a headline count of 23: 'French try third heart transplant' is active and has all the key words but is too long. But 'Third French transplant' would fit and it is worth using despite the omission of the verb, because it has nearly all the key words and it covers the news.

These are all instances where the label has been acceptable but second best. Very occasionally it is better, for instance on a story which relies on suspense:

> It looked like a big raid. Suddenly ten detectives including two chief inspectors moved into the garden of a semi-detached house yesterday. Methodically, they set about their business . . . with two motor mowers, garden forks, spades, rakes and clippers. But it was not a murder hunt. They were not looking for clues. The detectives were giving up a day off to tidy the overgrown garden of one of their colleagues who has been in hospital for six months . . .

An active news head on this story spoils the suspense and reads very flatly:

Detectives tidy garden

But a verb-less label can make something of the suspense idea using the familiar abbreviation CID for Criminal Investigation Department:

SECRET OF A
CID DIG-IN

The label head can be effective if deliberately teasing with mock suspense:

> An attractive ex-nurse told a conference yesterday that most girls know all there is to know about sex by the time they are nine.

The active head: 'Girls of nine know all about sex' is a bit bald. The label scores: 'What every girl of nine knows'.

Words like 'secret' and 'riddle', if used sparingly, can rescue a difficult label head: 'Riddle of Russian diplomat'. A combination of evocative key words may also be superior for a complicated story where no single news point merits a central position: 'The monk and the mystery of the Mussolini diaries'; 'The "lusty" life of Errol Flynn' (a tax hearing).

The choice between a label and an active head requires judgment. Remember it is the label which is the exception and which needs justifying. As I write, one British daily newspaper, for instance, has an unjustified label which rouses no curiosity at all:

MEDICAL HAZARDS
ON THE ROAD

I find myself reading another newspaper's version headed:

HEALTH TESTS URGED
FOR OLDER DRIVERS

Similarly, the active news heading 'Girl strangled with dog lead' is at once more intelligible and forceful with all the key words, than the confused label: 'The missing dog murder hunt'.

Headlines in Practice

But let us now take the concept of the key word and apply it to several stories here and in the next section, seeing what headline emerges. Note, incidentally, how frequently it is the verb which is the prime key word.

> A soldier, aged 18, got a barrack room friend to chop off his trigger finger with an axe so that he could get his release from the Army, Major M Clarke, for the prosecution, said at a Colchester court martial today.
> Privates M and B, both serving with The Prince of Wales's Own Regiment, pleaded Guilty to malingering. M was sentenced to 112

days' detention, and B to 126 days' detention, both sentences being subject to confirmation.

Major Clarke said that on December 29 six soldiers were in a room discussing ways and means of getting M out of the Army. Someone suggested he should lose his trigger finger, and B agreed to chop it off for him. M then lay down on his bed, put his right index finger on an upturned locker, and smoked a cigarette while B chopped the finger off with an axe.

Captain A B Bower, in a plea of mitigation for M, said he was anxious to get out of the Army because his mother had lost her job, and was not getting enough money on which to bring up a large family.

For B, Captain Bower said that he thought M was bluffing. When he realised however, that M was serious, he could not back down, otherwise he would have lost face with his fellow-soldiers.

The strong key words that spring from that story are:

> Finger
> Chop off
> Soldier

It is a simple matter to put these into coherent form and into a headline: 'Soldier got friend to chop off finger'. One English national daily handling this story managed this: and another, tight on the headine count, wrote 'Soldier got pal to cut off finger'. Here 'cut off' is distinctly weaker than 'chop off' because it suggests the action of a knife rather than an axe. Another, subject-less, heading was less satisfactory, with the unattributed, unquoted head 'Please chop off my trigger finger' (though the word trigger would just suggest the context). Two other national papers, however, headlined this story in this way:

| Soldier 'lost trigger finger for release' | Why a soldier lost his trigger finger |

We see at once how a head fails without the key verb 'chop off'. 'Lost' is dreadfully weak for the sudden violent action of an axe on a man's finger. The first head, incidentally, also illustrates the troubles that arise from trying to say too much. 'For release' so close to 'trigger finger' gives a momentary but disconcerting impression that the finger was somehow trapped and needed releasing. It does not convey 'to get out of the Army'. (And why the quotes in this headline?) The second head fails by resorting to feature-style treatment, which is all right on a featurish story without much news, but out of place on a hard news story. Why the soldier lost his finger is, in any event, less compelling than *how* he lost it.

How The Dailies Do It

Let us now try the same technique on two stories with rather more elements. How to weave the key words into a headline depends, of course, on the given headline pattern. I would argue that on certain important stories there are key words which so much go together that retaining their integrity should be a function of page design and headline typography (*see* pp. 36–7).

In what follows I give the text justification for the headline, and then I list what I consider the key words for the headline. Following each example I list the headlines that appeared in English national dailies and I give a comment on these to demonstrate how the absence or presence of a key word affects the headline. Of course, doing this in relative tranquillity after the rush of press time is easier for me than for my colleagues, but it is worth doing for three reasons. One is to show how, if one begins with a conception of what the key words are, an effective headline is easier to write; second, to show how failure to observe this discipline will prevent even the best professionals from achieving an optimum combination of key words; and third, to emphasise the wisdom of letting words dictate headline shapes, and not the reverse. Here is the text for the headline(s):

> Mr Adlai Stevenson, US Ambassador to the United Nations, died after collapsing in the street near the US Embassy in London last night. He was given the 'kiss of life' by Mrs Marietta Tree, a member of his UN delegation, on the pavement before an ambulance took him to St George's Hospital, Hyde Park Corner.
>
> Mr Stevenson, who was 65, had just left the Embassy in Grosvenor Square, where an office had been put at his disposal while he was on a private visit here to see friends. He had walked with Mrs Tree, who is on holiday here with her husband, Mr Ronald Tree, into Upper Grosvenor Street, and collapsed outside the International Sportsman's Club.
>
> A doctor called from the club gave Mr Stevenson an injection and cardiac massage.

These are the key words that should appear in the headline:

> Adlai (Stevenson)
> dies
> London street
> kiss of life
> woman

The Daily Telegraph had the head in three decks:

> ### ADLAI STEVENSON
> ### DIES IN LONDON
>
> ### Street Collapse: Vain
> ### 'Kiss of Life'
>
> ### Johnson's tribute to
> ### Voice of US

The space restriction meant the omission of the key word 'street' from the main deck. This considerably weakens it. A dramatic collapse in the street is quite different in news terms, from death in a hospital. When the word 'street' is properly introduced in the second deck the word 'collapse' has to be added to make sense, though 'collapse' adds little to 'dies'. Given the headline banking construction, it is an inevitable superfluity—and it entails the omission in the second deck of the key word 'woman' related to 'kiss of life'.

The Yorkshire Post had a main banner and second deck, with an overline in smaller type:

> Mr Adlai Stevenson collapses in London street
>
> ### WOMAN TRIES TO SAVE DYING
> ### STATESMAN
>
> Kiss of life and oxygen used

The banner does not contain any of the key words. Immediately the headline becomes vague. 'Dying statesman' might have sufficed for a foreign secretary from a banana republic but it will not do for Adlai Stevenson. It is an elegant variation introduced because the headline writer made the mistake of treating the overline as something read first and used the name there. Having done this he then has been forced to use the banner for the secondary point—the woman's attempt to save Stevenson's life. The real news, the death of Stevenson, has been subordinated.

Daily Mirror—overline and main banner:

'Kiss of life' bid fails

ADLAI STEVENSON DIES
IN LONDON STREET

Right on target with the first five key words. At once we learn the main news. The key word 'woman' is omitted, however, and with it an element in the drama.

Daily Mail—four-column banner in 72pt and a second deck across 1½ columns in 30pt:

ADLAI DIES IN LONDON

Woman diplomat tries
kiss of life in street

The banner misses by omitting the key words 'Stevenson' and 'street'. The name Adlai is not quite the instant signal that Adlai Stevenson is. And 'in London' might have indicated a normal death in a nursing home.

Daily Express—a top line in 42pt, then an 18pt line, and finally a seven-column banner in 60pt:

Adlai Stevenson dies

Woman envoy rushes to his
aid in London street

KISS OF LIFE FAILS

A serious failure: the outstanding weakness is that by trying for a striking banner the *Express* headline writer separated particles that go dramatically together. 'Dies' and 'London street' go together, and so do 'woman' and 'kiss of life'. This is an instance of essential news phrasing being tortured to fit a make-up formula. In any event the main heading misses because the 'kiss of life' is never certain to succeed—that is its implicit drama.

The Times in 30pt across two columns, with a second deck:

ADLAI STEVENSON DIES
IN LONDON STREET

Woman's kiss of life fails

All the key words are there, making a headline with force, directness and news sense.

The key-word theory applies especially to speeches where no positive action emerges:

> Mr Harold Wilson today told an American audience of nearly 2,000 business men that this Government had a 10-point programme for Britain's industrial regeneration, and he added: 'Given the response of which our people are capable, be under no illusions, we shall be ready to knock hell out of you.'

The news here is not the announcement but the unparliamentary language, which reflected the spirit and purpose of a speech designed to show a confident Britain. Therefore the key words are not '10-point programme' or 'business men' or 'response', but

(we) knock hell (out of you)
Wilson
US

Daily Express—30pt single-column heading:

BRITAIN'S
COURAGE
WILL WIN,
WILSON
TELLS US

later changed to a double-column:

WILSON
PROMISES
'EM HELL

The first heading is flat without the key words. The second attempt scores with the one word 'hell', but to promise somebody hell is not as vigorous as 'we'll knock hell out of you'.

The Yorkshire Post—two-column 36pt, with second deck

Britain hopes to
knock hell
out of US
Hidden reserves bolster pound

Directness is lost by rendering the key phrase into third-person, and 'hopes' also weakens the idea; it is, on the contrary, a promise. Omitting the key word 'Wilson' greatly reduces the news value of the headline.

Daily Mail—banner in 60pt across six columns, with a side deck in 18pt:

WILSON ISSUES CHALLENGE TO U S
We'll knock
hell out of you

'Issues challenge' is a pompous circumlocution. The omission of key words from the banner weakens the heading. In another edition the *Mail* offered a small confused overline saying 'National Opinion Poll with the Premier in America, a shock from the voters, see page 11', and a 36pt heading across two columns:

We'll knock hell out
of you—Wilson

This otherwise strong main heading is considerably weakened by loss of the key word 'US' and hence the news that Wilson was saying this to the Americans.

The Daily Telegraph in 18pt:

'KNOCK HELL'
WARNING BY
WILSON TO U S

Rendering the key phrase into headlinese spoils its flow. 'We' and 'you' are necessary to capture the directness of the attack, and so this headline's meaning is far from clear.

The Times in 30pt, with a second deck:

BRITAIN HOPING TO 'KNOCK
HELL OUT OF U S'

Mr Wilson's 10-point plan
for revitalizing industry

The separation of the key word 'Wilson' from the 'hell' phrase conceals that the Prime Minister said it to Americans. Omission of 'we' and 'you' loses the original directness. Again 'hopes' weakens the idea; 'means' would have been better.

Daily Mirror in 48pt:

BRITAIN CAN DO IT—
WILSON TELLS U S

Without the key words, another hesitant bromide.

The Guardian in 42pt, with second deck:

'We shall knock hell
out of you'

Premier tells U S of
British trade plans

It is good to have the full phrase together, but again the separation of attribution and key words is unsatisfactory. The introduction of the non-key words to fill the second deck softens the impact of the headlines.

The Sun in 18pt overline and 48pt main heading:

Wilson tells US leaders
We shall
knock
hell out
of you

A slight improvement on the *Guardian*: all the key words are there and though attribution is separate, the headline gains force by restricting itself to key words, thereby putting over a single idea with emphasis.

Daily Sketch in 24pt overline and 84pt banner:

Premier in lions' den
warns U S bankers

WE'LL KNOCK HELL
OUT OF YOU—WILSON

All the key words except 'US' in the banner, and therefore a strong main heading. The overline makes up for the omission of US, emphasising the confrontation with the imaginative 'lions' den'.

Daily Mail

No. 21,597   FOR QUEEN AND COMMONWEALTH   News Chronicle and Daily Dispatch   TUESDAY, OCTOBER 5, 1965   PRICE 3d.

'If you wish to be brothers let the arms fall from your hands... Swear: No more war'

THE POPE TO THE UN LAST NIGHT

Comment

Wilson and Aunty

MR. WILSON is treading a dangerous path in his relations with the BBC. and he should consider where this could lead him and the country.

The reason for his dissatisfaction is an assumption by some Labour leaders of a pro-Conservative bias in some of the BBC's documentary programmes.

But the same point could have been made, in an opposite sense, by Conservative leaders when they were in office. For it is the essence of this democracy that all authority be subjected to searching public scrutiny.

In reading too much into the sort of questions put to them by the BBC's political commentators Labour politicians are being far too sensitive.

Angry

From STANLEY BURCH
United Nations,
New York, Monday

POPE PAUL called on UN members today to swear an oath to change the world's future history: "No more war, war never again."

He presented his passionate plea for peace as "an appeal to the moral conscience of man."

"If you wish to be brothers, let the arms fall from your hands," the Pontiff declared in eloquent, rhetorical French to the General Assembly.

"One cannot love while holding offensive arms."

The world must get used to thinking of man in a new way.

Dog patrol alerted at train raid jail

By Daily Mail Reporter

A NEW security patrol was still on alert last night at Durham Prison after a tip that a bid was to be made to free the three train robbers.

Senior police officers in the anti-escape plan were alerted at breakfast time on Sunday.

By last night the watch was being eased. But a patrol of dogs was outside the prison wall.

Two vans of the dog squad were stationed outside the back of Durham Jail where the wall is at its lowest, about 15ft.

They were on guard in a lane beside the prison officers' club. Five handlers were on duty, one armed with a portable radio receiver much bigger than the normal midget equipment

NCB sacks 22 stay-home miners

By Daily Mail Reporter

TWENTY-TWO stay-at-home miners have

150 die in train crash

DURBAN, Monday.

AT least 150 people were killed and many more injured when three coaches of a passenger train were derailed tonight.

It happened on the North Natal coast railway line.

Two white railwaymen were attacked by incensed African passengers after the crash. One of them was battered to death.

More than 40 ambulances went to the scene.

Police find missing officer's car

Police and coastguards searching yesterday for Flight Lieut. Terry Peet, who vanished after leaving RAF Tern Hill, near Market Drayton, Shropshire, found his car parked near sea at Moelfre.

LATE NEWS

Daily Mail, Manchester. BLA 8600.

2 HANRATTY: Three women talk of the dark young man, of the green bath, the attic and the tiled back-yard

4 Free-style Headlines and other Specialities

It is often easy, but is nevertheless meretricious, to seize upon a minor point that is merely incidental to the main theme and base headlines upon because it is catchy; it is much more difficult, and much sounder journalism, to bring within the narrow compass of a heading the real purpose and significance of the story, and to express it as brightly as possible.

—F J MANSFIELD

We have been writing headlines to a strict discipline, as demanding as the form for a rhyming pentameter. The words we could use have been suggested by words in the text carrying the most important news point; and the number of words has been limited by the unit count, as it must be for a newspaper handling a multiplicity of news stories, the staple of the newspaper. There are clearly occasions when a news heading to a limited count is not suitable:

(*a*) When the ideas in the text are so rich and diffuse that a simple hard news head does not do them justice.

(*b*) When the natural headline wording is so attractive (so funny, so apt) that it should be given whatever space it needs.

These categories need a wide range of what I shall call free-style headlines. News-style heads always give information impartially. Free-style heads may not: they may ask a question or make a joke or be a general label. Most main features need free-style heads; but discussion under the traditional division of news and features is not really helpful to us. The text is primal. Free-style heads should appear wherever the text requires, on news or features.

Take first, a few free-style heads giving information on news text. Here is an example broadly in category (*a*):

A schoolgirl is told she has failed her advanced GCE examination. Her father complains, in a complicated series of events, and at the end of it all she has her marks approximately doubled to give an excellent grade B with merit.

Now reducing that story to a hard news head with a limited count produces this:

**GIRL'S 'FAILURE'
BECAME PASS
WITH MERIT**

But the story is suffocated by this condensed form. The story only really came alive in a detailed free-style headline:

It took six letters and four
examiners to switch Julia's
A-level failure into a pass
with merit

There are a lot of words in that free-style head but it is easy to read because it is a complete clear sentence. Of course, the typography has to be adjusted to that headline, but the convenience of a standardised news-style typography (and it is convenient) should never be a strait-jacket.

Example (**2**), opposite, was an adroit use of free-style on an even more complicated story which could have carried a limited-count news heading only at the risk of distortion. ('Hanratty: Three women talk' would have over-emphasised the elements of disclosure.) The free-style headline as a full sentence enabled the headline to overcome this difficulty and at the same time reflect the atmosphere of mystery and detection. But note two points: the free-style headline must read coherently like a sentence with punctuation marks—and no words omitted. This attempt at a free-style heading falls flat:

Now, can you think of name for London
motorway box?

The omission of the word 'a' quite spoils the ring of that headline.

Exceptionally vivid quotes are worth free-style treatment: when the Pope addressed the United Nations, the London *Daily Mail* soared over the commonplace news-style headlines of its competitors (POPE PLEADS FOR PEACE AT UN) by running his actual words across the top of the page (**1,** opposite).

Two more heads based on quotations illustrate the free-style range between emotional expressiveness and straight information.

A trawler goes down. The crew is given up for dead. But one man comes ashore alive in Iceland and his wife flies to see him. A straight news-style head (Wife rejoins 'dead' husband) would have failed to capture the richness of the reunion in the way the *Sun* did with a free-style head running beneath the reunion picture:

> Honestly, deep inside me
> I thought I would
> never see you again

And at a rail inquiry, the striking information is right to be given in a single original sentence and the typography made to fit:

> I'd have made it a 60 mph limit before
> if I had known of the danger . . .

Letting the Words Take Over

The examples so far would come under category (*a*) of free-style heads. It is relatively uncharted territory. Indeed, very few newspapermen anywhere have been experimenting in this direction—breaking out of formula presentation in an intelligent and not merely cussed way. Now let us venture into the disputatious area where it is the inspiration of attractive wording which breaks the bonds of the news-style head.

There is no limit to innovation here: puns proliferate and allusions abound. Of course, what I think funny you may regard as the bore of the century; and what both of us agree is hilarious may be a stroke of genius from which no general guidance can be drawn. Accepting that, it may be worth saying that pun, allusion, irony, wit, metaphor, alliteration and anti-climax are all acceptable fathers of free-style heads which are better than straight news heads. Borrowing a current catch phrase for a heading, be it from a pop song, an advertising campaign, a film title, a novel, or a TV comedian, requires superb timing. There is one brief flowering moment when more people appreciate the allusion than are likely to be irritated by it.

The moment perhaps lasts a week. Coming across the catch phrase in frequent heads long after that is like being locked with a prize drone in a corridor-less slow train to Plymouth. 'Wind of change', 'Room at the Top', 'No Room at the Inn', 'Hard Day's Night', and numerous others too painful to mention have seemed to survive as if pickled. But—and it's only my opinion—a very ancient

catch phrase may be revived successfully in a head. A small illustration will suffice. When a new hotel in Manchester was opened, small sections of the plasterboard ceiling fell down at a celebration lunch:

> The VIP luncheon was going with a swing. Waiters moved smoothly from tables amid the chink of wine glasses and buzz of chattering guests. Then it happened—somewhere between Delice de Sole Piccadilly and the Aile de Poulet Nicoise . . . down came bits of the ceiling.

These were the straight news heads:

Ceiling collapses at £2m hotel opening

Ceiling falls at hotel opening

Ceiling collapse probed at hotel opening

Crash goes ceiling at £2m hotel

These are all right as far as they go, but they suffer by being cast in the straight news mould; they tend to overdo the seriousness of the incident. 'Ceiling collapse' conjures up a calamity and this is why the label 'The day the ceiling fell in' would be softer, the Thurber-style being a hint that nothing really serious happened. But a free-style head with allusion to an old joke tells the news perfectly in harmony with a formal lunch:

> WAITER!
> There's part
> of the
> ceiling
> in my
> soup

One source of fun is to reflect the idiom of the text. For instance, this is a headline on a story about the teaching of English in the Army:

Educationising of Army a failure Englishwise

Another is intentional incongruity. When the British Aircraft Corporation announced a two-deck airliner to carry more than 300 people, 80 per cent on the top deck, the head neatly inflated the cry of the bus conductor:

ROOM FOR 260 ON TOP

And these also succeed:

> Losing by a whisker: some people's
> beards cost them their jobs

Wrigley fights inflation—by gum

All that's rolled gold
need not glitter
(a court ruling that rolled gold jewellery
need not be completely covered in gold)

London Bridge will fall—to
the highest bidder

The Adulterous Society

A good light head has a core of news; and its writer must not be caught giggling at his own joke by exclamation marks, quotes, underlining italic or any other of the red-nose devices of prose. The standard for coolness is set by the head on the story about a Russian hydrofoil which, on demonstration trials with hammer and sickle flying, went aground on a sandbank off Sandwich, Kent (to which of course the Vikings once came):

The Russians
land at
Sandwich

If you are in doubt about an allusion, a good test is to ask yourself whether the head, in making its joke, also indicates the news. If it does not, you have almost strayed too far in your enthusiasm.

Two players called Smith played a sharp attacking football game inspiring Glasgow Rangers to victory. The headline writer had fun with a play on the well-known brand of potato chips, Smith's Crisps:

CRISP SMITHS
SPUR RANGERS

But what would have happened to the headline if it had been pushed further? 'Crisp Smiths full of crackle . . .'; 'Crisp Smiths so untasty for some . . .'; 'Crisp Smiths put salt on tails . . .', and so on. Economy is a hallmark of wit and the original head gets all the gaiety there is out of the names in the first line. By wisely refusing to overdo the joke the line becomes an elegant throwaway, and is all the better for it. Tickle the reader; don't prod him in the solar plexus.

Good and bad puns

Most injury is inflicted by clumsy puns or ill-kempt metaphors. On a story about tyre regulations: 'Motorists "tyre" of these regulations'. On a story of a road offence: 'Kerbing his exuberance'. On an art show making a play with someone's name: 'Art exhibits are fun-nee'. On a story of cemetery vandalism: 'Two youths given grave sentences'; on a story about people being stranded in snow: 'The white paralysis'; on a weather report: 'Jack Frost's road toll'. And inaptness again on a story of money for coal mines: 'Pep pills for pits'. The metaphors are self-conscious and contrived—and puns which have to be trussed in quotes should not be allowed out.

Puns on people's names should be avoided. They and everyone else stopped laughing at that one at the christening. I am not against puns in heads. Let Fowler set the standard: 'The assumption that puns are *per se* contemptible, betrayed by the habit of describing every pun not as *a pun* but as *a bad pun* or *a feeble pun*, is a sign at once of sheepish docility and desire to seem superior. Puns are good, bad, and indifferent, and only those who lack the wit to make them are unaware of the fact'. So, some good puns: Four men accused of singing ribald songs in a harbour attracted the head:

Four vulgar boatmen

A book review:

Absinthe friends

A debate in the Indian Parliament on whether saris too revealing should be banned:

A sari without a fringe on top

A film review:

James Stewart faster on the drawl

And there are the famous London *Evening News* small paragraphs:

BORING DETAILS
He kept on and on about his job on an oil rig.—Lambeth witness.

HOST OF PROBLEMS
Things always go wrong when I hold a party.—Lambeth man.

LUNCHEON VOUCHER
The cafe owner can confirm I had a meal there at midday.—Herts man.

CHEQUE MATES
My wife and I have a joint bank account.—North London man.

Feature Headings

Most main features heads should be free-style heads in the sense that the wording should dictate the layout. This does not necessarily mean long wording. Two or three words may be the most apposite and then the typography should be adjusted to display them.

Many news subs seem all at sea writing feature heads. What can they grasp for projection? There is no news to tell in the traditional way, so the simplicity, urgency and stridency of the news head will be wrong unless it happens to be an exposé feature. A few guides may be offered. If the feature has an especially colourful phrase, let that be the head:

Review heads should carry opinion, which can come word for word from the text if it is pithy:

'I can imagine Camelot without the music . . .
but not without the red-blooded Miss Redgrave'

If the feature sets out to answer set questions, pose the questions. Just who are the speculators? Well, what really goes into a meat pie? What is the cost of a night out? Who killed Jan Masaryk? The question can be rhetorical: What do hippies wear in winter? The answer is granny's old fur coat.

For general feature heads, there are certain formula constructions which come to the rescue provided they reflect the emphasis of the text. These formula headings are based on the how, what, wherefore syndrome. For instance:

When it pays to live in sin
When love turned sour
Why young Germany exploded
How they planned the heart transplant
Why de Gaulle faces crisis in the streets
The truth about bust developers
What is wrong with racing
What made Johnson decide
Where Heath went wrong
The inside story of the Tiger talks

Making these formula headings live means choosing key words after the initial word sets the scope of the piece. It might be helpful to analyse a feature headline on text which told how Francis Crick and James Watson worked out the structure of deoxyribo-nucleic acid, universally called DNA. The paper they published won each of them a Nobel Prize; and the text says it has proved to be the key for unlocking some of the fundamental secrets of life. They were in competition at one stage with the celebrated chemist, Dr Linus Pauling. Here are some stages to an accepted popularised feature headline for two articles:

HOW THEY WON A NOBEL PRIZE

Too unspecific, could apply to all Nobel prizewinners.

HOW THEY DISCOVERED DNA

DNA will not signal a great deal to the average reader. Can we say: secret of life? A good phrase but needs care.

HOW THEY DISCOVERED THE SECRET OF LIFE

Too strong: the text says it was the key to unlocking some of the fundamental secrets of life. They have taken one stride, but others must follow, so the headline must not suggest we know all there is to know about life.

HOW THEY HELPED TO DISCOVER THE SECRET OF LIFE

More nearly accurate, but 'helped' is a weak word. So is 'aimed' which underplays their success. Can we make a feature of the competition with the other scientists? Yes, the text seems to support this even to the extent of the word 'race'.

HOW THEY RACED TO DISCOVER THE SECRET OF LIFE

Stronger wording, but 'raced to discover' is wordy and may be open to the objection again that 'discover' suggests all was in fact discovered. We need a head which retains 'race', which is one element of what they were doing and 'secret of life', which was their objective.

THE RACE . . . THE SECRET OF LIFE

becomes

THE RACE TO FIND THE SECRET OF LIFE

So much for the first article. The second can pick up that wording for a small identifying label, and there in the text is a vivid phrase which can serve as the full-sentence, free-style headline. Suddenly the pieces fit:

IT WAS ALL TOO BEAUTIFUL NOT TO BE TRUE

Feature heads, like news heads, are better when they have a specific element; where, when they are labels,

The war in Vietnam did not alter yesterday; it is simply that in Saigon it is easier to see what is being done and easier to understand what it means

they use key words. Just one piece of colour from the text will do. 'The deal in Chicago' is less vivid than 'The deal in Room 410'. A meeting of Governors aboard the USS Independence contains the paragraph 'To my considerable surprise I discovered that many of the Governors regard themselves as doomed men. They suspect that they face early political extinction'. The head: A shipload of doomed men.

If in addition to being specific you can make a play on words, so much the better:

AVIS v HERTZ: MADISON AVENUE'S FAVOURITE FEUD

('Madison Avenue' is more colourful than 'Advertising's' and 'Favourite' and 'Feud' make a nicely alliterative surprise union and pun.)

THIEU AND KY THINK ABOUT THE UNTHINKABLE

Addressing the Reader

Finally, while the newspaper's own identity is normally expressed through editorial comment, there are exceptional occasions when a free-style head can be used to address readers directly, simulating conversation. Over a set of agonising pictures from the Vietcong Tet offensive against Saigon, the traditional head would have been 'Shock pictures from Vietnam', but the *Sun* (**above**) took space to spell out the words in a way that emphasised the gravity of the war and seemed to unite reader and newspaper together to pause for a moment.

Opinion headings are simpler. Vigorous editorials are too often topped with a wishy-washy heading. The editorial head should on all classes of paper say something positive; if it can be witty, so be it, but at least let it be partial. For instance:

Keep Britain civilised
It *is* a moral issue
Save Stansted

Why it should be Rockefeller
An evil speech
Time for a change at the Treasury

The *Daily Mirror* blockbusters have set a record, some would say for vituperation, but certainly for vitality in popular projection.

My own favourite free-style headline salvo was the *Daily Mirror* using its page one like a poster to talk back to Mr Khrushchev in 1960:

Running Stories

The key-word concept is a help in headlining running stories, by which I mean stories that develop from the first reporting and appear in the newspaper over days, weeks or months. A single key word can then be used to identify the subject and act as a signal for summarising the past sequence of events, leaving the rest of the headline space for detailing new developments. On the first day of a trial, for instance, the headline will have to say 'Moors murder trial'. When the reader has been exposed a few days to this story, it can safely be identified in the headline as 'Moors trial', and later just by the tag 'Moors'. This word will then be used at the opening of the headline to give sense to what follows, but it will be separated from the other wording by a colon. For instance, this is how a key-word tag might develop for two different running stories:

First day :   Vietnam peace talks set for Paris
Second day :   Envoys chosen for Paris talks
Third day :   Paris talks: 'End the bombing' demand

First day :   British surgeons transplant heart
               into man of 45
Second day :   Thumbs up sign from heart man

The second-day heads make the assumption that the reader knows what the Paris talks are about and what 'heart man' means. They assume some carry-forward of knowledge by the reader. The text must not make this assumption; it must always include a theme paragraph or sentence which makes sense of the whole series of developments to a man coming across the story for the first time. But the headline must make the assumption of knowledge, since if it were to re-state the old information before giving the new it would become unduly wordy, and in turn that would make it impossible to stress what is new: 'Man who had heart transplant gives thumbs up sign'. The practice of compressing a long phrase into an adjectival noun 'man who had heart transplant' into 'heart man' is legitimate. It can be abused (see p. 99), but it is absurd to be snootily self-denying about a device which condenses so much useful information and which the reader now well understands. Later, as the man's name becomes well known, it would be right to begin using the name by itself as the symbol for the story:

West: I'm feeling fine

There comes a moment in all stories—from very early

on with fairly well-known people—when it is more helpful to the reader to use a man's name rather than subject tag. Nobody would now think of using the tag line 'Missing diplomat' in a story about Mr Kim Philby. And when the United States spy ship Pueblo was captured off Korea it was soon legitimate to label developments 'Pueblo. . . .'

The tag line need not always be a simple statement. When a proposal is made and is the subject of running debate, the tag can usefully become a rhetorical question:

Rent rise? 'It was only an idea'

As television takes more of the cream from the top of spot news, newspapers will have to develop more and more the practice of taking the story forward in the headline—even when the story itself has not already broken in the newspaper. When television, for instance, has the previous night devoted several news bulletins to the simple fact of a boy's death from poisoning, it is inviting suspicions of staleness for the newspaper the next morning to headline its report 'Boy of nine dies from poisoning', rather than, say: 'Man hunted in poisoned boy riddle'.

Of course the decision on whether the head should be a 'breaking' news head or a second-day head depends on the degree of broadcasting exposure it has had: and vice versa. Broadcasting, too, must change its treatment of the well-advanced press story. Both mediums of communication have to recognise that news is indivisible.

Some of the failures to write good second-day heads are due less to philosophical doubts than to neglecting to read one's own newspaper. Nothing more quickly reduces a news editor to tears or more baffles the assiduous reader than a follow-up story with a headline written on the original old news point. ('Thirty non-union men go on strike', said the headline on a strike which had already been announced two days earlier in the same paper as 'Sackings strike hits timber firm'.) On another occasion a newspaper showed initiative after an inquest on a woman who had gassed herself but lay dead for five weeks before anyone discovered her. The follow-up idea was to find out why five weeks elapsed. It was well done—but it attracted the heading: 'Forgotten' woman took gas.

A good deskman recognises that he must be familiar with every stage of the development of major stories, which means reading other newspapers and listening to broadcasts when officially off duty, but two kinds of item tend to suffer: local stories and inquest reports. Of course, a deskman cannot be expected to remember every turn in a local dispute, but if in doubt he can be expected to consult the library clippings or the reporter.

On inquest reports, it cannot be emphasised too much that the death has already been reported. What the inquest is about is to find the cause of death—and that is the focal point for the headline. 'Car passenger died in crash' is a useless headline on an inquest. We know it; there would not be an inquest otherwise, and there in the inquest report is the reason: 'Tyres caused death crash'.

Here is another which reached print: 'Two dead and 130 ill in outbreak of food poisoning at hospital'. We know it. The inquest has to find out why, and there in the text is the point for the headline 'Food deaths: Hospital cook broke rules'. And yet again—to show how widespread is the blight—there was the headline '41 Servicemen died in air crash'. We know it. And there in the text is the reason the inquest has uncovered: '41 died because of two broken bolts'. Neither should you give up if the inquest fails to explain the reason behind the death, but only suggests possibilities. That, too, can be a news point for the headline: 'Puzzle of pilot's death: did bird damage propeller?'

Court and Crime

The risks for the headline writer are clearly libel and contempt of court. They are serious, though clear guidelines can be drawn. (A helpful book is L C J McNae's *Essential Law for Journalists*, Staples, 1954.) In headlining news reports from a court case, avoid any headline which might be construed as commenting on the court's fitness. If the judge makes a joke, it is all right to report it in the headline. It is not all right to make a joke at the expense of the judge or jury. A headline which is regarded as offensive to the dignity of the court may lead to a fine or imprisonment. Of course, headlines in which the newspaper comments on a case will normally appear over editorial comment and not over the court report. These headlines are safe enough provided the language is restrained, does not impugn the judge's integrity, and provided also the case has genuinely finished. Newspapers do sometimes write comment while an appeal is pending or during the time allowed for an appeal, but it is a decision for the Editor.

These cautions should not inhibit you in writing a direct news headline when an appeal court comments strongly on the conduct of a judge in a lower court. The newspaper might not be safe in using such language itself, or reporting another lay comment, but it is safe enough reporting the comments of a higher court.

The second limitation is not concerned with the dignity of the court but its exclusive prerogative to try a case. In the United States it has been possible in some States to label a defendant the 'murderer' even while his case is pending, but the American courts are becoming stricter, and no British court would tolerate this in headline or text. Nothing must be published which would at all tend to prejudice a trial. For the deskman the trickiest implications of this are when the newspaper is running a crime story and an arrest follows. Say there has been a bank raid, a chase, and an arrest. The headline writer would be *grievously wrong* to write

Raider snatches £50,000: Caught after street chase

This immediately implies that the man who has been arrested is the man who did the bank raid. He may not be, he may be a perfectly innocent citizen arrested by mistake.

The text of the story must contain a break to avoid linking the arrest and the crime: the traditional phrase is 'Later a man was helping the police with their inquiries'. In the headline that can be:

Man at police station

But it would be wrong again to say:

The Man at police station

Similarly in heading a road accident where the facts may be in dispute in court, avoid anything which implies a degree of guilt. To say 'Car plunges over cliff' is all right, but it would not be safe to say 'Bus runs into car' because it suggests that the bus driver is at fault. For headlines it is a bus-car crash. You will not go far wrong here or in headlining actual court cases if throughout you remember and respect the principle that in English law a man is innocent until proved guilty.

There is no risk of libel in reporting court cases if the reports are contemporaneous, fair and accurate. Fair and accurate means that there must be a proper balance between the prosecution and the defence. This privilege does not apply to headlines, contents bills or extraneous comments in court.

You can only plead justification or fair comment for headlines, but if they follow the principles laid down for the text you will be safe enough. What this means on a court case running over several days is that you must show fairness and balance in the points you select for headlines. To give all the headlines to the prosecution statement, witnesses, and cross-examinations, would be gravely to put your newspaper at risk. But in a single case which opens and concludes in one day the headline need not strive to be 'balanced' in the sense that it needs to give both the defence and the prosecution. The headline can then be based on the court's findings. If these findings confirm the allegations, or all these allegations can be taken as proved, they can be written into a headline as a fact. If some of the allegations are found proven and some dismissed, the headline should make it clear that not all the allegations were proved. An imaginary example:

Bloggins guilty on
five counts

or

Bloggins cleared on four
charges: £500 fine for
falsification

You use the present tense to headline a court's findings, just as you do with other contemporaneous news stories: but headlines on allegations and evidence go in the past tense since present tense here would suggest that the man on trial was in a permanent state of recidivism.

The commonest failing of new deskmen is to headline as a fact what has merely been alleged and has not been proved to the court's satisfaction. The prosecution's opening statement may sound very convincing, but it is no justification for writing

DOCTOR DROVE
LIKE MADMAN

The doctor has yet to give his side of the case. Imagine how you would feel if it were you. There is real danger in the prosecuting counsel's opening statement; it is in fact only privileged if it is borne out by evidence, and there have been occasions when a prosecution counsel has not been able to substantiate his opening statement. In a long case it is always wiser to choose as a headline point something that has been corroborated in court—and, of course, it is essential to indicate in the headline that this is only one side of the story: It will not do to indicate this merely by quotes:

'DOCTOR DROVE
LIKE MADMAN'

Some newspapers do put their trust in quotes, but it is

thin trust and not really fair to the defendant. The proper way is to say:

DOCTOR DROVE
LIKE MADMAN,
COURT TOLD

There are only a few ways in which court attribution can be given in headings. The most common is a variation of allege, but there are other possibilities: Court/magistrates/ judge/JPs told; says QC/police. And if the defendant is well known he can appear as himself: 'Secretary to blame, says Bloggins'.

The attribution can be a tag line in smaller type than the main heading or an overline, provided the attribution is really closely related to the main heading. It must not be so small or separate as to escape notice. Even so, it is a good practice then to add quotation marks to the damaging section in the main deck of the headline. For instance:

Two company directors—one of whom later committed suicide—set out to strip a stores company of every possible asset. This was alleged at Blanktown court today when former City financier, Mr X, was charged with fraudulently misapplying £100,000 as a director of the stores group, with Mr Y. . . .

Court story of missing £100,000
DIRECTORS 'STRIPPED COMPANY'

Remands and adjournments need watching. It is all right to say 'Rape charge youths again remanded', though of course 'Rape youths remanded' would be defamatory. When a man is remanded you do not assume any headline based on the prosecution to be safe, without qualification, even if the man has pleaded guilty. The plea can be changed. For instance, this headline is imprudent as well as confused by trying to say too much:

Man grabbed
nurse's neck,
remanded

Since this was a first appearance before remand it would have been better to say simply:

Man grabbed
nurse's neck,
court told

There are a few other cautions which can be summarised. When a man *elects* to go for trial do not say in the headline 'sent for trial', since this has been held to imply that the magistrates considered there was evidence of guilt.

In juvenile cases avoid the harsher court words 'conviction', 'sentence', 'charge' (and, of course, anything which might lead to identification, though that should not be in the text either). Do not use Borstal as a synonym for approved school, remand home, remand centre or detention centre: use the precise description that the court used. In divorce and consent-to-marry cases, which are subject to statutory restrictions, headlines are most safely based on the decisions of the court and the summing up of the judge. And a whole host of traps ensnare the deskmen who use words loosely.

A man found guilty of a Customs offence is not necessarily a smuggler, or necessarily guilty of fraud. Never glibly write 'thief' in the headline on a man convicted of a theft, or use other criminal epithets, especially if it is a first offence. It could be held to suggest that the man is a professional thief incapable of reform. Never call a man a bankrupt until there has been an adjudication order.

It is as well to know all the inhibitions there are in headlining court reports, not simply for safety, though, this is paramount, but also to avoid needless pussyfooting. When the facts are no longer at issue—when the court has convicted—you can drop the tag 'court told', 'allegation', and so on. You can state baldly the most interesting fact to emerge and that is generally not the penalty of the court but the evidence it has accepted. A woman is ordered to keep her dog under control. That is unremarkable; the interest is in the evidence that a 2½-year-old boy was found lying on the ground screaming with the snarling dog over him. Since this is not an event of the immediate past, you use the past tense:

Dog attacked baby boy

Defence points in concluded convictions rarely merit a headline point since they have anyway failed. This was poor headlining:

TRADER 'IGNORANT OF LAW'

This was the defence offered by a man found guilty of selling firearms to boys under 17—in this instance air pistols to two 13-year-old boys.

The chairman said the magistrates were disturbed that almost lethal weapons had got into the hands of mere children. Clearly the headline fails on two counts. It omits a key word—gun. A headline about a vague 'trader' could be concealing anything from opium smuggling to selling balloons at street corners. Secondly, the defence, having failed, is a negative aspect of the story. A passable headline was:

SOLD BOYS OF
13 AIR
PISTOLS

The most defeatist type of court headline which afflicts many provincial papers all over the world like a pestilence, is the lift-and-dust 'Man fined. . . .' That formula, emphasising the fine, is only justified when the fine is colossal, and the case itself of excruciating boredom. What you should do is fasten on the liveliest evidence which has been confirmed.

Confirmation of the offence itself usually yields the most striking headline. Here is an American example.

> A court martial board has found a Poughkeepsie, NY, coast-guardsman guilty of causing the sinking of his ship and sentenced him to nine months at hard labor without pay.

Wrong:

GUARDSMAN FOUND
GUILTY IN SINKING

Right:

GUARDSMAN SANK
HIS OWN BOAT

Remember the injunction about restricting the headline to one thought. Court headlines frequently tempt a deskman into trying to cope with the crime and sentence in one breath:

Wrong:

Councillor fined £1,040 for expenses fraud

Right:
Councillor sent in bogus expense
claims for nine years

Because it is a formal court case, there is no need why—given accuracy and fairness—the headline should not contain some wit. When a High Court judge ruled against cricketers who hit a ball for six into a man's garden, it was a harmless metaphor to head the story:

JUDGE BOWLS 6-HIT BATSMEN

Specialised Pages

All the injunctions for active news headlines apply to sports and business headings.

Businessmen prefer restrained treatment of business news and they should have it. But confidence in the financial pages is not a matter of avoiding verbs and simple words. It is a matter of tone, moderation and simple accuracy. Business shares with sport one special headline requirement: names. The names of the companies and the names of their leaders are the essential signal. Shun the more general headings such as 'Pieman and the baker in merger talks' and write simple active specific headlines:

BOAC profit drops by £3m

£35,000 a year for Beecham's new man

Thorn Electrical Chairman calls for sales tax

Rank sells last of TV outlets to Rediffusion

Similarly with sports headings the names of teams, players, managers, and horses and jockeys, are essential headline material. Sport is vigorous and the headline should be vigorous. There is certainly no place in any newspaper for the kind of dead-hand sports editing still surviving in some 'quality' newspapers:

INTRODUCTION OF THE
STARTING STALL
Argument For and Against

ENGLISH AMATEUR CHAMPIONSHIP	Cameron Corbett Vase for H Frazer
No Seeding for M J Burgess	Match lacks atmosphere

Another report tells how in an angry game the referee was knocked out, whereupon the daredevil sub-editor wrote the heading: 'Rough and tumble in Cup match'. Sport is no place for euphemisms. A more common headline failing is euphoria leading to incomprehension:

Oh-so-softly Gary putt triumph 2 up

This is related to the other temptation in sport which is to crowd the head with too many ideas:

'Mike Who?' Wins for LA; Bosox Beaten

It should be possible to achieve vigour and comprehensible brightness and I would not want to squash the occasional lark within the limits of the English language, such as Hugh Cudlipp's celebrated head on the night the boxer Lee Oma had gone prematurely horizontal:

OMA, COMA, AROMA

The point you select for the head will depend on whether you are headlining a rush evening sports special, or a morning or Sunday sports page. With the first, you can safely assume that the head should concentrate on the result of the game, since the readers will primarily be buying the paper for that. In the second instance, with the results having been broadcast several hours before, the sports readers should be given headlines which concentrate on a feature of the game leaving the result to be implied:

Superb Osgood puts Chelsea in good heart

Wales pay dearly for three mistakes

The best way to avoid clichés in sports headings ('Feelings run high at Arsenal') is always to select an outstanding incident or player, rather than a generality.

5 Headline Typography

What type shall I use? The gods refuse to answer. They refuse because they do not know.

—W A DWIGGINS

Newspapermen, even if not destined to be dedicated typographers, will find a study of the history of type rewarding.[1] It emphasises the primacy of function, of legibility and utility over custom and aesthetics. The Italian humanistic lettering we call roman (the style of this book and all our printed matter today) ousted Caxton's Germanic Gothic in England and everywhere else because people found it easier to read. And the history of typography is populated by some remarkable people— William Caslon of London who cut his most famous type in 1720 had been an apprentice to an engraver of gun barrels. John Baskerville of Birmingham was a footman before he was a type designer. Giambattista Bodoni, who was inspired by Baskerville, made his fame from 1786 in the printing office of the Duke of Parma.

There is romance in type names; and considerable confusion. Bodoni designed a distinctive type, but today there is no such simple thing as Bodoni type. The types bearing the famous eighteenth century names were primarily designed as small-sized types for books; the development of display sizes was limited. When in the nineteenth century type manufacturers had to meet the huge demand for display faces for posters, shops, advertising, and newspapers, they produced strengthened versions of the book faces, and, later, wholly new designs of their own.

The differences between a display type with a famous name from one foundry or from one of the four machine composing manufacturers (Ludlow, Linotype, Intertype, and Monotype) may be insignificant in some instances, but immediately noticeable in others. Most of the modern Bodonis in newspaper display, for instance, are similar because they are based on a recutting by M F Benton for American Typefounders from 1907 onwards, but the Linotype and Intertype Bodoni Italic are much closer set than the Monotype Bodoni Bold Italic. Again, the Stephenson Blake typefounders' Caslon Heavy is wider and stronger than any of the machine-set versions. There is a further confusion. Types which look very similar have been given different names by the different manufacturers. Linotype's *Poster Bodoni* is a similar fat face to the Monotype *Ultra Bodoni* (Series 120), or the Ludlow *Bodoni Black*. Look at the two sets of very similar typefaces, all with different titles, shown here.

Pabst Extra Bold from Linotype

Ludlow Black from Ludlow

Goudy Extra Bold 214 from Monotype

Memphis from Linotype Cairo Bold from Intertype

Rockwell from Monotype Karnak from Ludlow

But there is no need for despair. The illustrations are meant to instil the need for accuracy in the specification of typefaces for newspaper display. And though there is today a vast range of display type, which may seem to present too bewildering a choice, the newspaper must select from a limited range. Speed of production alone requires that the headline type in general use in the newspaper should come, as metal, from the keyboarded machines of Linotype and Intertype, or the semi-mechanised Ludlow system, or as filmset characters from these and other manufacturers. An attractive hand-set type from a founder can only be contemplated for the larger sizes at wide measure, where hand-setting of the relatively few characters is as fast as a machine and redistribution of the few characters of used type not such a chore. In hot-metal newspapers, the Ludlow system of slug-casting from hand-set matrices is most popular for headlines: the keyboarded machines do not set above 36pt in upper- and lower-case.

Elements of Type Design

There are other requirements as well as speed which define the area of display type selection for the newspaper, but before we examine these we must begin by analysing the ingredients of type design. Five concern us at this stage.

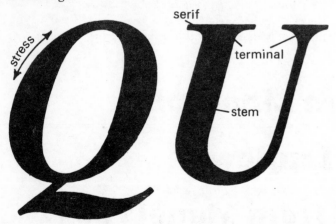

The serif

This is the line crossing the free ending of a stroke. It looks insignificant but its presence, its thickness, angle, and the way it is joined to the stem have a decisive effect on the appearance of the letter. 'It is in this manipulation of the serif that the human appetite for variety finds its satisfaction', said Stanley Morison.

The stress

Where curved strokes vary in thickness, the distribution of the thicks and thins is the stress or shading. If in any of the thickest parts they are directly opposite each other (as they are in the Bodoni family), the stress is said to be vertical. If you find this concept of stress difficult, try tracing a set of, say, Bodoni type characters and then place the tracing paper over Caslon or Century characters. It will help you to pick out the different stress.

Record
Franklin
Garamond
Bodoni Black

The weight

The range of weight is seen when you contrast the types above. Weight means the degree of blackness of a typeface. What is sometimes called 'colour' in a typeface is a combination of its weight and width. The relative weights are classified logically by names in British Standard 2961: 1967:

Extra Light
Light
Semi-light
Medium (being the weight the maker puts forward under the name of the family as representing the design in that normal weight from which variants in the family have been, or are, derived)
Semi-bold
Bold
Extra Bold
Ultra Bold

These British Standard names are not yet universal—some manufacturers designate their Bold as Heavy or Black—and, of course, not every type family can offer anything like this range of weights. But agreement on description and classification should gradually spread. Univers, identified at birth by only a series of numbers, is now identified by names, too. Filmset headlines can, of course, have their weight varied readily by the addition of a screen tint.

Record Bold Extended can say this

Record Gothic Extra Condensed says this much and more

The width

The range of width or condensation available to the letterpress newspaper headline typographer is between, say, Record Gothic Extra Condensed, which compresses a whole alphabet at 36pt into a line just over 18 picas long —and, at the other extreme, Record Bold Extended where the length of a lower-case alphabet in 36pt is more than double. (The samples above are 24pt.)

Again, manufacturers' names can confuse. The lighter version of Century which is called Century in British Linotype catalogues is called Century *Expanded* by Ludlow and American Linotype, though it is not an expanded letter at all. One can only hope that gradually manufacturers will adopt the British Standard. This is its proposed list of relative widths of typefaces:

Ultra Condensed
Extra Condensed
Condensed
Semi-condensed
Medium (the width the maker puts forward under the name of the family as representing the design in that normal width from which variants in the family have been, or are, derived)
Semi-expanded
Expanded
Extra Expanded
Ultra Expanded

One must not assume that this range of widths is available in every hot-metal face. Of course, the range of widths available photographically by filmsetting is extensive. Master film founts on a negative can be stretched or squeezed as the designer desires, though not always with happy results. Edward Ronthaler has suggested as a cold-type standard a grid of 2,300 different coded weight–width combinations.

x-Height

The Bodoni setting of Big News below looks smaller than the Franklin setting on the right. But both in fact are in 36pt. The point size is identical; the difference is in the x-height—the size of the printed image of the middle part of the face, exclusive of ascenders and descenders. It is the height of x and similar letters in the fount, measured on what is called the 'appearing' face. See Book Two, Text Typography, for a fuller discussion. It may seem odd to make the body the basis of the measurement of type when it is the type face, rather than the body, which one sees in print. A moment's thought will show that it is convenient to measure the body. It is the metal body which occupies the space in the forme.

Why do designers not use the whole body for the letter? Why waste that metal above the below the x-height? The answer is that the body has to bear the whole alphabet in continuous relationship—the capital letter and the eleven special letters which need extra space on the body.

The eleven lower-case letters that have space-consuming descending or ascending strokes are g, j, p, q, y (five descenders) and b, d, f, h, k, l (six ascenders). Fractions, commas, and parentheses also ascend or descend as do the capitals J and Q. Some types are designed with long ascenders and descenders, some with short. The types with long extremities leave less room on the body for the x-height. A type of great x-height is therefore bound to have compressed descenders and ascenders.

Capitals

The capitals of most typefaces sit on the same baseline as lower-case and are almost as tall as the ascenders of lower-case. A capital letter of a fount with caps and upper- and lower-case normally occupies two-thirds of the body depth. It takes the space of the x-characters plus the space of the ascender. It leaves, as white space, the area occupied on the body by the descending strokes of

Big News   Big news

the five lower-case descenders. There are some founts which are made only for setting titles in capitals—titling founts. Here the capital letter can take all the space on the body since, by definition, there are no lower-case descenders to worry about. The titling cap does not have to be on the baseline of lower-case characters, because there is none there for alignment. A titling cap is, therefore, normally full on the body so that a 36pt titling appears almost 36pt in print. There are also some typefaces which offer the reverse of titling caps: they offer small capitals which line up with the x-height characters.

So much for the characteristics of a piece of type. What matters equally, of course, is how the single image combines with other images to form integrated and readable units. Some definitions are necessary.

6 point
8 point
10 point
12 point
14 point
18 point
24 point
30 point
36 point
48 point
60 point
72point

A TYPEFACE: The face is the engraved image which is inked and prints. A typeface means a set of characters of a particular size designed to be used in combination. It is a design for a whole alphabet of printing. For example 14pt Bodoni Bold is one face, 14pt Bodoni Italic is another. You have not created a typeface if, using a filmsetter, you have your handwritten headline turned into a negative for printing, or even if you make a negative of a few words of typing. A typeface is not merely the printed letter. It is an integrated design.

A single typeface can be made in different sizes:

A SERIES is the size range of that typeface. The series of the Bodoni Bold typeface runs in Ludlow from 6pt to 8pt, 10pt and up to 96pt. **Below left** is the Ludlow Record Gothic Bold series.

A FOUNT (pronounced font) is all the characters of any one typeface in any one size that you will need for a piece of printing. A fount of metal type will consist of capitals, lower-case, punctuation marks, and numerals in varied assortments according to a 'founting scheme' based on the average frequency of characters needed in printing. This is a fount of 10pt Linotype Century:

ABCDEFGHIJKLMNOPQRSTUVWXYZ
abcdefghijklmnopqrstuvwxyz
1234567890
fiflffffiffl
[(-,.:;"—!?.../*†‡§‖¶)]
&£$ àèìòù áéíóú âêîôû äëïöü çñ
@·+−×='''°% ⅛⅜⅝⅞

ABCDEFGHIJKLMNOPQRSTUVWXYZ
abcdefghijklmnopqrstuvwxyz
1234567890
fiflffffiffl
[(-,.:;"—!?.../*†‡§‖¶)]
&£$ àèìòù áéíóú âêîôû äëïöü çñ
@·+−×='''°% ⅛⅜⅝⅞

A fount and a series describe what is available in one typeface. But typefaces beget. . . .

FAMILIES: A basic design which breeds a family is a 'model' typeface. The word family in typography means exactly what it means with human families. The members of the family will all have a resemblance to the common parent, but all will have individual variations. Some of a human family will be short, some fat, some dark, some

BODONI TRUEFACE

POSTER BODONI

Bodoni Trueface

BODONI BOLD

Bodoni Trueface

Bodoni Bold

Bodoni Trueface

Bodoni Bold Italic

BODONI TRUEFACE

Bodoni Bold Condensed

Bodoni Trueface

Bodoni Campanile

BODONI TRUEFACE

BODONI CAMPANILE

BODONI MODERN

Bodoni Modern

Bodoni Modern

light, but all may have blue eyes and a hooked nose. Some of a type family will be condensed, some extended, some bold, some light, but all will have, say, monoline strokes and square serifs.

There are a few display typefaces which are orphans and not members of families. For the contrast and variety we seek in newspaper display work, however, we will be working with typefaces which do belong to a fairly large family. We can obtain a rich variety of changes within one family. Let us assume, for instance, that the newspaper is based on Bodoni. Then, within the Bodoni family, **above** are some of the Ludlow variants on the primary design.

The qualifying terms attached to the name of the model design give some idea of the varying permutations of type within one family. Families of typefaces can be classified in periods and styles with varying degrees of refinement, the basic difficulty being that some characteristics overlap different groups. An attempt is now being made to gain universal acceptance for an international classification.[2] The British Standards Institution classifies type in nine basic divisions according to the axis of the curves, contrasts in the strokes, and the nature of the serif[3]. The German standard—DIN 16518 (1964) follows the same general plan but uses ill-assorted class names. Allen Hutt divided display types according to the formation of the serifs[4].

I will refer to the British Standard classifications in the section that follows, but since the old terms will for some time be the ones the newsman hears I will continue to use them. I begin by classifying the families, in three broad categories—*romans*, *sans serifs*, and *slab serifs*. These categories are not as esoteric as they might be to classify the variations and hybrids but they do cope with the dominant characteristics in a way which will help recognition and discussion among practical newspaper deskmen.

Romans
In the British Standard romans are subdivided into four categories (Humanist, Garalde, Transitional, Didone). The common characteristics are serifs and strokes with some contrast between light and heavy lines. Basically, the range runs from old face romans (called Garalde in the British Standard) through a transitional period to modern romans (Didone in the British Standard).

Old face
The *old face* romans—called *old style* in North America—have rounded shapes resembling the shapes made in handwriting; most book types are old face. There is a gradual transition from thick to thin. The serifs are short lines joined to the stem with a continuous curve—rather than with a sharp right-angle. Here is a letter in Caslon Old Face, with bracketed serifs, and the stress of the curves to the left:

B

Serifs like this are called bracketed serifs, because of the way they are linked to the stem and because they do support the serif of the actual metal type and prevent its breaking away. Bembo, Garamond, Caslon and Goudy Old Style are old face romans (Garalde in the British Standard).

Fournier, Baskerville and Bell are *transitional* faces, with thick–thin contrast increasing, serifs sharper pointed but still bracketed to the stem.

The *moderns*, fully developed by the end of the eighteenth century, are distinguished by a general note of precision and perpendicularity and abrupt variation of colour. Bodoni, Didot and Walbaum are the best known. The strokes are with a vertical stress to the curves—as if they were cut by a chisel rather than written by a pen. The body is less rounded and open than the old face. The transition from thick to thin is sharp, not gradual.

The serifs do not merge with the stroke. They are fine lines extended horizontally from the end. The modern face serif is also thinner and longer than the old face serif.

Here are some letters in Bodoni:

ABCDEF

Now look at a drawing showing the changes in stress from old style through transitional to modern.

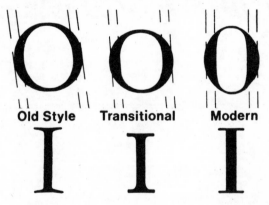

Old Style   Transitional   Modern

Types in the roman family blend the characteristics described above in different ways. Scotch Roman, for instance, is the British development of French–Italian modern. It avoids the extremes of Bodoni; the serifs are thin and sharp like a modern but they are finely bracketed to the stem. The thick–thin contrast is strong but not so abrupt. **Opposite** are some of the roman families, marrying old face and modern characteristics in varying degrees.

MONOTYPE'S CASLON TITLING

Monotype's Baskerville Bold

Monotype's Bodoni 135

Monotype's Plantin 110

Monotype's Scotch Roman 137

Monotype's Goudy Old Style

MONOTYPE'S TIMES BOLD TITLING 328

Ludlow Cheltenham Bold

Ludlow Garamond Bold

Ludlow Bodoni Black

Sans Serifs

The British Standard term for the group of sans serifs is Lineale. They have no serifs, and strokes in most of the types appear to be of equal thickness with little or no contrast.

It is worth distinguishing four forms of sans type:

Geometric sans

Geometric sans is derived by compasses and set-square from two elements only—a circle and straight line. The letters do not follow roman proportions. Paul Renner with Futura and Rudolf Koch with Cable set the pattern in the 1920s following the functional aesthetic of the Bauhaus (though some individual letters in these faces have had to be adjusted to give the optical impression of austere geometry and uniformity). The strokes are usually monoline and often have a single-storey 'a'.

Spartan, the most widely used sans in American newspapers, is a geometric sans, similar to Intertype's Futura with uniform size of circles and areas and junctions with stems. Erbar and Eurostyle are two more.

Note the geometry, please

Styled sans

Sometimes called *modern sans*. Edward Johnston in 1916 and Eric Gill in 1927 created unserifed monotone designs based on the classic old face roman letter. These sans types have personal touches such as the slanted terminals in some, but not all, of Linotype's Metro by W A Dwiggins.

This is Metroblack

Grotesques

These types stem from a German development this century of the first sans serifs ever shown in England in the early nineteenth century. The Germans developed this range by varying the width of the letter and by replacing some of the squared ends with tapering strokes. They have squareness of curve and generally curling close-set jaws. These sans types were first called *grotesques*, and later in Europe *new grots*, and in North America, *gothics*. Typical specimens are for Franklin, Record, Univers and Helvetica. Such grots, it has been well said, 'avoid the

Monotype's Univers

brutally dogmatic geometry of the Futura school. They are still designed for the eye, not for the mind'.[5] They are the most viable of sans types for newspaper display.

Stressed sans

Serifs are still absent but the monoline character of the sans group of types is softened by giving a thick and thin contrast in lines. Albertus, for instance, has strokes thickened towards the end.

Albertus

Slab Serifs

Slab serifs are monotone in stroke character, like many of the sans serifs, but there are serifs—heavy, square-ended serifs, with or without brackets. These serifs are usually the same thickness as the stems of the letter and there is not much differentiation of colour.

d d d

This category is sometimes called *antique* or *egyptian* because of their early association with exhibitions of Egyptian antiquities. The serifs are most often unbracketed but there is a related family of typefaces called *clarendons* (last **d** above). The first clarendons followed the egyptians in the 1840s but softened the exaggerated harshness of the egyptians. The serifs are gently bracketed and the better proportioned bear some thick–thin contrast. The clarendons bred the famous range of open text-type faces—the ionics—and still have display potential.

Choosing a Basic Type

Let us now recall what we said in Chapter 1 were the all-round requirements for a basic newspaper headline family: a clear signal; swiftly readable; economical in editorial and production time and in newsprint space; proportionate to the news; and flexible.

Production considerations

The production qualifications should come first. Speed and flexibility are required in headline setting. It is no use choosing a general news headline face which can be produced only slowly and in limited sizes and weights. A newspaper needs a type which has in its family at least a change of bold and light; or of upright (usually called roman) and italic; and in sizes from 14pt to 48pt for tabloids and up to 60pt for broadsheets.

One of an executive's first ventures on joining a publishing operation should be to discover precisely what can be offered. If working with filmsetting and web offset, speed will not be a limitation and on a film machine like the PhotoTypositor of the Visual Graphics Corporation a fantastic range of sizes up to 144pt can be produced at will by instantaneous photographic enlargement of characters. A single film fount can yield about 2,800 different type sizes and setting styles.

In the news operation of a web offset newspaper it is normally more convenient to work in accepted point sizes. (In features, given the need, you can escape from the limitations of fixed point sizes. If the wording fits well at $32\frac{1}{2}$pt you can easily summon up $32\frac{1}{2}$pt photographically.) But if you do not need to worry much about size or speed you do need to know what typefaces are available from the photosetting machines.

On all newspapers the deskman should ask the head printer to show him the machines he has and discover how they are stocked. (In newspapers, headline schedule cards are often out of date and rarely indicate what sizes are available from which methods of production.)

The very largest headings (over 60pt) may acceptably be set in movable original type, hand-set into a composing room stick, transferred to the forme, and redistributed into the type case after use. But this is too slow for the run of news headings, especially when time is included for distributing (dissing) the used type. Letterpress newspapers today prefer a type which comes in slugs—solid lines in which the letters and spaces are joined up together and are hence easy to handle. These are provided either by:

(a) Linotype or Intertype keyboard machines, similar to those used for setting text type but with a different stock of matrices.

(b) The Ludlow machine which provides slugs from hand-assembled matrices.

There are two other machines which follow the Ludlow principle, but can cast headlines from Ludlow matrices or the matrices of any other slug machine. There is the British SAM (Suit All Matrices) machine and the Italian Nebitype.

Setting headlines with the Ludlow is more flexible than the Linotype and Intertype machines, which have limitations on the range of size they can offer.

The second production consideration is economy in editorial time and newsprint space. The headline face should yield enough characters to make 11-pica headlines easy enough to write in two or three lines.

The third production consideration, most important for letterpress, is to avoid a type unless it is rugged enough to emerge unscathed from the cruder processes of hot-metal stereotyping. Other things being equal, a newspaper display type should have good open counters (the full or semi-enclosed space within a letter). Newspapers should avoid a type where, say, the letter e has a small eye (as it has in Garamond), especially in the smaller display sizes, and should not be seduced by the fine lines of a face like Truecut Bodoni Italic.

Fine but delicate

The fourth production consideration is the method of setting and printing and the paper and ink used. One cannot account for all the variables here—types should be judged not by their catalogue finish but by printing them on newsprint. But a warning can be given that photosetting or web offset printing and especially the two together produce a different image from hot-metal letterpress on some important display faces. Old style faces like Caslon, for instance, were designed for printing that would force (sock) the face into the paper. The ink would spread and thicken the image. But printed offset, where there is no permanent indentation of the paper, where the image is simply deposited on the surface, Caslon seems emaciated. So does Bembo. And I have seen filmset display lines of Century Bold look quite thin by comparison with hot-metal Century Bold, despite being sadly squeezed of traditional letterspacing to give a more compact image. Experienced printers[6] using filmset-offset report that sharp clear modern faces designed after the Industrial Revolution are best in photo-composition (the trend in British offset papers has been to choose, at the risk of monotony, ultra heavy condensed sans types).

Legibility

All newspapers have to consider the other requirements for a satisfactory headline type which is to be published after being printed at high speed on rough porous paper with thin inks.

First, a clear signal. It means we must have a face which has enough weight (i.e. enough black printing surface)

Specialization, the keynote of surgical endeavour over the past 50 years, has meant that the pace at which kno
On these two pages some of these specialties are examined by fellows of the Royal College of Surgeons and a
anonymous. Each specialty has been selected not because it is necessarily more sophisticated or more drama
and the medical and social implications for those whom its techniques are designed to heal—give it either a to

BIO-ENGINEERING 1. HIP PROSTHESIS

An exercise in organized collaboration between two disciplines opens

Bio-engineering, the new medical discipline of this decade, is an organized collaboration between graduate engineers and medical scientists. It replaces the dabbling in mechanical matters which was the only way in the past by which surgeons

centre specializing in artificial hip joint surgery at Wrightington, near Wigan, Lancashire. Over the past 10 years this exercise in specialization has involved consultations and collaborations with a multiplicity of research engineers in widely

nature had evolved an extraordinary means of lubrication in animal joints. Past failures of surgery undoubtedly were in part due to failure to incorporate factors of lubrication in the design of implants. Though probably coincidental, this col

only superficially and in no case with the sophisticated techniques which are now commonplace in engineering circles. The gap in knowledge was filled by work in the University of Strathclyde, in the University of Manchester Institute of Sci

could not be succe bonded to the living bo each side of the joint. implant became loose und load of the weight of it would cause as much p the original diseased jo which the surgery had

Family Today —

Make stuffing a sp

IT'S WHAT'S inside that counts in your Thanksgiving turkey. Here's a trio of delicious stuffing suggestions.

¼ teaspoon poultry
　 seasoning
¼ teaspoon salt
2 cups chopped, peeled
　 apples

1 tablespoon lemon juice
¾ cup water
1 cup coarsely chopped
　 oysters, drained

to contrast with the grey of the text even at small sizes. This (1) is too grey.

Types of this lightness need to be used fairly big to be noticed: and in a newspaper space is precious. A light face is useful for a variant in headline display but it should have somewhat more strength than this. And a type can also be too black for general use. A heavy black face can only be used effectively at small sizes. Used generally on a news page at the usual range of sizes it sets an unhappy tone scale for text and half-tones. It can raise the pitch of display too much. In Stockholm's lively *Expressen* (2) the big Bodoni headlines are powerful in themselves but they kill the pictures.

Readability

If it is to be readable it needs extra white; and black faces, at the bigger sizes, tend to look smudgy and scruffy. Pabst for instance is acceptable at 18–24pt but obtuse at 36–48pt. Secondly, the typeface should be both legible

and readable. Legibility and readability describe different characteristics of type. A typeface is *legible* if it is easy to tell the different letters one from another. This is not:

aoilij tl I

A typeface is *readable* if the eye moves easily along the line of type: if the individual letters knit well together in words and phrases. Since we read by words and phrases rather than by individual letters readability is the more important criterion. Legibility is only one factor in readability. Some typefaces have letters which are legible enough as individual letters but which spring out from the rest of the typeface when it is set as a line. And it is not the individual letter we want to see; it is the word shape. Individual letters stand out too much from this mannered feature display face in *Chicago Today* (3).

1

l techniques have advanced has varied widely
the Royal College of Physicians. For profess
y of a dozen others but because the particular :
representative significance

v horizons

ty led to the introduc-
self-hardening methyl-
late cement. Many
dic surgeons consider
e an outstanding tech-
development which
n up new vistas in
dic surgery.

ing prototype implants of all
kinds, a bio-mechanical laboratory in the hospital precincts,
staffed by two full-time research technicians, has been of
paramount importance. This
laboratory has been financed
by the Research Committee of

safely ;
amount
concentr
implante
always p
would l
mechani
body. A

day, Monday, November 24, 1969 **27**

ialty

3

An exaggerated prominence for individual letters may be because there is a thickening of some downstrokes, as here; or perhaps a change in one of the curved letters in the distribution of 'stress' (the thickening in a curved stroke as the line changes direction). It may be that an individual ascender has a slightly different terminal. It may be that the word has been opened out by excess spacing so that individual letters are emphasised, or that some upper-case letters stand out awkwardly with some lower-case combinations. And, of course, in some faces there is a technically illegible letter which will impede readability.

This is the point behind the aphorism of Beatrice Warde of Monotype that 'printing should be invisible'. If the type distracts you it has hindered your reading and hence the communication of the message. Headline type should draw attention to the news not to itself. For read-ability (which, remember, is only one test of a face) judge the superb Linotype Helvetica against another line from a different face.

A pure linear pattern

Not so readable

When judging readability of a face read it set in a long line and in different sizes. Glimpse it quickly through half-closed eyes; and then examine individual letters, especially the letters s, a, o, j, g, f, and the consistency of spacing. Condensed types in particular are weakened by excess white between the letters. The letters themselves have small counters and white between the letters weakens the horizontal unity of the typeface. Newspapers using filmset headlines can easily overcome this weakness in an original metal design, if it is consistent, by pushing the letters closer together in filming.

Overseas_____ Middle East_____

Mr Sato certain to stay leader of the ruling party in Japan

From Michael Hornsby
Tokyo, Sept. 29

Mr. Eisaku Sato, Prime Minister of Japan since 1964, is now certain to be reelected to a fourth term as leader of the Liberal Democratic Party (L.D.P.) at its national convention on October 29.

It is part of the peculiarity of Japanese politics that this can be stated without Mr. Sato's ever having announced that he intends to stand for the office.

Japanese politicians have dogged Mr. Sato's footsteps for weeks on end in the hope of some titbit of news can now at last get some sleep.

It has been an uphill assignment all the way. Most newspapers have been obliged to present speculation about the state of Mr. Sato's health as scoops. It was a sensation when someone disclosed that the Prime Minister had strained his left hand while playing golf ; it was a counter-sensation when someone else was able to quote culinary chapter and verse to

Israel security forces on alert as Arabs in occupied territories lament the loss of their leader

From Eric Marsden
Jerusalem, Sept. 29

Security forces throughout the west bank and in the Gaza Strip were out in force today as a million Arabs in the occupied areas were plunged into mourning for President Nasser of Egypt. The intensity of feeling shown surprised many observers of Arab affairs, especially as the Egyptian leader had been criticized lately for his role in the Jordan crisis.

Demonstrations were held in several towns, mostly without serious incident, but in a Gaza

also come in for criticism because of his support for the King.

President Nasser's death is another unsettling factor for the people of the west bank, already in a mood of shock and confusion over the Jordan civil war. It is likely that talks which have been going on about the future of the area and of the Palestinian people as a whole will be suspended during the mourning period.

Informal meetings of west bank notables have been held recently

would see to it that Parliament would not pick them to rule.

Mr. Yigal Allon, the Israel Deputy Prime Minister, discussed President Nasser's death in a lecture to secondary school students in Haifa today. He said the Egyptian leader had introduced agrarian reforms and had initiated tremendous industrial and agricultural development programmes but he had also squandered Egypt's resources on arms and wars and the Egyptian people were now as wretched as they had been during the regime of King Farouk

Cholera in Amman amid stench of death

From Ibrahim Noori
Amman, Sept. 29

The stench of death and rotting bodies hangs over Wahdat refugee camp on the edge of Amman where soldiers today used a bulldozer to shovel earth over nearly 50 swollen corpses sprawled in a ditch. Cholera has broken out in the area, with several cases already confirmed, Red Cross sources said.

Wahdat, stronghold of the Popular Front for the Liberation of Palestine, was heavily shelled by

New leader in Egypt is well prepared

From Paul Martin
Beirut, Sept. 29

Mr. Anwar Sadat, who has been sworn in as provisional President of Egypt following the death of Gamal Abdel Nasser, had begun to assume the role of heir apparent in the Egyptian leadership over the past year. However, like all of those at the heart of the Egyptian regime, his role was only relative to the degree of power leased to him by the late President.

Mr. Sadat was one of the inner circle of the Free Officers who overthrew the monarchy in 1952.

anxious to unload many of the less pressing burdens of office on to shoulders he knew he could trust. He was known to be been more than satisfied with Mr. Sadat's handling of these affairs of state.

Mr. Sadat had been one of four joint Vice Presidents from 1964 to 1967. From that period until he was singled out as the heir apparent he played a leading role in the country's Parliamentary life, particularly relating to Egypt's relations with friendly countries and the third world.

Like all of the free officers, Mr. Sadat is an ardent Egyptian

---

Economy and crispness

In width we seek something for news heads which is not an extreme. It might seem that the extra condensed faces should be preferred for newspaper headlines, but useful though a condensed face is for single-column headlines, the extra condensed face can easily become illegible, and especially in multi-column measures where it also produces a wordy, flabby headline. This is a difficulty with the comparatively condensed Times Roman 334 when used in multi-line horizontal display **(above)**.

With the trend to horizontal layouts and multi-column headlines, compactness looks like being even less of a necessity compared with weight and colour. Hence the attraction of a wide set bold and open face such as Century Schoolbook (as seen in Long Island's *Newsday* and the London *Observer*).

There should certainly be vertical economy. The display type should have a big x-height. And the newspaper news display type should have a further quality—crispness. It should be clear-cut and emphatic. The news headline should not be a fat letter like:

Ludlow Black

Taken together all the specifications described above severely limit the choice. For news headline purposes we have to eliminate several entire categories of type—those that imitate cursive writing; old English or blackletter faces; decorated, outline, shaded and three-dimensional letters. None of these remotely meets the regular requirements of a newspaper. We have to eliminate typefounders' faces not yet available on line-casting machines. We have to eliminate thin grey faces.

Of course we have to recognise that what is right for *Reveille* will not suit *The Hindu*. Newspapers do have different attitudes and personalities to express and headline typography is one of the ways they can express it. Neither can one ignore reader habit and associations which have built up over a long time. The public in Britain at least will need careful indoctrination before it

will accept that a quality paper can be headlined throughout in sans (as it might very logically and handsomely be in, say, Univers or Record Bold). Clay Felker has reported an American experience :

'Recently the *World Journal Tribune* changed its typeface from Spartan to Bodoni. Not only was there a noticeable change in morale in the office staff, but circulation improved immediately. But the more important, long term effect for the paper is likely to be a changed image, and all that goes with such a change. For example, it now looks more like a New York instead of a small town paper. It appears to be more of a quality and less a popular paper. If my suspicions are correct, this should mean that its writers will begin to produce more sophisticated material, which in turn will bring in a more sophisticated audience, and perhaps even further gratify its present audience.'[7]

Even a new design, alas, could not save the *World Journal Tribune*, but the point survives. The associations and alleged aesthetic appeal of a type cannot be ignored.

Mixing Typefaces

I have been referring to 'the' display type for a newspaper, which begs a question. Why not have several display types? The American preference is to keep to one typeface, or at least one family, throughout a whole newspaper (news, features, different sections); in Britain, the serious papers have on the whole preferred one display dress, certainly for news, but the popular and local papers have tended to mix types throughout the paper and on the page as well, almost as much as some of the Europeans (*see* Book Five, pp. 103–28 for international comparisons.

There is a lot to be said for a change of family between sections of a newspaper, whether the sections are separately folded or not. Sport and the leader or feature page have their identity emphasised by a different family of type (say Bodoni for news, Goudy for features and sans for sport). And there is something disconcerting when the same type which has told you on page one of an earth-shattering event is used elsewhere—with similar style and emphasis—to headline a page of recipes.

Changes of type within a news page, and especially

The Visual Arts

apparently arbitrary changes, are another question. The choice must be determined by the nature of the newspaper and its audience (and the facilities of the plant). But I have no doubt that where the main purpose of the paper is to communicate information clearly and authoritatively (and that can sometimes mean communicating in an entertaining way), then the anarchy of mixing several different families higgledy-piggledy in news headlines is unwise. Consistency in news values requires consistency in news display dress. Newspapers in this are no different from other crafts: 'In all great epochs of history the existence of standards—that is the conscious adoption of type-forms has been the criterion of a polite and well ordered society; for it is a commonplace that repetition of the same things for the same purposes exercises a settling and civilising influence on men's minds.'[8]

The standard for newspapers is typographic—one basic type family for news headlines. It offers consistency. It unites news pages and issues of the same newspaper. Of course this judgment can be challenged. It may be that a serious newspaper will adopt the type anarchy of the popular newspaper. But the reader will need a period of indoctrination to take it seriously, such is the influence of good typography and of the association of ideas.

There are otherwise two kinds of type mixing. The first is the razzmatazz effect of a typographic cocktail which may be suitable for a newspaper depending less on coherence and continuity and more on shock and entertainment and whose purpose is to dazzle and entertain. Here anything goes. Variety is the plague of the aesthete's life. The *Daily Mail* of London gave an example in 1963 when it coloured its basic Century Bold and Bold Extended with a weird variety of Monotype faces such as New Clarendon 617, Grot 215, Victoria Condensed Titling 181 and Placard Condensed. It had all the consistency of a Victorian showbill. The other kind of type mixing is the judicious mixture of faces within one small typographical unit to achieve changes in colour. This is especially hard to accomplish. Most of the mixes one sees are bizarre, and the worst effect is when the mixed families are unrelated and are run beard to beard—Pabst, say, run as an overline or kicker to a Franklin headline. This is more than a mixing of faces or a mixing of families. It is a mixture of types from different categories, different heritages, different sympathies. It is (see **above**) like putting a thatched roof on a London penthouse.

That is a bizarre example, but (1) is another exhibiting the same fault over a narrower range of type changes. The display in the Business News of *The Times* mixes Bodoni Black, a sans, Times Roman 327 and there is just nothing in common between the flat wide letter of Bodoni Black and the over-condensed grey sans (and the Bodoni Black heading 'The Group of 4' makes things worse, especially the contortions thought necessary for the numeral 4).

The skilled typographer who feels he needs to mix types for colour contrast or spot emphasis for a feature panel, say, or a news page, looks for sympathy between the faces, sympathy in the stresses or serifs. He avoids mixing a geometrically derived sans with a roman old face, avoids mixing an old face and modern face.

Carefully done in this way, with good white around the different faces some type mixes can create cool and effective colour contrast, even within a single unit as in this example of running Record as a light sandwich between the reverse block and the Franklin (2).

Helvetica and Century mix effectively; Helvetica and Bodoni are not so good, and the clumsier sans faces like Tempo Heavy kill serif types. But one comes back to the warning that successful mixing is rare by comparison with the daily examples of unhappy marriages. All too common is the kind of clash produced by this hypothetical transfer (3) of display type from the London *Daily Mirror* to *The Times*.

The injunction to prefer one type does not of course rule out by any means the possibility of variety and contrast on a page. There are other display elements besides type (white space and half-tones, for instance) and there are enormous possibilities of variety even with one normal news display family. There are all the changes of size, style and weight. Indeed exploiting all the range of changes within one big family on one page would be too much.

Selected News Faces
Romans

It is now time to consider representative newspaper display types. There is no point in showing the full range. Availability and range change within countries and between countries and over different periods. Ludlow faces are universal; but Linotype and Intertype display faces are subject to the limitations that the machines made in Britain and North America (and Germany) produce type struck to different depths.

The current appropriate catalogues—always available from the manufacturers—are the best guide to any newspaper reconsidering its display dress and repay browsing by any newsman. What I hope to do here is comment on a representative selection as guide-lines.

CASLON

Today's Caslons (4), based on the famous old style roman introduced in the 1720s, are bigger on the body than Bodoni, and crisper than Century or Cheltenham. From the smallest to the largest faces, Caslon shows a superb graduation of strength and colour. Caslon is above everything an honest face. Peter Palazzo chose it for the New York *Sunday Herald Tribune* 'because of the instant impression of integrity it gives to the news'.

It is not as condensed as Century Bold, but reasonable, especially in the narrower Heavy from Intertype. (There are condensed versions which are more compact than Century Bold but they are not as readable.) A colour contrast can be obtained by mixing one of the lighter Caslons with the Heavy. A quiet weekly paper (right) could base its news headings on Ludlow Caslon, mixing the old face heavy roman with italic on the light–bold variation. But Caslon works better with letterpress than offset (and my photographed page inevitably does it less than justice).

4

LUDLOW'S CASLON OLD FACE HEAVY
This is Ludlow's Caslon Bold
Ludlow's Caslon Bold Condensed
Here is Ludlow's light italic
Ludlow's fine Heavy Italic

1
2

CENTURY

The front page of the old *News Chronicle* (1) shows some of the wide range of Century Bold—Roman, Bold Extended, Italic, Italic caps, and Bold Extended caps for a punchy streamer. *The Guardian* (2) is a serious paper dressed in Century Bold, demonstrating its wide appeal in Britain. It is odd that it has not been more widely used in the United States.

Century Bold is big on its body. It gives a large black printing surface with the largest possible areas of white in the hollow letters. Century Bold is of modern style but it is more rugged than Bodoni, and x-height for x-height (as distinct from point size) has a usefully more condensed lower-case.

The mix of Century Bold and the light Century (Ludlow's Expanded in the settings) is not very effective because the Century Light is too thin in letter form and has a large beard. If using Century Light as a contrast to Century Bold care has to be taken to make it one size bigger than would otherwise be chosen.

The disadvantages of Century are few. It is not as handsome a letter as Bodoni but it survives better than Bodoni with the excess interlinear white so common in newspaper display. In the large sizes, 48pt and up, the Bold Roman looks too tall for its width, which is a reason for preferring the Extended at these sizes.

CENTURY SCHOOLBOOK: A squarer, heavier face more related to the clarendons. Because it is wider it makes narrow-measure headlines harder to write, but when lower-case headlines are used extensively across multi-column as they are in horizontal layouts, it gains by being easier to read.

The lighter Schoolbook provides an excellent weight contrast to Schoolbook Bold—*see* the London *Observer* (3) or the *Daily Mail*.

The Nixon doctrine has them guessing

Dayan: No new peace talks without a real cease-fire

3

THIS IS THE FAMOUS CENTURY BOLD

Here is a showing in lower case

This is Century Bold Italic from Ludlow

HERE ARE CENTURY BOLD ITALIC CAPS

This is Ludlow Century Bold Extended

But this is called Century Expanded

And this Ludlow calls Century Modern

This is Ludlow's Century Bold Condensed

Ludlow calls this Century Modern Bold

Here is the Schoolbook Bold

This is Intertype Century Schoolbook

THIS IS SCHOOLBOOK BOLD IN CAPS

BODONI

The attractions of Bodoni are that the Bold is black enough for news headlines, it is reasonably condensed, and the modern style gives vivacity. Within the family there is a full range for variety so it is easy to standardise a whole newspaper or a news-or-feature section on Bodoni as many American papers do. The Bold Italic is exceptionally handsome, mixing well with most other typefaces in the roman group. Bodoni Modern is a useful light face for weight contrast. The Black (as in the *Herald Tribune* **below** for the Pentagon Papers) is emphatic in small doses, though Stockholm's *Expressen* uses it widely for colour and excitement.

Some think Bodoni too mannered for newspapers thriving on a sense of urgency, but there is no doubt of its brilliance and dignity.

The typographical disadvantage of Bodoni is that its x-height is small. The 30pt Bodoni is only as effective as a 24pt Century Bold. Bodoni Bold needs great care in the spacing. Since it is small on its body it carries its own white: too often in newspaper work the lines are well leaded and then Bodoni can look weak.

THIS IS LUDLOW'S BODONI BOLD CAPS
This is a showing of the lower case
This is Ludlow's Bodoni Bold Italic
Light contrast from Bodoni Modern
And this is the fat Bodoni Black

INTERNATIONAL

Herald  Tribune
Published with The New York Times and The Washington Post

No. 27,506   *   PARIS, WEDNESDAY, JUNE 23, 1971   Established 1887

Britain and EEC In Compromise On New Zealand

By James Goldsborough

LUXEMBOURG, June 22 (IHT).—Britain and the Common Market fought out a compromise agreement on the difficult New Zealand issue here tonight, clearing the way for British entry into the European Economic Community.

Negotiators continued meeting into the night to work out the details.

With New Zealand out of the way, Britain's financial contributions to the community, the only remaining problem, was earmarked for quick settlement later tonight.

The New Zealand agreement came only after a difficult day of negotiations that saw harsh words exchanged on both sides. At times it seemed the day would end with terms that New Zealand would denounce.

Though terms still were not known early tonight, informed sources said that Britain had accepted only after consultation with New Zealand and that therefore the terms should be acceptable to Wellington. New Zealand's acceptance has been held indispensable for Prime Minister Edward Heath to win parliamentary approval.

U.K., Russia Match Envoy Expulsions

London Says Moscow Acts Over Defector

By Joseph Frayman

LONDON, June 22 (NYT).—The British government has ordered out of the country two

The Pentagon Papers

- **Appeals Court Again Extends Ban on Times, Post, Pending Security Ruling**

- **FBI Agents Visit Rep. McCloskey to Investigate Documents He Holds**

- **U.S. Seek Restraining Order After Boston Paper Prints Revelations**

Congressman Invites Press Into Meeting

WASHINGTON, June 22 (AP).—Rep. Paul N. McCloskey Jr., R., Calif., met today with two FBI agents who, Mr. McCloskey said, wanted to know what kind of papers he had on a secret Pentagon study and where he got

U.S. Proposes Quick Review To Declassify Some Parts

By Fred Farris

WASHINGTON, June 22 (IHT).—U.S. Courts of Appeals here and in New York today continued indefinitely the temporary restraining orders against The New York Times and The Washington Post barring the newspapers from publishing further documents from or articles based upon a secret Pentagon study of U.S. policy in Vietnam.

The temporary restraining orders were to have expired today. The courts which have been hearing arguments upon the federal

CALEDONIA

Designed by W A Dwiggins and available from Linotype, this is a modified Scotch face. It is modern in atmosphere, with vertical stress, but less abrupt than Bodoni and there is somewhat less contrast in the thick-and-thin strokes than in Baskerville, Bodoni and Scotch. In set-width and x-height it is very similar to Bodoni. Caledonia has attractions as a display face for a quiet newspaper; the Bold is distinguished, the Italic runs well, and there is

also some possibility of colour contrast between Caledonia and Caledonia Bold, though the Caledonia (and the Italic) are just a bit thin. John Dreyfus in fact chose Caledonia for the new London *Sunday Telegraph* in 1961, which later went to Bodoni. One current major trouble with Caledonia for other than local weekly newspapers, is that the largest size in the Bold is 36pt. (The *Toronto Star's* bigger Caledonia headlines **below** have been cast from specially cut Ludlow matrices.)

THIS IS LINOTYPE'S CALEDONIA
This is Linotype's Caledonia
Caledonia has an Italic face
This is available up to 36pt
There is also a Caledonia Bold Italic

Toronto Daily Star

FAMILY SECTION

SATURDAY, JANUARY 30, 1971—PAGES 57 TO 64

Many men shaken by feminist cause

★ *Women's Lib has given family life a big jolt during the past couple of years and the world of the male has been shaken. Many men are made frankly nervous, or even apprehensive, by scenes like 'the one of the right, showing Canadian feminists raising their clenched fists in front of the Parliament Buildings in Ottawa, demanding free abortions.*

Star staff writer Wendy Dey has obtained the views of three husbands—a traditionalist who calls extreme feminists "a bunch of nuts," a moderate who approves the changing status, but with reservations, and a man who works alongside his wife in the fight for women's rights.

Three men give their views on women's liberation

Man should rule roost says school principal  *Moderate believes in 'freedom by machine'*

TIMES

Commissioned by *The Times* of London in 1931, and designed in Printing House Square by Stanley Morison, Times Roman is at its best as a headline face in the superb titling caps. The letter has much of the colour and economy of Century Bold, much of the crispness of Bodoni, with a large x-height. The serifs are small and sharply cut and Times Bold is strong and black. Times Roman 327 provides a possible, if thin, contrast with 334.

There are problems with the lower-case but it is puzzling it has not been more competitive with Bodoni. North American editors wanting to break out of the Bodoni pattern while retaining dignity might consider it more favourably. The main difficulty with Times Bold

334 is that it is excellently condensed for single- and double-column headlines but not for horizontal layouts. Beyond three columns, especially if there is prudence in headline sizing, the 334 produces too many words, and the serifs begin to intrude, so that it is not easy to read. There is difficulty, too, for the headline writer, in filling out the space. The smaller sized headlines in horizontal layout justify the cartoonist who had a headline writer approaching the reporter: 'Got any more facts to fill out the headline?' (See **above, right**).

These problems are not insuperable. The little used Semi-bold 421 is usefully wider set as a variant. And if caps are acceptable, then Times titling faces, especially the extended 339, are the best there are for restrained newspaper display.

ROYAL EDITION

MONDAY APRIL 24 1967

No. 56,923 NINEPENCE

THE TIMES

IN BUSINESS NEWS
TODAY: BANKS READY
TO LEND MORE

GREEK KING 'UNDER HOUSE ARREST'

New regime sends five generals into retirement

The National Broadcasting Company reported today in New York that King Constantine of Greece had been put under house arrest for refusing to sign decrees concerning the military takeover. The report quoted "sources in Athens." It gave no further details, said a Reuter message.

More people suspected of being hostile to the new military-backed regime in Greece were arrested by troops yesterday. Many were reported to have been sent to the island of Gavros, south of Piraeus, where Mr. Andreas Papandreou, son of Mr. George Papandreou, the Opposition leader, is believed to be detained.

Officials were reluctant to say how many people have been detained since Friday's Army coup, but reliable sources said that troops had been given a list of between 2,500 and 3,000 names and were working their way through it.

In a move designed to consolidate its position the new regime yesterday retired five generals from the supreme military council and appointed five others in their place.

Mr. Constantine Kotlias, the new Greek Prime Minister.

INSIDE STORY OF THE ATHENS COUP

From A. M. RENDEL—Athens, April 23

The main outline of the military coup in Athens and of the possible future course of government in Greece can now be deduced with reasonable certainty from the events of the weekend pieced together from many sources.

The coup itself was staged by a small group of officers of senior colonel rank without the knowledge of King Constantine and in open defiance of his wishes once he learnt of it.

King Constantine, who is 26, first heard of the coup by telephone either from Colonel Arnaoutis, his military secretary, or more probably from someone in Colonel Arnaoutis's household, while Colonel Arnaoutis was himself being forcibly arrested.

The King was at the palace at Tatoy, 30 miles outside Athens. He drove in at once to Colonel Arnaoutis's and then to the home of Mr. Bitsios, his political counsellor, who had also by then been arrested. He then went to the Ministry of National Defence.

Determined men

Here the sequence of events becomes more obscure, but it seems from all that is known of

it. The United States Ambassador had been to see the new Prime Minister two hours after he was sworn in.

Mr. Farmakis also said that the coup was carried through because Mr. George Papandreou had declared that he would call for a popular revolt at the first opportunity which he was to have addressed in Salonika today.

Information had then been received that the Communist Party had started to move militant cadres to Salonika. The security forces, therefore, feared that they could not maintain order and requested help from Lieutenant-General Zoitakis, the corps commander in Salonika. General Zoitakis told them that he could help but that this would lead to bloodshed. The coup leaders then decided to take preventive action.

He added that many people supported the Government, while the rest were waiting to see what happened. There is much truth in this. On the right, there is relief; on the left resignation. No one wants a return to the cruel days of 1944 and the civil war that followed.

The King's aim meanwhile—and

Labour MPs' concern on Ulster

BY THE NEWS TEAM

The Prime Minister is to get a report, probably today, from three Labour M.P.s about gerrymandering, discrimination, and unemployment in Northern Ireland. The M.P.s say they found evidence of these during a visit to Ulster a week ago.

The report, which is to be made public, was prepared by Mr. Paul Rose (Blackley), who is a barrister, Mr. Stanley Orme (Salford, West) and Dr. Maurice Miller (Kelvingrove). It coincides with an investigation of electoral practices in Northern Ireland by The Times News Team.

Demonstrators parading near the Greek Embassy in London yesterday in protest at the military coup in Athens. Another picture on page 4.

State seats for German extremists

FROM OUR OWN CORRESPONDENT
BONN, April 23

The Christian Democrat Union (C.D.U.) are clear winners tonight in the state elections in Rhineland Palatinate and Schleswig-Holstein. In Rhineland Palatinate they increased their seats in the Landtag from 46 to 49, and in Schleswig-Holstein from 34 to 35.

The Social Democrat Party (S.P.D.), which is in coalition with the Christian Democrats in the Federal Government, increased their seats from 29 to 30 in Schleswig-Holstein, but dropped from 43 to 39 in Rhineland Palatinate.

The extreme right-wing National Democratic Party (N.P.D.) did less well than expected in both states but managed to win four seats in both Landtags, thus entering the parliaments for the first time. German political leaders breathed a sigh of relief tonight that they had not repeated

SOVIET SPACESHIP IN ORBIT

Passenger switch possible

From KYRIL TIDMARSH—Moscow, April 23

The Soviet Union has launched a manned space ship, its first for more than two years. Circling the earth on board the space ship, Union 1, is Colonel Vladimir Komarov, who is thus the first Russian cosmonaut to make a second flight into space.

No information about the size of the craft or type of booster rocket has been revealed but it seems possible that this flight is part of a multiple exercise such as docking with another craft still to be launched.

According to the official announcement, Union 1, which went into orbit at 00.35 GMT, is different from craft previously launched. The object is to test the new ship, continue medical and biological studies on human reactions on space and to hold " extended scientific and physical-technical experiments and studies ". This seems to indicate walks in space or even transfer of passengers from one craft to another. The blast-off on Lenin's birthday and in advance of the traditional May Day holi-

Decision on gaol strike today

A decision will be taken today on whether to force out the eight prisoners who barricaded themselves in their cells at Leicester prison on Wednesday, the Govt.

Deadlock on equal pay for women

No agreement after months of joint talks

By ERIC WIGHAM, Labour Correspondent

A tripartite working party on equal pay for women, set up by the Minister of Labour, has been in existence for nine months without agreement on any of the four things they were asked to examine : definition, cost, methods of implementation, and timing.

There is to be a final meeting next week but unless there is a change of mind somewhere, which seems unlikely, the Ministry chairman can do little more than report the different arguments of the Confederation of British Industry and the T.U.C.

The eventual cost to industry will be so enormous that the employers' representatives are inevitably digging their heels in.

It is estimated that the direct effects of the change will add about 2½ per cent to 6½ per cent to the national wage bill. The official view apparently is that it would be from 3 to 5 per cent, according to how it was operated, but the employers think it would be 6 per cent, which would mean a cost to industry of £1,200m. a year without any consequential increase in productivity.

Conflict over definition

Perhaps the most intractable conflict of view is over definition. The employers say we should use that definition in Article 119 of the Treaty of Rome which can be summarized as equal pay " for the same work ". The T.U.C. want ratification of I.L.O. Convention No. 100 which provides for equal pay for work of equal value.

The latter would mean not only raising the pay of women doing men's work but also of women doing " women's work " if of equal value to that of men earning more. But that, critics say, would imply paying all men the same for work of equal value, which would involve nothing less than a national job evaluation programme. This, it is contended, would not be practical.

Job segregation

On the other side the Treaty of Rome definition is criticized on the grounds that employers would more and more segregate men and women in different jobs.

As for timing, the C.B.I. think that talking about equal pay is unreal in present economic circumstances. Their attitude is that we should wait to see whether we go into the Common Market.

Mr Nutting's Suez story in 'The Times'

Mr. Anthony Nutting, who resigned from the Eden Government in 1956 at the time of Suez, is to break his 10-year silence on the affair. Mr. Nutting, who as Minister of State for Foreign Affairs was closely involved in the events leading up to the British military landines in Egypt, has written his own account of the crisis in a book, *No End of a Lesson*, which is to be published by Constable later this year. Extracts from the book will appear exclusively in *The Times*.

No explanation

Mr. Nutting points out in a preface to the book that at the time of his resignation he offered no explanation of his decision, other than a brief letter to Sir Anthony Eden dissociating himself from the Government.

" I made no statement to the House of Commons", Mr. Nutting writes, " although it is an almost invariable custom for a Minister who resigns on an issue of principle to do so, and, in all the newspaper articles and books which I have written about Britain's relations with Egypt and the Arab world, I have avoided discussing the Suez debacle in any but the most general terms.

Reasons for silence

" The reasons for this long silence are very simple. Either I had to tell the whole story as I saw it, or say nothing at all. And so long as any of the chief protagonists of the Suez war still held high public office in Britain, it would have clearly been a grave disservice to the nation, which they still led and

Resentful applicants ask if the Six intend to take selfish decisions while the negotiations are going on

Fish rise to the surface of the EEC bargaining

From Our Own Correspondent
Brussels, Sept. 29

One of the more surprising aspects of the negotiations for the entry of Britain and other coun-

The point that most upsets the applicants about the present plans among the Six is the provision that after five years any fisherman from any member country will be allowed into the territorial

tance, of course, to fishermen of the 10 countries concerned, from the North Cape to Sicily. But it also has a broader significance for the negotiations as a whole, because it raises the question of

without modification when they do join, allowing only for a period of adaptation.

How all this will work out in practice remains to be seen. In the case of fish the Six clearly

This is Monotype's famous Times Bold 334

Times Bold Condensed is filmset

And this is the italic of 334

Here is Monotype's Times New Roman 327

It comes in an italic as well

Another weight from Monotype is semi-bold 421

MONOTYPE'S TIMES TITLING 329

THE SUPERB EXTENDED TITLING 339

CHELTENHAM

Once all the rage, Cheltenham has fallen out of favour and is associated in the mind with the fustian Thirties. It was first fully exploited by the new *Daily Herald* in 1930, which based all its news heads on this one family (something of a revolution). One attraction is the range of the family. The blackness of the letter is adequate in Bold; there is good colour contrast from the Medium; the Extended has the weight and appeal in multi-column settings of Century Schoolbook Bold; and of course the Extra Condensed is a fount in which a chimp could write a heading to fit (16 letters to an 11-em 24pt compared with 12 for Century Bold). The stress is modern but it has a larger x-height than Bodoni, with short descenders and bracketed serifs. The stress is vertical, the serifs flat and stubby. The type is widely available—as Cheltenham from Ludlow, Gloucester from Monotype, and Cheltonian from Intertype (Linotype having abandoned the display sizes). The basic disadvantage of Cheltenham is the monotony of the design which as a family lacks any vitality and urgency.

LUDLOW'S CHELTENHAM OLD STYLE

This is Cheltenham Bold from Ludlow

It is also in a Condensed version

And this is Cheltenham Wide

Cheltenham Bold Extended

There is a Medium

THE SUNDAY TIMES, JULY 25 1971   The Arts/Films/Television /Ballet/Art/Books   25

Monsters of the deep
FILMS □ DILYS POWELL

IT IS A question of how much is too much.

First, the abdicating king, his arrogance swollen with age, who rejects the daughter who loves him and exposes himself to the vicious ambition of the two who don't and who throw him out to die in the madness which awaits the habit of absolute power. Shakespeare's **King Lear** (A) is now to be seen at the Prince Charles Theatre in a version directed by Peter Brook. Death by poison and the sword, a hanging, a

Mr Russell. At the start that shows. Everything moves with desperate slowness; he has even had recourse to a kind of chapter-heading.

But as the plot gathers force one sees him turning the difficulties to advantage. The screen has been used to elucidate the characters, not to fog them; the imperiousness, the uproar in Goneril's palace makes the impetuous rejection of Cordelia more comprehensible. The vast deserted beach (the film was shot in Denmark) where Lear and Gloucester, broken old men,

Riley's line
ART □ JOHN RUSSELL

THE Bridget Riley retrospective at the Hayward Gallery marks a further stage in the emancipation of British art from the defensive, cap-in-hand attitudes which were current until not more than seven or eight years ago.

Those attitudes were broken down in individual practice by Moore and Nicholson in the 1930s. By defying anyone to regard them as second-class citizens of the world of art, they broke the spell of the submissive posture. Bacon did the same thing, from 1946 onwards. Caro, Hamilton, and arguably one or two others

Status Quo Vadis?
TELEVISION □ MAURICE WIGGIN

OH DEAR, how disconcerting. It really isn't fair of the BBC and ITV to switch roles like that. So unsettling.

Despite abundant evidence to the contrary, it is still widely believed that ITV is the channel for bland pap and the BBC is the place to find the thought-provoking stuff. At the back of this gullibility, I shouldn't wonder, is the easy (and naïve,

enjoy the deep satisfaction of corporate achievement, and who are there to be called on. This was a refreshing change from the message which usually comes across.

ITV's two advertisements for revolution were both exceptionally vivid and entertaining, in their very different ways. The play *After a Lifetime* was written by Neville Smith, directed by Kenneth Loach, produced by

DEREK JEWELL COME IN NUMBER ONE, YOUR TIME IS UP.

"Ought to

Sans serifs

Sans serif types have still to be fully exploited in newspapers. The best are emphatic and clean. The worst are self-conscious, ugly and strident. The best have a look of boldness and integrity; and they are economical. They are large on the body. They are robust. They are the best types of all for reversing as a white letter in a block. Yet sans has been neglected or indifferently employed. In Britain no serious newspaper has ever based itself on a sans family. Among the populars, the tabloid *Daily Mirror* and *Daily Sketch* have used bold sans with variable skill; the *Sunday Express* and, after a bad start, the old broadsheet *Sun*, have demonstrated how effective they could be in broadsheet. In the middlebrow newspapers of the United States, sans has been accepted as respectable, but the most widely used display type (Linotype Spartan) is one of the less satisfactory sans. In Europe and Australia sans has been abused with bad mixes and exaggerated weights. In Britain it will take some time to overcome the association of sans with glaring popular treatment, but it will happen.

Robert Harling and Edwin Taylor at *The Sunday Times* and Raymond Hawkey at the *Observer*, have already shown the effectiveness of a well-chosen sans—Harling's choice of Franklin and Record on the leader page, and Taylor's use of Record Bold Medium Extended for his redesigned arts pages **(above)**.

Undoubtedly for newspaper display, the best sans are among such grotesques (grots).

The geometric sans types have two detractions. First, some individual letters are irritatingly eccentric or ambiguous in their letter form and frequently do not knit well into words: the letters do not combine closely enough into words; the geometric style for each letter results in forcing undue white between some combinations of letters.

was   design

Secondly, the geometric sans (like the slab serifs) are severely restricted in the possibility of letter variation; modification is limited by the need to maintain the appearance of geometric order in the letters, so that there is less scope for satisfactory variation of weight and compression.

This is the biggest single weakness of American newspaper display with so much of it dependent on boring geometric sans in roman, or ungainly italic variations.

The other large group, the styled sans types (such as Metro) are also open to question. Attractive though individual letters may be, when used in the frequent permutations required in headlines they often do not combine easily into words. Where the letter is not coterminous with the body undue white appears between letters, hindering reading by producing a spotty effect.

Moreover, as Allen Hutt has noted with Gill[9] just 'those individual letter points of fineness, which gave it its note of urbanity in good job or advertising display, irritate in a headline, where there cannot be the delicacy of composition needed to give Gill its full effect'. The second drawback with the styled sans types is that, deriving from classical styles, they depend for their quality on the subtle proportional relationship between the height and width of the letters, and variations in the styled sans have so far had difficulty in maintaining these proportions as satisfactorily as in the parent design.

By contrast with these two broad groups of sans types, the best grots have a basic letter form which is neither dependent on geometry nor on fidelity to exquisite original proportions. The letters are individually subdued to fit unobtrusively into words subdued, it has been put rather poetically, 'to the purity of linear pattern'. Moreover, the basic letter form in the grots can be expanded, condensed, thickened or fattened over a very wide range—and that is a distinct asset to a newspaper basing itself on one family. For photoset papers Univers, for instance, has twenty different faces of carefully judged weights and proportions and clean lines, and they are all readable.

SPARTAN & OTHERS

GEOMETRIC SANS: Spartan (1951–4) is the most widely used sans in the United States and very similar to the earlier (1927–30) Futura, by Intertype, and Erbar. They represent the archetypal German geometric sans, a monotone with no stress and letters which do not follow roman proportions, being made, instead, to appear in uniform in the sizes of circles and curves and the treatment of joining stems and apexes. Erbar attempts to relieve the geometric sans with some styling. There are seven weights of Spartan from Mergenthaler Linotype (Light, Bold, Medium Bold, Heavy, Black and Extra Black, and Book), of which the recent Bold and Heavy are best for general news display, with Medium for light contrast. The Extra Black may be all right for posters but it is not a starter for a newspaper (and the 'j' is irritating). Spartan is somewhat more compact than Century or Bodoni, and similar to the grot sans, Record.

Futura has six weights, also a Condensed in three weights and an in-line (which is the same as outline). In these types the splayed 'M', the crossed 't' and the one-storey 'a' are noticeable.

TURKEY TIME — These two pretty young ladies didn't have the heart to scare a live Tom Turkey with their brilliant red hatchet, so an artificial one was used for the picture. Miss Diane Sanders (left) and Miss Karen Cleoson, both of Aurora, wear headgear reminiscent of the first Thanksgiving. Although the attire has changed, the main item on most tables Thursday will be the same as that which the Pilgrims and Indians had — a turkey. (Beacon-News Photo by Terry Popeck)

AURORA
BEACON-NEWS
Final Edition

122nd Year—No. 341   WEDNESDAY, NOVEMBER 27, 1968   34 Pages   10 Cents

Miner's Wife Clings to Hope
'He'll Come Out of That Mine'

Boycott of Talks Ends
Thieu Cautions Viets On Over-Optimism

Festive Feast Will Help Ease 'Sting'

NLF Says It Wants Equal Status

B-N to Publish Morning Edition On Thursday

This is Spartan
Black Condensed

This is Spartan Bold from Mergenthaler Linotype

This is Spartan Medium from Mergenthaler Linotype

Here is Spartan Black from Linotype

Here is Futura Bold from Intertype

TEMPO & OTHERS

STYLED SANS: Tempo (Ludlow), Metro (Linotype) and Vogue (Intertype) are representative.

Tempo is a rich family—the *Sun* here is in Tempo Heavy Condensed. Tempo has no fewer than five weights, condensed faces and also a heavy in-line, so that a newspaper can easily standardise on this face. It would not, however, be as attractive as standardising on the Record grot by the same designer (R H Middleton).

The weakest link in the family is the Tempo Heavy. It is exceptionally heavy, wide and abrasive and the design does not carry it. The capitals are too big for the lowercase letters and the size and weight relationship of some of the lower-case letters to each other is uneasy. The 'e' here jumps out as inadequate:

New speed
Beat men

The Tempo Bold Extended is too square and stretched for news headings, but the Tempo Heavy Condensed Italic is one of the best sans condensed italics.

Here is Ludlow's Tempo Medium

This is the useful Tempo Bold

It is available in Italic as well

And an attractive Tempo Heavy Condensed Italic

THIS IS TEMPO HEAVY

There is also Tempo Heavy Condensed

And there is Tempo Bold Extended

METRO

METRO is a styled sans, designed by W A Dwiggins. There are three weights (and from Mergenthaler Linotype an exceptionally light Metro thin which I do not recommend for letterpress newspapers). It would not be satisfactory to standardise a newspaper only on Metro, but it is a useful ancillary type, most notably in the smaller sizes where it is popular in Metroblack for intros and captions. The Metromedium makes a good type for overlines and other subsidiary display lines and mixes well with some of the commoner serif display types which have old face affinities. Metromedium makes an excellently sharp overline, for instance, with Century: but Metroblack mixes badly with a modern such as Bodoni. Metro has a one-tier 'a' (an ambiguous character) for which an alternative is offered, and is noted for its sheared terminals; the sheared stem at the top of 'F', and the foot of 't' and 'j' are too intrusive.

This is Metrolite No 1 in the Metro Family

This is medium weight, Metromedium No 2

The heaviest weight is Metroblack No 2

VOGUE

VOGUE comes with standard and alternative characters: the standard should be specified because the alternative 'g', 'e', 'M', and 'W' are too eccentric for newspapers. The smaller sizes of Vogue Bold Condensed are useful where a great deal has to be packed into a small space, but should be used in a very few lines in any one place. Vogue does not knit as well into words as the grotesques do, especially in the extra Bold where the letterspacing is not consistently tight and the Vogue Oblique stumbles at the 'g'.

The larger sizes of Vogue are for use with an Intertype composing-stick attachment.

Here is Vogue Bold from Intertype

This is Vogue Light

And here is Vogue Extra Bold

The italic up to 30pt is called Oblique

Finally, Vogue Extra Bold Condensed

The grots

The grots (or gothics as they are called in North America) offer the best choice for newspaper display. The outstanding examples are the American face, Record, designed by R H Middleton for Ludlow; Franklin Gothic designed for American typefounders by M F Benton; and the European Univers, Helvetica and Mercator. *The Minneapolis Tribune* re-dressed itself from Futura (**1**, in the right-hand six columns) to Helvetica throughout (**2**). *The Southside Virginian* (**3**) is another example. Franklin Gothic is seen in *The Sunday Times Business News*, mixed with Record; and its arts pages are based on Record.

RECORD

RECORD has more than a dozen variants and a newspaper could easily be based on four:

Bold

Bold Medium-extended

Heavy Medium-extended

Record Gothic as occasional colour contrast

Alternatively, since Record Gothic is somewhat thin, Gothic Bold Italic could be chosen for variety. The other italics should all be avoided for headlines.

Record Gothic Condensed or Extra Condensed might

be useful in sport or semi-display classified (the thin line Condensed not shown here is too thin altogether for newspaper work). The Bold lower-case letter runs well into words but not quite so well as the excellent Bold Medium-extended lower-case, which is altogether preferable to the over-stretched Extended. All the Records are better above 18pt than below, and for the very large headlines, such as 60 and 72pt, the squarer Medium-extended should be specified. Record is big on its body (similar to Century Bold and bigger than Tempo), and the Record Bold is just that bit more condensed than Century for easy (but readable) headline writing. Record mixes well with other grots. Record Gothic and Ludlow's Franklin are excellent foils.

This is Ludlow's Record Gothic

RECORD GOTHIC BOLD FOR HEADLINES

Here is the Gothic Bold Italic

This is Record Gothic Medium Extended and note how well it runs

Record Gothic Heavy Medium Extended

The Bold comes in a Medium Extended
And also in an Extended version

The Record Extended Bold has an Italic

There is a Record Gothic Condensed

And for a tight squeeze an Extra Condensed

UNIVERS

UNIVERS, unlike many type families which 'just growed', was conceived as a unified family from the beginning with the same character through all weights and variations.

It was started in 1952 by Adrian Frutiger, the Swiss typographer, and is available in metal—for setting from the case for headlines—from Monotype and in filmsetting from Monophoto. It was designed to be an unobtrusive grot, a concept which weakens the larger display sizes (in metal the series runs 14, 18, 22, 36, and 48pt). For newspaper work, as with Ludlow's Record, three or four variants would suffice, of which the best are:

Univers Bold for standard news headlines
Univers Medium for colour contrast
Univers Bold Expanded for multi-column headlines
Univers Extra Bold for occasional strong statements

Univers Medium 689 is good for newspapers

Univers Bold 693 is excellent for general news

EXTRA BOLD 696 FOR EXTRA PUNCH
As well as this Roman *there is an Italic*

Compare Univers
Extra Bold Expanded 695

Univers Ultra Bold Expanded 697

Compare Univers Bold Condensed 694

Here is Univers Medium Extra Condensed 691

FRANKLIN

FRANKLIN GOTHIC is based on the early English sans. It is a heavy sans serif designed for American Typefounders, with the somewhat taller Ludlow version shown here.

Franklin comes in one weight only, though there are style variants in the one weight. A newspaper could not be based wholly on Franklin's bludgeoning effect, but it mixes well with other lighter grots such as Record or Ludlow Square Gothic or Ludlow's Grot 215. For readability banner headlines in Franklin should preferably be specified in the plain Franklin—available up to 72pt—rather than in the condensed versions. Ludlow also offers a Gothic Bold Condensed titling caps fount and this is better for banners than the Franklin Gothic Extra Condensed (too cramped in the bigger sizes and without much impact at 72pt).

This is Ludlow's Franklin Gothic: it is available up to 84pt.

Here is Franklin Gothic Italic

This is Franklin Gothic Extra Condensed

OTHER GROTS

There is a wide range of other grots. *Helvetica* is best in its light and medium weights in which it is splendid (and less successful than its bold, condensed and expanded versions). *Mercator*, designed by Dick Dooiges in Amsterdam, comes in several useful weights. *Folio*, designed by Konrad F Bauer and Walter Baum for Intertype (Frankfurt), has not been available in Britain because of the different depth of strike but could be used on American machines and is a useful family with three weights and a condensed and expanded.

And there are numerous condensed grots, of which *Placard* from Monotype is perhaps the most striking. The condensed grots mix well with other grots but they should be used sparingly. The more condensed varieties, in particular, can become very difficult to read, especially in the smaller sizes and especially in multi-column settings.

This is Linotype's Gothic Condensed No 25

Compare the Ludlow Condensed No. 2.

Compare the very condensed Intertype Alternate Gothic No1

Monotype's Placard Bold Condensed 506 is notable

This is Ludlow's Square Gothic

Slab Serifs

Only in the United States has there been any use of the slab serifs in newspaper display. This is because letter forms have not been expanded and varied, like the grots, and because the heavier ones are square and slow. This stolid character seems out of sympathy with the vivacity associated with news, though the slab serifs can be of use as a distinctive signal for a separate section. Where the bolder egyptians are used for news they require plenty of white. Slab serifs have the advantage of being large on

This is Ludlow's Karnak Intermediate

Compare the Linotype Memphis

Here is Ludlow's Karnak Medium Italic

This is Memphis Bold from Linotype

This is Cairo Bold from INTERTYPE

This is Karnak Medium from Ludlow

A mule kick from Karnak Black

Similarly from Memphis Extra Bold

Ludlow offers a Karnak Black Condensed with Italic

There is also a Memphis Extra Bold Condensed

the body, but in the normal set widths are too wide for easy single-column headline writing, forcing recourse to the less attractive condensed. (The lower-case alphabet length of Karnak Medium, for instance, is 351 points in 24pt compared with 307 points for Century Bold.)

The intriguing faces in the group of type families are the clarendons. The clarendons (or ionics) first appeared in the 1840s as a sophistication of the egyptians and have been prolific progenitors of text types. They have more colour and verve than the egyptians; the serifs are gently bracketed; the letters are solid but there is plenty of white space within, which helps letterpress reproduction, and the x-height is larger. Century Schoolbook is their sophisticated descendant. One feels there is still newspaper display potential in adaptations of the clarendons, though the choice in existing faces, other than from typefounders, is limited in size and variation, and there are weaknesses in the way some letters form loosely into words (*see* for instance the New Clarendon Bold 618 from Monotype).

This is Ludlow's Clarendon Bold
This is Ludlow's Clarendon Heavy

Monotype offers New Clarendon 617
HERE ARE THE CAPS OF MONOTYPE'S 617

Monotype also offers New Clarendon Bold 618
THE CAPS OF 618 KNIT TOGETHER

Consort is from Stephenson Blake
Consort comes in a Light version

There is a Consort Condensed
This is Consort Bold Condensed
And here is a line of Consort Bold

Angry parents campaign for a new school

Evening Standard Reporter

Angry parents are campaigning for a new village school to replace one that was burned down —20 years ago.

They complain that the tem- proper school. There is only an outside toilet and no hot water. Meals come from Wantage about

other urgent projects in the area.

"The fire officer has not

61 IN AIRLINER DOWN AT SEA

A time now for self-help

AFTER six years of hard thinking in opposition, the Conservatives are preparing to roll

ARTHUR SELDON

And none of them recalled that W. E. Forster envisaged "tickets" (a kind of luncheon voucher or

Spacing

Type is changed by white space. There are three places where white space can go wrong in headlines—between letters (see **above**), between words, and between lines.

Between words and letters excess space is the commonest fault. The habit on some newspapers of letterspacing the headline to make it fill the line is a guaranteed wrecker of words; the letters which form a word should not be erratically separated by white. Condensed letters in particular should never be letterspaced. The small white counters of condensed type should be reflected in small space between the letters. And generally the amount of space between words should be proportionate to the amount of space between letters. A rough guide is to say that the thickness of the lower-case of the type should be the thickness of the space between words. But always spacing should be judged visually. If it looks wrong it *is* wrong.

Inter-line spacing

There are four places where the amount of white should be watched:

1 Between first line and cut-off
2 Between lines
3 Between decks
4 Between last line and start of text

As a general rule, the maximum white should be over the headline (1); and between decks where they exist (3). The minimum should be between the lines of headline (2). The spacing between the last line and the start of the text

(4) should be more than between the lines but less than above the first line. The aim is to aid legibility and to use white space to unite the headline and relate it to its text. If there is more space at point 4 than point 1, the headline is related too closely to the cut-off. If there is more space at 2 than 1, or 4, the head will not stand out as a unit. It will merge with the text or the cut-off.

Always remembering that it is a visual matter, depending on the type and the run of the lines, it is possible to suggest some rough mechanical guides:

Between first line and cut-off: 12 points

Between decks: 9 points

Between block and headline: 12 points

Above down-page multi-column heads: 9 points

Above shorts: 6 points

Between nearest touching lines of headline: 3 points

But spacing remains essentially visual. An old rule was that the space between lines of caps should be *nearly* equal the appearing face of the type being used. But where you have, say, 30pt Bodoni caps, putting 30 points of white between the lines would be excessive, since Bodoni being small on its body already carries a big beard of white. Between 30pt Bodoni caps, which is an appearing face of 24pt, 12–14 points of white looks about right.

One cannot be too dogmatic about this. A lot depends on the purpose of the headline, how tight it is, its degree of blackness, the character of the newspaper. For routine headlines the newspaper cannot do better than to try different spacing, pick which appears most legible and attractive and follow it as a rough guide.

Here are some examples from which we can begin to build a judgment of good and bad spacing.

1 Hopelessly cramped to the point of illegibility (note also that space between lines varies, which it should not do in caps).

2 Excessive white between the lines—and between decks. The space between the lines of the first deck is more than the appearing face of the caps.

3 Too much space between decks.

4 Too little over first line. Transposing or removing a thick lead from between the lines would have made all the difference.

5 Not nearly enough white between decks, and main lower-case head is too tight.

6 First deck correctly spaced but second too close—and too great a contrast in size.

2

PILOT SAVES CREW

IN 90 mph GALE

Rig battered in North Sea

FROM OUR CORRESPONDENT—Scarborough, March 6

A helicopter pilot battled through winds gusting up to 90 m.p.h. to rescue 45 men from the stricken £2,500,000 oil rig Ocean Prince off the Yorkshire coast today. The rig's superstructure had been torn off during a gale in the North Sea.

The incident began at 2 a.m. Within four hours one-third of the rig, valued at £1m., had disappeared under the 60ft. waves.

3

FIGHTING SALINITY
& WATER-LOGGING

——

German team assures all
possible financial aid

The four-man West German technical mission to Pakistan is understood to have assured all possible financial assistance required for the various schemes prepared by the West Pakistan WAPDA and the Provincial Government to fight water-logging and salinity and increase food production in the Province.

1

COUNCIL IN CASH ROW OVER PLAY CENTRES

A £100,000 row has broken out between the borough council and a group of social workers and residents over play centres for the children of Southwark . . . to keep them off the streets.

The council is blamed for a tight-fisted attitude to the problem of where children can play.

The Camberwell Adventure Playground Steering Committee

the steering committee, at little cost to the council.

One has already been set up in Peckham, and the council has given £100 towards it.

4

BUTANE CYLINDER
WAS FIRE 'BOMB'

OUR THORNABY REPORTER

REPORTS of an explosion

John L. Hopper. "A cylinder of

NEWS IN THE AIR
by JAMES STUART

The jet hopping executives are buying British

5

DEVALUATION A SHOT-IN-ARM FOR OVERSEAS SALES

Devaluation has given a tremendous shot-in-the-arm to overseas sales of British jet executive aeroplanes. In the first two months of this year, thanks to the lowering of the

Another price rise for the motorists

6

CAR BATTERIES GO UP BY 4 PER CENT

DEARER car batteries will follow a Prices and Incomes Board report published today.

Because of a post-devaluation rise in the price of lead, PIB chief Mr Aubrey Jones has given battery manufacturers

Safety

Let us now look in detail at the very troubled area of inter-line headline spacing. We have moved, rightly, to more lower-case headlines, but what was satisfactory automatic spacing for caps will not work with lower-case because of ascenders and descenders. Compare these two lower-case headlines which are identically spaced:

Watch white between lines

Watch space between lines

The first looks all right. The second looks all wrong. Because there is no ascender in line 2 there is now too much space between first and second lines. But the clash of ascender and descender in line 3 makes that bit look cramped. Here the space is adjusted visually:

Watch space between lines

Spacing between the lines of headlines is bad on most newspapers, and especially on modern photoset newspapers where the comps and editorial men have apparently not yet learned to trust their eyes.

If heads are crammed in with erratic horizontal white, they become harder to read, especially in caps. If they are over-whited, their impact is reduced and space wasted.

The commonest fault is to run too much between the lines. The irregular ascenders and descenders create their own white space and adding formal spacing, irrespective of the visual need, spoils the read-on effect of the headline as well as dissipating its blackness. Where you have a type small on its body, like Bodoni, or Century Light, it is safer to remove leads between the lines and let the type stand solid. But other display faces, too, are frequently over-whited. So many times there is too much space between the lines and too little over the headline unit. Look at these examples:

1 Uneven effect because of excess white between lines 2 and 3—and how it was corrected.

2 Too much white.

3 Too much between line 3 (where there is no descender) and line 4; and between lines 4 and 5 where there is neither ascender nor descender.

4 Too little over the head, too much between the lines.

5 Too much between the lines, spoiling read-on effect.

1

Crowds riot as King 'sacks' Greek Premier

MR. George Papandreou, the Greek Prime Minister, handed his resignation to King Constantine last night while thousands of young pro-Government Greeks

Crowds riot as King 'sacks' Greek Premier

MR. George Papandreou, the Greek Prime Minister, handed his resignation to King Constantine last night while thousands of young pro-Government Greeks

2

State steel extension

Inspectors to check on two more firms

By MICHAEL COOLING

The two inspectors investigating three cut-price motor insurance companies were yesterday appointed by the Board of Trade to look into affairs of the London and Midland Insurance Company and a "dormant" investment

Marsh 'in favour of wider take-over'

By GRAHAM CAWTHORNE

The Minister of Power, Mr. Marsh, has let it be known to Mr. Richard Winterbottom, Labour MP for Brightside, Sheffield, that after steel nationalisation he would be "favourably inclined" towards the State corporation extending their diversified activities beyond those which they acquire with the 14 companies.

Last night Mr. Winterbottom commented: "Under this, there is nothing to stop the Steel Corporation taking over any firm in the steel and en-

3

Chelsea killing – 'FBI trace a man'

From RICHARD EVANS NEW YORK

A man who Scotland Yard think can help inquiries

4

Highgate critics of new Act

The new Civic Amenities Act—which may make Highgate a protected area next year — was criticised by members of the Highgate Society last Thursday, after they had heard a speech from Mr. Peter Robshaw, one of the experts who drafted the Act.

One member, Mr. Walter Bor, former planning officer with the LCC, said that there

Commenting on Haringey Council's plan to make Highgate a conservation area under the Act, Mr. Bor said: "They are doing this at a time when there is no viable traffic management scheme for the area and this is putting the cart before the horse.

"Then there is the second question on the vast GLC

doubt the effectiveness of the Civic Amenities Act."

Mr. Robshaw, of the Civic Trust, said he agreed with much of what Mr. Bor had said.

"We must get to terms with the problem of the car in a conservation area," he added. "My view—as a keen motorist—is that we have

5

Ambulances, buses, autos crash, I dead

PETERSBURG, Ind. (P) — Collisions involving a Greyhound bus, two autos, three ambulances, and a loaded school bus left a baby dead and 31 persons injured today

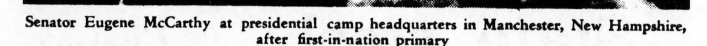

Senator Eugene McCarthy at presidential camp headquarters in Manchester, New Hampshire, after first-in-nation primary

THE NEW HAMPSHIRE PRIMARY

A landslide for Mr Nixon

From ALISTAIR COOKE : New York, March 13

THE voters of New Hampshire, a tricky compound of

But this morning Rockefeller has a bare 11 per cent of the

Rockefeller-Reagan combination as a dream ticket. The Governor

·30 *The Daily Telegraph, Friday, October 11, 1968*

Hogg gets Conference ovation after his Greek tilt at Powell

MODERATION AS 'GUERDON OF OUR CONSERVATIVE FAITH'

—●—

CLASHES ON IMMIGRANTS

BY OUR SPECIAL CORRESPONDENT

BLACKPOOL, Thursday.

STORMY debates on immigration ended in a personal triumph for Mr. Hogg, Shadow Home Secretary, at the Conservative party Conference here today.

He received a standing ovation after pleading with Mr.

Underscores

Three final typographical details about headlines. First, deskmen should shun the temptation to underscore. It is a mark of failure in type choice if you feel there is insufficient emphasis without underscore. There is only one legitimate use for underscore and that is with expanded faces where the continuous line links the words and makes them more legible. For instance, the well-spaced *Guardian* headline (1), on Mr Nixon.

If one is to underscore, however, the thickness of the underscore must approximate the thickness of the stems in the type underscored. Too thin a line is pointless; too thick a line competes with the type. The thickness of the stems is not, of course, the same thing as the point size: a 30pt Century Bold, for instance, has strokes about 6 points thick, so any underscore should exceed 6pt.

Especially to be shunned is the underscoring of lower-case. It leads to all sorts of horrors when the underscore meets a descender: if the underscore is low enough to avoid the descender there is an ugly rivulet of white between rule and medium letters; if the underscore is broken at the descender the effect is broken.

For instance (2), taking out the underscore would increase clarity.

3

THEATER/ARTS

Denise LeBrun / a new

By Paul F. Kneeland
Globe Staff

Since it opened here last

between dainty bites of souvlakia at the Athens-Olympia — "I am enjoying the Greek food very much

slowly shaking her head "No!"

As a sub-teenager, Den-

4

New bank to be opened in Hong Kong

LONDON, Wed — Schroeders and Chartered Bank, two big city banks, announced yesterday they are to form a new merchant bank in Hong Kong — Schroeders and Chartereo Ltd — in co-operation with the financier Lawrence Kadoorie, who will become

Here are examples of the bad use of rule: underscoring from the *Bangkok Post* **(4)** where it never, anyway, has enough white; and oblique dividers too solid for Bodoni from the *Boston Globe* **(3)**.

Buckets and bonnets

A word on hoods, bonnets, buckets, boxes, curtains—all names for the different ways one may be expected to put headlines within fine column rules, or thicker rules, usually to cut off one headline from another in an adjacent column, or to fence in a headline whose wording floats it in too much white.

It is rarely worth the fuss to do this—especially for a single-column open-ended box which needs fiddly bits of rule at the end—and above double-column boxes and hoods looks absurd. But these are the styles:

MAN IN BANK RAID	BANK MAN SHOT IN RAID	RAIDER SHOOTS MAN IN BANK RAID
Bucket	*Hood or curtain*	*Open-ended box*

Reverse blocks

Finally, when making a reverse block (a white letter on a black or tint background) always choose an open bold face without fine serifs. Even Century Bold will reverse badly. And open sans or a slab serif is ideal. Contrast the way the sans in **6** has reversed cleanly with the muddy filling in of the Pabst fat letter **(5)**.

5

IT'S A MAD,

BUS CLIPPIE Doris Smith, formerly wall-of-death motor-cycle rider Marjorie Dare, passed her moped driving test yesterday—at the 20th attempt. Doris, aged 54, of Lawrence-close, Hertford, took 19 tests at Hertford, then applied to take one at Stevenage, Herts.

MAD WORLD

6

There comes a time in every man's life when he starts slipping.

Whenever you aim to hit 'em with full colour, be sure it doesn't go off at half-cock

Photo-composition

All the observations on spacing apply equally to film-setting routine headlines. But, of course, filmset feature headlines are emancipated from the rigid spacing of metal typesetting. For colour or shape or to suggest a theme, letters can be placed very close together; they can be placed so that they actually join or overlap or they can be printed so that they appear to curve or wobble or dip. These effects are occasionally acceptable in features and the features designer can learn something of the potential of filmsetting from the more adventurous advertising. But ten thousand warnings are required about misusing photosetting to run ordinary headlines without good spacing. Overcrowding as here (and especially **above**) should be avoided.

Newsmen moving from letterpress to filmset news-papers should have one small care about the system of measurement. Leading in filmset newspapers is not measured, as in letterpress, as the space *between* lines. There is no beard in filmset headlines and it is more logical to measure from one baseline of type to the next—from the foot of the first line to the foot of the second.

Culver: Nothing will stop anti-war movement

6 Headline Miscellany

Punctuation

Since headlines are truncated sentences they need punctuation just as prose does, but for headlines there are a few conventions for clarity and ease of expression.

Every headline once concluded with a full point, but it is now recognised as dispensable (except in the middle of a free-style head). It is clear that the last word in the heading is the end of a 'thought'. Where two thoughts are joined together in one deck, they are separated by a colon. The separation of two thoughts by a dash is less pleasing, especially at the end of a line, and the dash should be reserved for creating extra emphasis:

> Shares see-saw: Only   Johnson gets
> Bank buys £   his surcharge
>   through—but
>   at a price

The American practice is to use a semi-colon where the British newspapers use a colon. The British practice is against the use of semi-colons at all on the grounds of simplicity, typographical neatness and ease of read-on.

But ration your colon or semi-colon headlines in any event; the simple self-contained single thought unbroken by punctuation is the easiest reading in a headline.

Full stops are falling into disuse, too, in abbreviations. They survive in places after Dr. and similar abbreviations, but thin spaces are better than full points between the initials of organisations such as U N. Thin spaces are more economical and they escape the awkwardness of U.N.: unless they are as familiar as UN, abbreviations should be avoided in headlines:

> RIBA's
> 'anxiety' over
> future

How many readers recognised what RIBA was? It is the Royal Institute of British Architects and the head would have been better: 'Architects worry about North-East'.

Exclamation marks

Exclamation marks should be used very sparingly. Sub-editors sometimes make the mistake of giving themselves a medal with the exclamation mark—using it after a clever heading so that buffoons shall not miss their wit.

> A BARE LIVING!

The wording is all right over a story describing how difficult it is for strippers to make a living wage; but sub-editors should practise modesty and only use the exclamation mark after an exclamation: 'Halt!' cry saved girl's life, or 'Owzat!' over a picture of a wicket-keeper exclaiming to the umpire.

Commas

Use the comma in the headline in the normal way to separate clauses, but only in a tight corner should you adopt the practice of using it to indicate the omission of the word 'and'. There are times when this is barely tolerable (left) and others when its omission leaves the chance of misunderstanding:

> Shops, hotels, reel   Heart Transplant Man
> from riot's impact   is Tired, Resting

When quotation marks are used, the comma normally separating quotation from attribution can be dropped for the sake of typographical neatness.

> 'Preposterous',   'Preposterous'
> says Councillor   says Councillor

But when the quotation marks are dropped the return of the normal comma is essential:

> Preposterous,
> Councillor
> calls new
> rates rise

Quotation marks

You will see how much depended on the comma in the headline above. Quotation marks around the word 'Preposterous' would have been better if they would fit. Quotes should be used when the actual words are important. Quotation marks are very helpful in a number of ways in headlines (and space-saving single quotes will suffice). First, of course, you indicate external authority for a statement in the ways I indicated in the discussion of attribution in headlines. Secondly, quotes should be used to indicate doubt (spoken or unspoken) when headlining news assertions which are not yet confirmed:

Ferry sinks: 'Over 100 die'

Here the newspaper is not yet prepared to lend its authority to this estimate from agency reporters. The same implication attaches to quotes round allegations or rumours or where a strong word needs toning down. Without the single quotes the following headlines would be less detached than they should be:

Gold 'flood' denied

'Leak' exam scrapped

The quotes tell the reader to take care, the word is not what it might seem:

'Arctic' schoolrooms will be heated

The word 'Arctic' in quotes indicates that the school is very cold, not that it is in the Arctic. Fourthly, there are occasional uses for quotes to reverse the meaning of a word:

'Missing' wife in hotel job

Finally, quotes can bring into one unit two words which are needed to form an adjectival noun:

'Don't wed' couple missing

Question marks

Like the exclamation mark, the question mark is generally to be avoided in headlines. It is most properly used after genuine questions and then the text must *answer* the question. These headlines should turn up more often on the feature pages than news pages:

Do we do enough for unmarried mothers?

The question mark has also been used to indicate doubt about the preceding statement:

Income tax up in Budget?

However, the question mark in such contexts is an advertisement of weakness. It is better to rewrite the head (City expects income tax to go up). The question mark has, however, one exceptional value for heads, and that is

How Britain and France be

By Philip Howard

Nearly 1,000 pages of the previously unpublished raw material of British foreign policy between the wars are published today. The latest volume in the

Nazi regime, initiated in the period of this volume, was to continue in one form or another until after Munich in 1938. During the years covered by this volume, German rearmament,

High comedy of Göring's n

Continued from page 1

role, which has been distorted by propaganda.

Throughout the year British policy was dominated by the lingering, although dwindling,

with, we now know, were by no means rational men.

This sombre story is illuminated in flashes by the brilliant telegrams and dispatches from Sir Eric Phipps, the British Ambassador in Berlin, a shrewd

in the developing story where by imitating dialogue it can economically take the news forward:

Banished from Bisley? It's ridiculous says major

Numbers and Percentages

It is desirable, but not essential, to spell out figures below ten. For clarity spell out 'one' at all times: in several type founts the numeral 1 is indistinguishable from the letter l. And, of course, you should never use the figure 1 as a substitute for the word in constructions such as:

The big one that got away

Million and per cent can be spelled out (the style 10,000,000 consumes space and is less easy for the reader to grasp). But, such is the inflation of modern life, and so commonplace is the million-pound story that the abbreviated 'm' for million has arrived and should be welcomed. There are two conditions: it must be related to a figure and not used as an abbreviation on its own. For instance, 'Rail freight extensions will cost £12m' is fine, but 'Tories say £ms wasted' is not. The abbreviation should be a lower-case 'm', set without a full point, and set close to the figure without spacing. Newspapers which set their heads in caps should avoid the clumsier and wasteful abbreviation 'M.' and opt for lower-case for this at least. Similarly for percentage, the lower-case 'pc' is acceptable, provided it is related to a figure:

39pc leap in Shell income

(The fussy % sign is better avoided, even when it is

rying to tame the Nazi tiger

...e spring of 1934. By ...November those res... ...t the Foreign Office, ...Sir Robert Vansittart, ...aded Sir John Simon, ...en Secretary, that a

that all their demands must be met before any general agreement could be concluded.

Hitler professed his desire for an agreement with England, but showed little enthusiasm for

cided t... Simon ... Berlin. their c... printed

So ar...

I

...ge to an actress

...being would wish to ...eekend. This perora...minating and reveals ...rity of his highest

...ipps reports on a disas-...rview with Hitler, his

devastating description of Göring's unbelievably vulgar engagement party, a Foreign Office colleague wrote him a private letter (published in this volume) to tell him that the Foreign Office had decided that

**Pla...
shot
by p...**

From O...
Berlin,
Victo...

2

available: often it is not, and the use of odd sorts from the printer's bottom drawer can have ungainly results.)

The degree of precision for figures in headlines depends in part on the story. If the headline is reporting the total raised by a charity, detailed figures should be given—to the nearest £ if the sum is any size:

Minster Appeal raises
£2,845

The exact figure in a contentious tender or political dispute should be given but in other stories involving large sums, it is simpler for the reader if you go to the nearest round figure: it is better to say '£450,000 for new roads' rather than '£451,826 for new roads'.

Some stories have two figures to give an estimated range:

Between 130,000 and 150,000 attended. . . .
The raiders took between £500 and 800 . . .
Estimates of casualties ranged from twelve
to thirty wounded.

The best advice here is to take the more conservative estimate (while, of course, leaving both figures in the story). This may seem to weaken the story: but it is better to take that chance than to weaken the reader's credibility by consistent risk of exaggeration.

At all times, incidentally, avoid gimmicks with figures in headlines, especially the play with the £ sign: 'Britain gives big £oan' (or 'Everybody wants £££s') and also with the dollar 'Stadium costs two million$.' Caxton's apprentice may have won a few smiles with these, but nobody since.

Turn Headlines

Asking the reader to turn from one page to another for the story to continue is sometimes an unfortunate necessity. The text to read on the turn should always be worthwhile. Some North American newspaper will turn a mere two or three lines of type to another page (under a 24pt continuation heading!) instead of cutting to keep the story on one page. But even when the turn is worthwhile no reader likes turning and no sensible newspaper will let him feel neglected as he makes the expedition.

Far too few newspapers and magazines provide proper signposting on the continuation ('turn') page. Some give no headline at all on the turn, merely a weak line 'continued from page one'. This will not do. The turn should stand out, particularly on a crowded turn page. This means it needs a headline, and it should be a reasonably bold headline even for a down-page turn. The next worst thing to having no turn headline ('jump head' in North America) is to provide one with wording which fails to echo the theme of the main heading, as **at left (1, 2)**.

Conscious of these follies, some newspapers have a rule that the wording of the main head should be repeated on the turn. This is good general practice, though there are disadvantages to it. For instance, where a page one headline says:

POPE ARRIVES IN ISTANBUL
Reception polite but cool

the same words may be repeated as the turn heading. This is relatively easy to find on the turn page but there is nothing in the text there to justify that head. The odd reader beginning the story on the inside page might feel disappointed.

A second slight worry is that this formula produces turn heads which are not distinct enough from the rest of the news heads on the page. One way round this is to use only the top line of a two-line main head—and set this one line up a size on the turn. That is more economical than using two lines, and yet more noticeable among the turn page's traditional multi-line heads. The Pope turn would be headed: 'Pope arrives in Instanbul.' It is of course still open to the objection that the text underneath has gone beyond that point.

There is another way of headlining turns which has some attraction. That is pick up a few key words from the main heading and feature these boldly on the turn. If you take only a few words 'POPE IN TURKEY' or 'RHODESIA' there may be two gains. Firstly, the words will sit

more happily on the text than the example just given. Secondly, with fewer words, it is possible to increase the size of type of the turn head. The distinctions of size and limited wording will help the turn head to stand out from the other news heads on the page (1).

The turn words have to be key words. It is no use turning from 'Callaghan stakes his future' to 'The gamble'. That should have been a turn to 'Callaghan'. And again the turn from 'Expo 67 puts you in the picture' should have been to 'Expo 67' and not to the weaker identification 'in the picture'.

When the turn is long and detailed, the turn head should give the key words and then it may legitimately carry the story forward—preferably in a tone to match the first headline:

Page One:

How Comrade Schulz joined
the SS and won the war

Turn:

Comrade Schulz: When Hitler called him
'the good soldier'

A white-on-black block saying 'continued from page . . .' is a good ancillary signal on all turns. Miscellaneous blobs, stars and other symbols are useful for additional signalling of turns: the important point is that the same symbol should be used in both places, where the story turns and where it is picked up. Different symbols must be used for

different stories, to avoid misleading the eye, and they must be used sparingly, so as not to become mere fussy ornaments.

Contents Bills

There is a cartoon which shows a heavily muffled and overcoated newspaper seller holding a poster:

Heat Wave

The cartoon tells us two things about writing these posters (called contents bills or newsbills in Britain) to persuade people to buy a newspaper. First, the promise in the bill should be fulfilled. If it is cold and we read a bill saying Heat Wave, we will not be amused if we buy the paper only to discover the story is about a heat wave in a distant land. Secondly, a bill is useless unless it stimulates curiosity. If it is hot weather, we are not going to buy a paper because a contents bill announces 'heat wave'. We might if it promised rather more: 'Heat Wave Surprise'. But the story inside the paper would then have to meet our first rule. It would have to tell us something surprising.

There has been devaluation in the effect of the contents bill because of over-selling. 'Famous star dies' may tempt some casuals to buy the paper but if the story supporting it is one obscure paragraph, and the name of the star sadly forgotten, the next bill does not seem too persuasive.

Both the quality of the billed story, and its position in the paper, must justify billing. The reader must not have to search every corner of the paper for a story which has been billed. It will pay newspapers to restore the integrity of the contents bill because it is still a valuable selling aid (curiously neglected in the United States). Words like 'sensation' and 'shock' will be used sparingly. Nothing will be billed unless it has a strong position in the paper. The contents bill must be based on the slogan of honest temptation.

For an interesting discussion of the history and graphics of the British news bill *see* Sarah Whitcombe in 1969 *Penrose Annual* (Lund Humphries, London), pp. 177–187, from which the illustration **opposite (2)** comes.

In most newspaper offices the deskman's instruction to write a bill will come from an executive. The word 'Bill' or 'B' may be scribbled on a corner of the copy to be edited. Where a newspaper is nationally distributed the deskman will be told whether he is required to produce a general, local or special interest bill. The deskman writes the wording for the bill in caps boldly and clearly on a blank folio which will go back to the executive or direct to the circulation department (not to the printer). There is normally no need to indicate type sizes: many of the bills will be handwritten or stencilled anyway.

The bill folio itself should indicate the kind of distribution intended. One story in a paper can yield several bills because bills can be distributed to small areas of potential readership. Unless the billed story is of overwhelming national interest every story billed generally should be exploited for its appeal to smaller groups of potential readers. Deskmen should not need to be told to do this. For instance, a general bill in a city centre would be:

HONOURS
LIST
IN FULL

But the same honours list story would yield innumerable local bills:

REDHILL
MAN
KNIGHTED

And there would be bills for other concentrations of readership, such as universities, conferences, factories. The man selling newspapers at the factory gate might be provided with a bill:

FORD
MAN
KNIGHTED

Those are examples of general, local and special interest bills from the same story. Never forget this fact that the same story appeals in different ways to different layers of readership and therefore justifies different contents bills. Ask yourself: have I exploited the general, special and local interests of this story? To take another example, there is news that subsidies to farmers are to be cut. In farming areas itself that would be the basis for a special interest bill:

FARM
SUBSIDIES
SHOCK

That approach could itself spawn more specific special interest bills for display in special areas:

TOMATO
GROWERS
HIT

But in non-farming areas, the readers are only remotely

THE DAILY MIRROR

LIGHTNING FLASH KILLS SEVEN PICTURES

interested in farm subsidies. They are more aroused by the general bill which springs from the same story:

FOOD
PRICES
WARNING

Local bills can proliferate from a single local story. Place names, the death of many a headline are the lifeblood of the local contents bill. A national or regional newspaper can bill the story first with a regional tag, then a county or town tag, and possibly with a village tag:

SOUTH WEST	SOMERSET	BATH
FACTORY	FACTORY	FACTORY
CLOSES	CLOSES	CLOSES

And, of course, there can be cross-fertilisation from a

local bill to a special interest bill. A story about a Birmingham council ruling on a militant university student's grant will be billed 'Birmingham grant ruling' in Birmingham, but every other university city should be billed 'University grant ruling'.

The commonest mistake editorial deskmen make in writing a news contents bill is to treat it like a headline. Thus they scribble 'Barmaids' strike over' when they should write:

BARMAIDS'
STRIKE
DECISION

The bill is like the bikini. What it reveals is provocative; what it conceals is vital. That barmaids' bill is a label—a form condemned as a news headline but reprieved for bills. The crucial thing is to provoke curiosity without satisfying it—to tease. Just what question you leave unanswered depends on the news story. The barmaids' bill leaves unanswered *what* the decision was. Other bills might leave unanswered the *why, who, where and how*. For instance, at the beginning of the barmaids' strike, it would have been hopeless to write a bill:

BARMAIDS IN
SURPRISE
ACTION

That reveals too little. Very few people would have been stirred by barmaids' negotiations for a rise. Here it is necessary to arouse more interest by telling more of the story in the hope that more people will be provoked into finding answers for some of the other questions:

BARMAIDS
TO STRIKE

That tells more of the news but it still leaves the drinking reader anxious to buy the paper to discover when the strike starts, for how long it is thought it will go on and whether anybody else will be serving.

The skill in writing the contents bill is just in deciding what to reveal and what to conceal. If a Member of Parliament or a Senator has to stand trial, that alone would be provocative enough for a bill, without giving the charges. The unanswered 'why' would be the reason people bought the paper. But if the charge was against a relatively humble local Councillor, then it would be necessary to spice the bill with the alleged offence and change its emphasis.

MP
FACES
TRIAL
(Unanswered: Why, who?)

BRIBERY
CHARGE
AGAINST
COUNCILLOR
(Unanswered: Who bribed whom, and how?)

Only on very special occasions should the contents bill give the news and those are the occasions when you can naturally expect a rush of public curiosity over and beyond the mere event—say the birth of a royal baby, the death of a leading politician. During Churchill's illness the contents bills said 'Churchill: 4 p.m. bulletin', but on his death the bills rightly announced the news like a headline:

Churchill Dead

Don't be shy of writing labels for contents bills. Label wording is common because it is easier to write a teasing bill. This is especially so with feature bills which can pick up the main theme line of the feature or series.

THE PILL: WHAT
EVERY WOMAN
NEEDS TO KNOW
Exclusive

CECIL KING'S
CANDID
MEMOIRS

But the rules for headlines apply in two particulars. It is better to write an active bill 'Minister Resigns' than 'Minister's resignation'. And the contents bill follows the rules of the headline in requiring a few short, simple words. The bill is bigger than a column but the size of letters is correspondingly bigger. The bill must be capable of being read at a glance from across the road or from a moving bus. An overcrowded bill is a waste of everybody's efforts.

7 Headlinese

*Mr J A Spender puts on record a prize heading as a master-
piece of summary:*

OYSTER BARS JAM QUIZ
*He was assured it would be perfectly well understood in
America.*

—F J MANSFIELD

The words individually are harmless enough, but in
certain combinations there is a mutation which twists the
headline horribly, and produces headlinese. Readers who
expose their gaze to it are not exactly turned to stone, but
there is a distinct glazing of the eyes and a buzzing
sensation between the ears. The headline Mr Spender
collected meant to convey that a Congressman named
Oyster had opposed an inquiry into alleged mishandling
of a crowd by police. Try this British headline:

SKYSCRAPERS PROBE HUSTLE

or:

HOMES PLAN FACTORY HOPE

We will come back to these in a moment. Even for
them there is a diagnosis and a cure. The road to recovery
begins by recognising the fundamental reasons for headlinese: compression plus haste. In the headline writer's
soul there is no malevolence for the reader he is about to
assault; he does what he does because, as Theodore
Bernstein[1] put it, he has a desperate need to fit size 7 ideas
into size 2 spaces. So absorbed is the headline writer in
this, so precoccupied is he with extracting its essence in
half a dozen words, so deep does every detail impress itself as he searches the copy again for the unique combination of headline words, so familiar with the facts does he
become, in short, that the headline he writes does not
mean a thing. What he should do when he emerges clutch-
ing the six words of truth is lay them aside for a moment,
pause, and try to read them as if he were the man next day,
who, with a train to catch and his mind preoccupied by
his overdraft, comes across them for the first time.

If the headline writer did this, few of the choicer
varieties of headlinese would survive with their ambiguities
and gobbledegook. Even the slightest doubt in the headline writer's mind should suffice to consign that headline
to oblivion. But doubt should be reinforced by diagnosis
and, as a warning to others who pass this way, the main
inspirations of headlinese will be set out here.

The Seven Deadly Sins

There are ways of dealing with them if you know what
they are: careless use of nouns as adjectives; the creation
of the plural adjective, hitherto unknown to the English
language; extravagant extension of metaphor; excessive
omission of words; confusion of tenses; abuse of headline
catch words; and slang. The latter can be dealt with sum-
marily. It passes in a light heading when the slang is indeed
common parlance and is one splash of vulgar procession
of subject, verb and predicate. It fails when slang is piled
on slang as in the classic *Chicago Tribune* announcement
that Professor William Craigie was joining the University
of Chicago to direct the compilation of the *Dictionary of
American English*:

MIDWAY SIGNS LIMEY PROF
TO DOPE YANK TALK

Nouns and verbs

The most serious begetter of headlinese is unquestion-
ably the abuse of the noun as an adjective. I have ex-
plained that I approve of calling the man who has had a
heart transplant 'heart man' in the headline, letting the
noun 'heart' do the work of an adjective and identify the
man. This is clear enough. The trouble comes when the
word which is used as an adjective *can also represent a verb*.
There are any number of words which can be either noun
or verb according to sentence structure, whose role is
revealed only by other words in the sentence. When these
other words are omitted to form the compact headline
sentence, the key word may become ambiguous. The first
defence against headlinese then must be to have an early

warning system which cautions the headline writer as he deploys the noun–verb words as adjectives. In the headline vocabulary these are conspicuous:

> tax, ban, plan, drive, move, probe, protest, bar, share, watch, cut, axe, ring, bank, rises, state, pay, pledge, talks, riot, attack, appeal, back, face, sign, jump, drug

It is the confusion of noun and verb which makes us stumble at this one:

POLICE STATE TAUNT BY HOGG IN ROW ON SEIZED PASSPORT

'Police state' we read here as subject and verb. So they gave evidence did they, about a taunt made by Hogg? No. The story tells us that during a row about a seized passport Mr Hogg accused the Government of setting up a police state. It is Mr Hogg who is using the word state and using it as a noun in the position of an adjective. He is quite entitled to do that, not because he is a Privy Councillor but because in his sentence the position of the words 'a police state' and the retention of the word '*a*' make it clear that 'state' is being used as a noun and 'police' is a noun being used adjectivally to qualify the noun 'state'.

The headline writer cannot use Mr Hogg's 'police state' unless he, too, indicates clearly what it means: and there are ways of doing this even within the limited space of a headline. First, the headline could hyphenate police-state to indicate that it is a compound and not noun and verb. Or secondly, and preferably, the words should be enclosed in quotes:

'POLICE STATE' TAUNT BY HOGG IN ROW ON SEIZED PASSPORT

Very many of the wildest headlines, created by the confusion of noun and verb, can be tamed if the headline writer recognises the beast as double-headed. Armed only with a hyphen or quotes he can then bring the troublesome words to useful service, though some examples are so ferocious they have to be put down altogether.

PUNJABI WHO RUNS STREET PROTESTS

And so do all of us. The headline is supposed to indicate an article about a Punjabi who organises protests in the streets. Street is being used as an adjective. Hyphenating street-protests might just rescue this one.

'SPEED PROBE NEED URGENT'

It is not a call to speed a probe (heaven help us). It is a call to hasten an inquiry into speeding in a town. The two initial nouns as adjectives with a third which could be a verb take some digesting; quick work might just about produce a survivor, coupling speed-probe and leaving the quotes for the one word which needs them:

SPEED-PROBE NEED 'URGENT'

NIGERIAN TALKS IN LONDON

Did they grill him hard? 'Talks on Nigeria in London' would fit. (If tight, you might just get away with 'Nigeria talks in London'.)

DISASTER PLANNING THE EUROPEAN WAY

One asks 'is it a disaster planning the European way?' But the article does not tell us. It is about the way the European Civil Defence plans for disaster in nuclear war. Disaster, you will have guessed, is a noun used as an adjective. Rather than create a hyphenated monster heading it should be written simply: Planning for disaster in Europe.

Plural adjectives

The English language does not recognise a plural adjective. We never say 'Ten beautifuls women' or 'Plums tart'. Absurd headlines like 'Skyscrapers probe hustle' are produced when we use a noun as an adjective—and then put the adjective into the plural. Here is another:

WHITE LINES EXPERIMENT ON ROADS

Very irresponsible of them. 'White lines' is being used adjectivally to describe the kind of experiment (just as 'skyscrapers' is being used to describe the kind of 'probe'). All such must be in the singular. 'White-line experiment on roads' is intelligible and not ludicrously ambiguous. And, of course, we understand there is more than one white line, just as we understand there is more than one road in road safety. Putting the noun being used as an adjective into the correct singular prevents many a nonsense, but sometimes this is only one fault. The most grotesque headlines occurs when in addition to a plural adjective we have to cope with not one but three nouns as adjectives.

NUCLEAR PLANT DAMAGES PROBE BY POLICE

can be swiftly treated for its painful pluralisation:

NUCLEAR PLANT DAMAGE PROBE BY POLICE

This inactive headline with three initial nouns to describe the probe is best recast positively

POLICE PROBE NUCLEAR PLANT DAMAGE

Let us take our courage in both hands and tackle

COLOURED TEACHERS

PLAN DOUBTS

Now you don't catch us imagining for a moment that this headline means what it says—that coloured teachers plan to create doubts. The headline, as we should have guessed, is trying to say that an education director is not very happy over an idea that coloured immigrants should be recruited as specialist teachers. Snipping the 's' off the noun–adjective indicates that we are not dealing with the verb 'to plan'. And putting the whole phrase in quotes might help further:

'COLOURED TEACHER PLAN' DOUBTS

But here again the three nouns bolted together make a formidable hurdle to instant intelligibility. They can be unlocked to provide 'Doubts on plan for coloured teachers' or we can fall back on the subject, verb, predicate construction: 'Official doubts idea of coloured teachers'.

When we are using a word in an unusual way the onus is on us to make sure the reader is with us all the way.

BEXLEY SCHOOLS BAR ROW SPREADS

The bar rows most people know about are not very pleasant. Is this an instance of alcohol being smuggled into the teachers' room? No, it is a decision to refuse to admit children to two schools—to bar their entry. 'Entry row' would have made some sense. And again:

PRODUCTION OVER MINE SAFETY, CLAIMS INSPECTOR

does not mean that output is over the level needed to keep the mine open. 'Over' here means 'put first': Pit output put before mine safety, says inspector.

North American newspapers are consistently guilty of the ambiguous use of the 'see' to mean somebody's opinion. This leads to all sorts of follies:

Johnson sees Hanoi weakening

McCarthy seen losing Indiana

Careless of him really. As the *New Yorker* magazine said when confronted with 'Many seen failing to enjoy their jobs', they might at least keep out of sight.

Excessive omission

You read the text, you chisel out an acceptable headline, then it fails to fit by a few units. This is the moment of temptation. If you omit just that one word, it still makes sense doesn't it? Why, of course, anybody who had read the story would appreciate

WALKOVER LONDON

As sports followers, we know it is a reference to Brian London, the boxer, but what do we learn? London has walked over somebody or somebody has walked over London? The clue is in the omitted word 'by' which would not fit the first line. A good test for excessive omission is to see if there is a chink in the wording where you can reasonably insert alternative pronouns or prepositions and change the meaning:

Signals at red, said nothing

The omission is between the 'red' and 'said', and what might we legitimately imagine in there? 'They' said nothing? 'He' said nothing? 'I' said nothing? 'We' said nothing? 'Police' said nothing? 'Archbishop' said nothing? I suspect that what was originally written was:

'Signals at red, I said nothing'

The text is that a fireman of a train which collided with another told the inquiry that after the train had begun to move he saw a signal gantry with all the signals at red—but he did not say anything to the driver about it. This admission is worth the headline, but the subject of the sentence cannot be omitted. Instead of trying to cope with the exact quotes here, the headline could have been:

Railman saw danger, said nothing

Two more with the missing word supplied (in brackets):

St. Paul's tribute to Luther King (Cathedral)

Vietcong flags over Saigon (fly)

Abuse of catchwords

The ugliest headlines gives the impression that a handful of words thought to be powerful in headlines have been taken at random without any attempt to create an intelligible headline sentence. Words like shock, ordeal, pledge, probe, are potent symbols, but like soup concentrates they need water. They cannot be served altogether and raw:

TRAIN RUSH HOUR SMASH ORDEAL

CAR PLEDGE MOVE HIT

FOOT AND MOUTH BAN BLOW TO DREAPER PLAN

In this category we must analyse our opening shocker

HOMES PLAN FACTORY HOPE

We have a noun-adjective double, Homes plan, which means a plan to accept industrialised housing in a new town; and factory hope, which means there may be an industrialised housing factory.

All these words are acceptable if used in a less constipated context. In addition, we have excessive omission. If we could insert a verb to separate the two sections of the headline we might just make sense:

HOMES PLAN RAISES FACTORY HOPES

But the truth is this headline is guilty of a further offence: two thoughts in four words. Headlinese is best avoided here by settling for the main news thought. So, too, with this monster created by coupling five nouns together:

Corned beef on 'secret' sale storm

This was also an instance of too much in the headline and of the headline overtaking itself. The news was:

'Typhoid' corned beef in shops after all

Extravagant metaphor

Escalation robs headlines of authority. People who are worried about through traffic find they are living in 'terror road'; a mild disagreement becomes a storm; and anyone who makes a criticism is in danger of being pictured in the most ferocious posture:

Bishop flays modern girl
Director slashes seats
Teacher lashes meals issue

Related to this source of headlinese is the escalation of metaphor until it loses touch with reality.

KLONDIKE RUSH FOR WHITE GOLD

'White gold' is a metaphor here for uranium. And the rush is not in the Klondike. It would be all right to say:

'Klondike' rush for uranium

This use of the metaphor would give an image of frenzy similar to the gold rush in the Klondike, and losing the 'white gold' metaphor hardens the headline without emasculating it. What happened was that the headline writer built on a good idea but left the reader behind.

Confusion of tenses

We use the present tense in heads for contemporaneous events; but we cannot retain the present tense throughout when there is a clear time-change built into the headline:

CID SUSPECT ARSON AFTER BABIES SAFE

I do not agree with the view[2] that when a past time element appears in the head the only thing to do is use a verb in the past tense. That would produce 'CID suspected arson after babies saved', as though they no longer suspect arson. What we should do is recognise that in this clumsily constructed head, the word 'after' enforces past tense on what follows: 'CID suspect arson after babies saved'. We could avoid the past tense: 'CID suspect arson after baby rescue'. But it is also better to avoid the 'after' construction. This would fit:

BABIES SAVED IN FIRE: CID SUSPECT ARSON

Clumsy construction

To make heads fit their line counts there is some juggling you can do with word order without sacrificing meaning. But a halt must be called when the word shuffling produces heads such as:

London model is strangling victim with City man

The news can and should be expressed in normal sequence:

London model and City man found strangled

or

London model found strangled with City man

And again:

Tenant hit raider with bottle on head

Who bottle on head had?

8 Headline and Intro Exercises

The National Council for the Training of Journalists in Britain has developed a number of practical exercises for journalists. If we take two of the sub-editing exercises set by the National Council and see how they were tackled by a group of journalists in training, it will emphasise the principles elaborated in the chapters on headline writing and highlight common errors. The aim is to edit this material for a hypothetical evening newspaper published in the city of Hull. After you have read the text you might yourself produce an intro, and try writing the headlines specified.

The intro is to be one paragraph in 12pt bold across three columns, with a drop letter, so you have to judge the number of words carefully. Too many words produce a slabby intro, too few leave the drop letter 'uncovered', i.e. hanging uneasily in white space.

Mark your folios correctly and stick strictly to the maximum unit counts indicated for the headlines. Do your own intro and headlines before studying the efforts of the trainees and my comments on them.

Headline instructions

Strap or overline in 36pt u/lc × 9 cols   Maximum count: 66

Streamer in 60pt caps × 9 cols   Maximum count: 25

Third deck in 48pt u/lc × 4 and × 3   Maximum count: 21 and 14

HEADLINE AND INTRO EXERCISES

Exercise One
Unedited text
The original story, catchlined Rain, was followed by
several add paragraphs which are indicated:

Rain 1.

"I'm singing in the rain". That was the theme song today
for Mr. Thomas Pickering, Hull's water engineer, as the rain came
down in the city to register the highest monthly figure in nearly
70 years of records, and Corporation water reserves came up to dash
every fear of the undertaking's 410,000 consumers.

Exulted a happy Mr. Pickering after wending his way to work
through this morning's downpour: "They say I am the only happy
person in the city today".

mf

Rain 2.

He had every reason for satisfaction, for earlier this year
Mr. Pickering warned that if the lack of rainfall continued, Hull
could be facing a serious shortage in later months.

So anxious was his department that they asked the government
for special powers to take more of their legal share of water from the
River Hull, and following a public inquiry, were given powers to extract
up to an extra 3,000,000 daily gallons on top of the 12,000,000 they
were already allowed to take from the river.

"But I don't think we will be forced to take such action the
way things are now," said Mr. Pickering.

mf

Rain 3.

"September has been very abnormal," he added "with five
inches of rain fallg durg the month, two-and-a-half times the normal.

"This hs certainly saved the day for us. The flow in the
river is increasg already followg this heavy rain -- the highest figure
for September in our records which date back to 1897."

Out of the month's 30 days, 21 of them were wet. Between
ydy morning and today (10 a.m.), .33 of an inch fell on the city, well
below September's highest of 1.02 inches on the 8th, but enough to
push the total to the five inch mark.

                              mf

Rain 4.

This is dramatically up on the same month last year which
registered .75" and so far brings the total for 1965 to almost 19½ inches-
compared with the 17.68 inches total for the whole of 1964.

Naturally sunshine figures have lost their warmth, dropping
from last year's 1,179.4 hrs up to September to the present 1,058.5.

"If we now get a normal winter rainfall we should have
plenty of water," sd Mr. Pickering.

But the recent heavy falls will take two or three months
before registering at the corporation pumping stations.

                              mf

Rain 5.

"It takes abt that time for the rain to perculate through the chalk to the pumping stations," added the water engineer, "whereas the river feels the impact immediately. The more water there is in the river, the more we can take out"

Goole, too, had its wettest September on record, rain falling on 23 days of the month to produce a total of 5.48 inches.

It was the town's wettest month since August, 1956.

Rain 6.

Mr. G.W. Hutchinson, senior engineer of the Yorkshire Ouse and Hull River Authority, sd the 6.22 inches recorded at South Bullock pumping station was the highest for the month since records first started 80 years ago.

"It ws three times the September average and 30 per cent higher than any previous September rainfall," he sd.

Only four times previously has six inches bn recorded by the authority, and their all-time record stands at 7.41 in July, 1940.

ENDS

Add rain   Platt, Goole

Goole's September rainfall was a record 5.48 ins.
Rain fell on 23 days of the month, and it was the wettest month that the town hs experienced since August, 1956.

Add rain   Thomas, Leconfield.

There were 7½ in. of rain at Leconfield, the highest since
records started and an inch more than the previous highest.

Add rain   Blair, Bridlington.

There were only ten days without rain at Bridlington,
which hd one of its wettest-ever Septembers with 5.9 ins., 3 ins.
above the normal.

Add rain   Jones, Beverley.

Beverley's 6.22 in. was three times the normal monthly
total.

Sunshine   Blair, Bridlington.

Bridlington's September sunshine figures will never be
known because the lens recording apparatus was stolen.

Police traced the missing lens and returned it, but it
had been damaged to such an extent that it cd not be used and it will
be impossible to maintain records until a replacement, which hs bn
ordered, is delivered.

The sunshine figure was near the 100-hr mark last Sunday
before the lens ws stolen.

                         ENDS

Clearly the text has to be edited hard to the news point: not even the most leisurely paper can afford to have Mr Pickering 'wending his way to work through this morning's downpour'. The news is that it has rained hard enough to end all the worries produced by the drought.

Trainees' answers

What the trainees produced are now given, and you might compare your own efforts with theirs. My own comments follow each answer.

Corporation's water reserves saved by sudden rainfall

GALLONS OF LUVERLY WATER

Hull will not need river water

'I'm singing in the rain'. That was the theme song today for Mr Thomas Pickering, Hull's water engineer, as the rain came down in the city to register the highest monthly figure in nearly 70 years of records, and Corporation water reserves came up to dash every fear that the undertaking's 410,000 consumers. . . .

COMMENT: Hopeless. The streamer 'luverly water' is banal: The place for a joke in this story, if any, is in the overline not the streamer. The overline is inaccurate: the text makes it clear the rainfall is not sudden. The third deck is newsy enough but by then the word 'water' has appeared three times.

This man left the wordy intro as it was which means it missed the news and in 12pt was too slabby. He aggravated these errors by submitting a careless second paragraph:

Exulted a happy Mr Pickering, after wending his way to work through this morning's downpour, said: 'They say I'm the only happy person in the city today'.

MECHANICS: There were no catchlines on the folio sheets. The upper- and lower-case heads were written in caps without any indication of where the printer should set initial caps.

No rationing for 410,000 as the rain comes down

WATER SHORTAGE AVERTED

(Third deck not submitted)

The threat of a water shortage in Hull ended today with heavy downpours of rain. The water reserves went up as the city registered its highest monthly figure of rain in nearly 70 years.

COMMENT: The streamer is right on the news (though the wording could be improved). The intro also slings the news point, but a little crudely. It is not the day's rain which ended the drought.

MECHANICS: The overline was written in two lines without any indication that one line was wanted. The head was written in block capitals without any indication in the upper- and lower-case heads of what would require initial caps. The overline was very short, some 16 units shy of the maximum unit count.

The folios were not numbered. The drop letter requirement was not marked on the intro.

September deluge saves city from serious water shortage

RAIN, RAIN, GLORIOUS RAIN!

Now no need for extra raid on river?

It rained two and a half times as hard as usual over Hull this September—and that was the best news the city Water Engineer, Mr Thomas Pickering, has had all year.

COMMENT: Intro misses the news by a mile. What matters is the good news for the people of Hull. It has been raining for a long time: for the evening paper to headline that as though it was news is ludicrous. The news is buried in the overline—that the city has been saved from a serious water shortage.

The third deck is more pointedly newsy. Raid is a good word—but question mark headings should be avoided.

MECHANICS: Three barely legible heads written on one folio instead of on three.

East Coast holidaymakers and Hoteliers call it 'a washout' as it's a case of

RAIN, RAIN and STILL MORE RAIN

Hull Water Board happy river 'loan' not needed

Fears of drought were removed today when the rain came pouring down creating the highest rainfall in Hull since records were begun nearly 70 years ago.

COMMENT: The intro begins on the right lines but wanders off into the record books—and inaccurately at that. The figures released were for the month; but the implication in the intro is that the day's figures were a record and they were not.

The streamer, succumbing to a weak play on words fails to tell any news at all: everybody knows it's been raining. The news is that it has rained enough to make water supplies safe. The overline, reading on to the streamer, is wrong: it is the streamer which is read first.

MECHANICS: The overline is absurdly over the maximum unit count. There is no indication of initial caps in the heads marked upper- and lower-case. The full point after Happy in the second deck should be a colon. The intro is hardly long enough to cover the drop letter. One good point: each headline folio is numbered and catchlined.

I'm the only happy man in the city today, says water engineer

RECORD RAINFALL ENDS DROUGHT

Rivers rise in wettest September ever

September rain figures for Hull and East Riding were the highest in nearly 80 years of records, soaring three times above normal in some places.

COMMENT: The heads are all active but the streamer and intro falter by focusing on the subsidiary news—the record rainfall ending the drought. The news is what affects the reader and that is the firm announcement that the fears of water shortage are definitely over. The overline is properly on a subsidiary point and nicely exploits one of the lighter passages in the text.

MECHANICS: The trainee failed abysmally. The streamer bounces (RECORD RAIN(S) would fit). The third deck was marked 43pt instead of 48pt. The three folios for the decks were rightly catchlined 'Rain', but illegibly, and without any numbering or other indication of the sequence of headings. The layout would do that, of course, but so should the sub as additional guidance on the stone.

Conclusion

The intro and headlines should have been something on the lines of:

Cheer up: all that rain—a 70 year record—has ended the drought

PLENTY OF WATER AGAIN

Raid on River Hull looks unlikely

Worries of water rationing for Hull are over. September's rainfall, the highest in 70 years, means that with normal winter weather there will be 'plenty of water', said the city's water engineer, Mr Thomas Pickering, today.

Exercise Two
In this exercise, set on a Westminster Press course for
reporters, the trainees were allowed to nominate varying
headline specifications according to a page they were
planning. The text, really raw, was for a Downtown City
evening newspaper:

Unedited text

1. Part of a flyover bridge being constructed in the city of Downtown
   today collapsed and trapped four workmen who were working on it.

2. The bridge is part of an ambitious scheme to drive a new road
   through the city to ease the congestion caused by the existing
   "one way at a time" traffic flow through the Market Place, where
   a policeman sits in an observation box controlling traffic lights
   with push buttons and closed circuit television.

3. The flyover will eventually take internal town traffic over the
   pier, which is now also being built.

4. A doctor and ambulances were at once called to the scene, and with
   the aid of other workmen and police, the doctor, Dr. William Jones,
   who has a practice in Drury Lane, Downtown, and lives at 110
   Sunderland Road, crawled into the wreckage. It took him almost
   ten minutes to reach the first man, who was trapped under the
   twisted mass of wrecked concrete and metalreinforcing rods.

5. He was rushed to hospital by one of the waiting ambulances
   immediately. But not before Dr. Jones had examined him. Later
   the doctor was asked how the man was, but shook his head and
   refused to answer. A police sergeant at the scene said: "The
   man Waterson is obviously very badly injured. I suggest you phone
   the hospital".

6. Two other men are known to be buried. It is feared that they
   are dead. Carefully the crane began the painstaking task of
   removing the shattered bridge in the search for the victims.

7. Piece by piece they removed the shattered concrete.

8. Meanwhile a workman said: "This should never have happened. Obviously something is very far wrong with the design of the bridge. You won't catch me working on this contract from now on."

9. A sign near the collapsed bridge states that the main contractor is the firm Johnston, Bainbridge and Whiteside, and the joint architects Messrs. Thomas Delong and James White, of Queensbury Square, London.

10. It is believed that the men who were trapped were all from Downtown. The contractors make a practice of employing as many local men as possible on all their contracts.

11. A foreman, Mr. Jimmy Scott, of 21 Lower Elvet - who hails from Scotland, and came to Downtown six months ago to work on the site from another contract on which the same firm is working - said: "Yes, that is true. We do employ a lot of local men. In fact these men were in my squad, and I know for a fact that they live in the city."

Presenting the news

The trainees were working for a single edition with an assumed monopoly of the news for the bulk of the readership. This makes the exercise a relatively simple matter of presenting the main news points. It is a practical assumption for an evening paper, even with broadcast competition, because most of the readers would not be following radio and TV throughout the day. It is certainly a bad mistake for an evening paper to overtake itself—updating the headlines so much that the original news point is obscured. (If the exercise had been for a morning newspaper, of course, the news emphasis would have had to be different. Assuming most people had heard something of the flyover collapse, the headline and intro would have had to concentrate on the fate of the trapped men and the reasons for the flyover collapsing.)

Trainees' answers

FLYOVER TRAGEDY
Local men buried
as bridge collapses

Four workmen were trapped today when part of a flyover being constructed in Downtown collapsed. One man brought out of the wreckage was dead. Two more, still buried, are feared dead.

COMMENT: Tragedy is a wasted word. In the headline 'Local men' is irrelevant parochialism on an obviously local story. In the space provided the head could have been more direct.

FLYOVER COLLAPSES
Man Dies: Rescuers dig
for two in debris

The intro was pithy, but again it would have been better to say more positively: 'Rescue teams are searching for two other men still buried in the debris'.

FALLEN BRIDGE
KILLS ONE,
TRAPS TWO

A construction worker died under the wreckage of a new flyover bridge which collapsed at Downtown today. Two others were still trapped at 4.30 p.m. It is feared they are dead.

COMMENT: Tenses are mixed up in this head. Putting 'fallen' into the past tense (wrongly) and the rest of the headline (rightly) into the present tense suggests that it was a bridge which had already fallen which caused the deaths. On this unit count the head should have been:

MAN DIES AS
FLYOVER
COLLAPSES

The intro is pithy, but 'under the wreckage . . . which collapsed' is clumsy. The collapse of the bridge should not be a mere subordinate clause.

In the second and third sentences the emphasis should have been on the more positive and active rescue effort.

TRAGEDY HITS DOWNTOWN FLYOVER
One Killed—Two Men Still Missing

The flyover bridge at High Corner, Downtown, collapsed this afternoon at 2 p.m. and one man was killed, another injured, and two men are still buried somewhere beneath the debris. It is anticipated that an inquiry will be held and allegations of faulty design investigated.

COMMENT: The main deck is much too vague. General words like 'tragedy' should be kept out and the space used to tell the news. 'Tragedy hits' does not tell us even that the bridge has collapsed. It could be a traffic accident. In the space this trainee allocated for his headings the following wording would have fitted:

FLYOVER COLLAPSES: MAN DIES
Flight to rescue two trapped in debris

In the intro the first sentence does not read well, with all its conjunctions. The allegation of faulty design is a trap in the exercise copy which all the other trainees avoided. The un-named workman's statement, in paragraph 8 of the unedited text, clearly defames the designers, and the trainee invented the idea that allegations would be investigated. This trainee also left in the copy the paragraph 5 reference to the doctor shaking his head, which could be a refusal to talk but might be read by the worried relatives as an indication that the man will not live. It should be deleted.

Conclusion

All the trainees avoided the obvious narrative trap in this exercise: the intrusion of background paragraphs 2 and 3 which delay the story too much at this point. Clearly expendable are the police sergeant's comment in paragraph 5 and the second sentence of paragraph 10.

9 Headline Vocabulary

Everyone must, for the most part, be his own analyst; and no one who does not expend, whether expressly and systematically or as a half-conscious accompaniment of his reading and writing, a good deal of care upon points of synonym is likely to write well.

—H W FOWLER

The headline writer must have an armoury of synonyms. 'Can you think of another word for "requisition"'? Pleas like that are common as deskmen try to avoid the long words and the abstractions which kill headlines. Practice in headline writing enforces acquaintance with a wide order of synonyms. The deskman will be his own analyst: in half a dozen synonyms only one may be quite right for the idea to be expressed.

For writing and editing there are a few useful dictionaries of synonyms[1]; Roget's rich *Thesaurus* is especially valuable once its method of presentation is mastered.[2] For headline writing, however, a different kind of vocabulary is useful—a list of the words which commonly give difficulty in headline writing with headline alternatives. These must be shorter and, preferably, more specific. It is these that the headline writer needs to store in his mind, and which the following vocabulary attempts to supply.

The main headings throughout are the nouns, verbs and adjectives which give most trouble, followed by shorter alternatives. With the troublesome abstract nouns listed it is often better to change the headline thought so it can be expressed with a verb. The list is not a list of synonyms. It is a list of headline ideas. Some of the alternative words suggested will not fit the shade of meaning in every case, and the deskman must judge.

It is a good idea to make your own additions when a moment of headline inspiration finds a new way round a familiar tortuous abstraction. Words in italic should only be used in difficulties and then only if the style of the newspaper permits.

A

abandon (v)
drop
give up
skip
quit
yield

abatement (n)
cut
decline
drop
ebb
easement
fall
slump

abbreviate (v)
chop
cut
lop
shorten
slash
squash

abduction (n)
capture
kidnap
seizure

abolish (v)
ban
bar
block
close
cut
drop
end
foil
kill
squash

abolition (n)
ban
bar
end

abscond (v)
flee
leave
run

accelerate (v)
bustle
dash
drive
hasten
hustle
push
press
race
rush
scramble
speed

acceleration (n)
drive
flurry
hurry
push
race
scramble

accident
(nouns)
blast
collision
crash
horror
pile-up
smash
terror
(verbs)
blast
collide
crash
gut (fire)
ram
raze
smash
strike

accommodate (v)
fit in
house
hold
put up
take in

accumulate (v)
add (up)
amass
acquire
build up
gather
grow

accurate (adj)
exact
right
true

accusation (n)
allegation (n)
blame
charge
citation

accuse (v)
allege
blame
charge
cite
indict

achieve (v)
get
gain
grab

achievement (n)
gain
triumph
victory
win

acknowledge (v)
admit
agree
ok/okay
recognise

acquisition (n)
benefit
bequest
find
gain
legacy
win

acquire (v)
buy
choose
gain
get
grab
inherit
pick
reap
take

acquittal (n)
clearance
freedom
release
reprieve

adamant (adj)
enemy
firm
hard
rigid
tough

administer (v)
control
direct
manage
run

adjustment (n)
change
revision
shift
switch

advantage (n)
benefit
gain
help
plus

aggravate (v)
annoy
excite
kindle
inflame
provoke
spark
vex
worsen

agreement (n)
accord
bargain
bond
deal
pact
treaty

agriculture (nouns)
crops (or be specific)
farm
food
farmers
land
(verbs)
farm
harvest
plant
reap
sow
till

alleviate (v)
ease
lessen
let up
reduce

alleviation (n)
aid
help
let up
lighten
relief
remission
rescue
succour

allocation (n)
cut
dole
quota
ration
share

amalgamation (n)
link
merger
tie-up
team

amalgamate (v)
combine
bond
fuse
join
link
merge
mix
team up
tie
unify
unite
weld

ambassador (n)
envoy
minister

amendment (n)
change
revision
rewording
shift
switch

announce (v)
notify
proclaim
report
reveal
tell

announcement (n)
disclosure
news
record
report

apartment (n)
flat
home

apathetic (adj)
aloof
cool
calm

appeal (v)
ask
call
plea

appoint (v)
choose
invest
name
pick

appointment (n)
duty
job
mission
place
post

apologise (v)
climb down
regret
repent
rue
say sorry

apology (n)
regret
remorse

apportion (v)
allot
divide
give out
share

apportionment (n)
deal
lot
part
quota
ration
share

appreciate (v)
grow
increase
rise
value

appropriate (v)
grab
loot
take over
seize
snatch

arbitrator (n)
judge
referee
umpire

argument (n)
dispute
fight
quarrel
row

arraignment (n)
case
charge
indictment
suit
trial

ascertain (v)
find out
learn
seek

assistance (n)
aid
back (up)
help
relief
rescue

attain (v)
get
reach
secure

authorise (v)
adopt
agree
allow
approve
back
favour
let
pass
permit
ratify
sanction
say yes to
sign
vote

B

bankruptcy (n)
crash
collapse
failure
fall

barrister (n)
counsel
lawyer
QC (not always)

beginning (n)
birth
dawn
debut
onset
opening
start

bequeath (v)
give
leave
will

bewilderment (n)
awe
puzzle
shock
surprise

business (n)
company
firm
trader

business premises (n)
company/plant
firm
shop/store/office

C

calculate (v)
assess
estimate
rate
value

catalogue (n)
details
name
list
record

ceremony (n)
display
fete
pageant
parade
party
review
spectacle

cessation (n)
end
gap
lull
pause
rest
stop

challenge (v)
contest
dare
defy
doubt
dispute
flout

championship (n)
award
crown
title

circumvent (v)
balk
beat
cheat
defeat
dish
foil
outwit
stop

clergyman (n)
minister
priest
rector
vicar

clemency (n)
mercy

close (v)
call-off
conclude
end
finish
shut

coalition (n)
alliance
band
group
league
syndicate

comfortable (adj)
cosy
fine
good
snug

commendation (n)
acclaim
applause
backing
eulogy
good record
homage
praise

committee (n)
body
group
party

commodious (adj)
fit
roomy
spacious

communicate (v)
pass on
reveal
tell

competition (n)
fight
race
rivalry

complain (v)
accuse
growl
grumble
object
protest
resent

completion (n)
end
finish

conciliation (n)
good offices
peace move
talks
truce

confront (v)
face

congratulate (v)
commend
praise

conjecture (n)
guess

co-operate (v)
combine
help
join with
side with

consider (v)
discuss
look at
probe
report on
study

consolidate (v)
bland
cement
combine
fuse
mix
unify
unite
weld

construct (v)
build
form
make
put up

continue (v)
go on
persist
run
remain
stay

contradict (v)
deny
dispute
disown
dissent
reject
refute
slap

contradiction (n)
denial
rebuff
rejection

contribution (n)
award
donation
gift
grant
present

criticise (v)
abuse
censure
challenge
chide
condemn
decry
deplore
flay
rap
rail at
slap
slam

criticism (n)
blow
censure
rebuke
rebuff

D

damage (v)
harm
hit
hurt
ruin
spoil
wreck

defector (n)
rebel
refugee
runaway

deflate (v)
contract
crush
cut
pinch
squeeze

deflation (n)
cut
squeeze

demonstrate (v)
march
parade
protest
riot
sit-in

demonstration (n)
demo
march
parade
protest
riot
row
scene
showdown
sitdown
sit-in

denomination (n)
name
religion
school

department (n)
civil service
office
ministry
office

deprecate (v)
attack
belittle
discount
discredit
knock
run down

description (n)
account
story
tale

designate (v)
appoint
name
select

destruction (n)
damage
havoc
ruin
waste
wreck

determine (v)
agree
find out
fix

disagree (v)
argue
differ
fall out

disagreement (n)
battle
clash
conflict
dispute
fight
fracas
quarrel
rift
row
rumpus
wrangle

disapprove (v)
ban
bar
block
deny
disallow
reject
say no to
throw out
turn down

discriminate (v)
bar
block
favour
penalise
screen
segregate

discrimination (n)
bias
favouritism
injustice
leaning
prejudice

discriminatory (adj)
biased
partial
undue
unequal
unfair
unjust

dissolve (v)
end

distribute (v)
deal
dispense
give
issue
scatter

distribution (n)
dispense
issue
supply

**domestic
appliances** (n)
devices
gadgets

E

earthquake (n)
'quake
shake
tremor

emergency (n)
aid call
crash
crisis team
disaster
SOS

employment (n)
job
work

endorsement (n)
acclaim
approval
backing
sanction
support

endowment (n)
donation
gift
legacy
offer

enfranchise (v)
give vote to
liberate
set free

enjoyment (n)
delight
glee
joy
pleasure

entertainment (n)
fair
feast
fun
show

equivocate (v)
delay
dodge
evade
shuffle

essential (adj)
key
main
must
necessary
needed

establish (v)
fix
prove
secure
settle

estimate (v)
conjecture
fix price
guess
judge
value

every (adj)
all
each

exacerbate (v)
irritate
vex

exaggerate (v)
amplify
blow up
enlarge
increase
magnify
overstate
swell

examine (v)
inspect
look at
question
quiz
search
study
view
watch

examination (n)
inquiry
probe
quest
scrutiny
study
trial

exemption (n)
exception
immunity

exhibit (v)
display
show

exonerate (v)
absolve
acquit
clear
free
uphold

expedite (v)
ease
hasten
help
hurry
press
rush
speed
urge

explanation (n)
account
answer
comment
reply
tale
version

explosion (n)
blast
shock
spasm

F

fabrication (n)
falsehood
lie
tale
untruth

facilitate (v)
advance
ease
expedite
impel
relieve
smooth

fallacious (adj)
false
untrue
wrong

fashionable (adj)
in vogue
modish
stylish

fraternise (v)
befriend
help
mix with
side with

foundation (n)
basis
base
beginning
charity

fundamental (adj)
basic
primary

G

govern (v)
command
control
direct
manage
rule
run

government (n)
Britain (i.e.
nation where
paper published)
Cabinet (if
Cabinet involved)
country
ministry
minister's name is
often aptest
nation
state
Whitehall
White House
(For provincial
and state papers
in federal country,
the capital:
London/
Washington/
Canberra/Delhi,
etc.)

grievance (n)
grouse
grudge
hardship
injury
injustice
wrong

guarantee
(nouns)
bend
mortgage
pledge
secure
support
(verbs)
endorse
go bail
insure
pledge
surety
sponsor
warrant

guillotine (v)
chop
cut off
gag
silence

H

hallucination (n)
delusion
dream
illusion
mirage

harmonisation (n)
accord
bargain
compact
pact
peace
truce

harmonise (v)
accord
agree
conciliate
heal
pacify
patch
settle
smooth

hazardous (adj)
bold
perilous
risky
unsafe

I

illegitimate (adj)
illegal
illicit
unlawful
wrong

illimitable (adj)
boundless
infinite
immense
no-limit

illustrate (v)
explain
picture
show
reveal

immaterial (adj)
flimsy
thin
trifling

imminent (adj)
near
soon

important (adj)
big
grave
great
high
key
notable
prime
signal
serious
top
vital
weighty

improve (v)
amend
better
bolster
ease
enhance
mend
patch
polish
promote
refit
refresh
remodel
renew
repair
restore
revamp
touch up

improvement (n)
advance
betterment
progress
recovery
reform
repair
relief

inaccurate (adj)
false
untrue
wrong

inaugurate (v)
begin
install
open
start

inauguration (n)
debut
opening
start

incomes (n)
cash
money
pay
salary
wages

indemnify (v)
balance
compensate
cover
make up for
redeem
set off

independent (adj)
free
impartial
neutral
unbiased

influence (v)
induce
lead
sway

information (n)
advice
details
facts
news

injunction (n)
order
writ

inquire (v)
ask
examine
look into
question
search
sift

instigate (v)
impel
incite
provoke
spur
start

instruct (v)
educate
guide
teach
tell

insurrection (n)
rebellion
revolt
riot
uprising

intercept (v)
balk
hold up
impede
obstruct
stop

interfere (v)
hinder
intrude
meddle
oppose
thwart

interrupt (v)
delay
disturb
hinder
stop

interrogate (v)
examine
fathom
grill
probe
pump
question
quiz
vet

interview (n)
dialogue
face-to-face
meeting
pow-wow
talk

introduce (v)
guide
teach
tell
start

investigate (v)
check
delve
examine
inquire
plumb
pry
scan
seek
sift
study

investigation (n)
analysis
check
hunt
inquiry
probe
quiz
quest
screen
search
study

invitation (n)
call
request
summons

invite (v)
ask
beg
bid
call on
petition

J

jeopardise (v)
endanger
hazard
imperil
risk

jewels (n)
gems (preferably
specify rubies,
diamonds,
pearls, etc.)
stones

journey (n)
hike
jaunt
outing
run
tour
trip
walk

judgment (n)
decision
decree
finding
result
ruling
verdict

justify (v)
bear out
clear
confirm
defend
endorse
excuse
explain

K

kidnap (v)
abduct
capture
carry off
grab
seize
snatch
steal
take

kidnapping (n)
abduction
capture
seizure
snatch

kingdom (n)
empire
land
realm
state

knowledge (n)
learning
skill

L

leader (n)
boss
chief
head
master
ruler
tsar

legacy (n)
bequest
gift
present

legalise (v)
allow
enact
ordain
permit
warrant

legislation (n)
Act
Bill
code
law

locality (n)
area
district
region
zone

luxurious (adj)
costly
cosy
lush
plush
rich

M

machinery (n)
machines
plant

magistrates (n)
Court
Bench
JPs
justices

maintain (v)
assert
back up
carry on
keep up
insist
support

maintenance (n)
support
upkeep

majority (n)
most

malefactor (n)
criminal
culprit
killer
thief
vandal

management (n)
board
company
directors
firm
owners

manager (n)
boss
chief
head

mannequin (n)
model

manoeuvres (n)
dodges
exercises
plots
ruses
tricks
wiles

manufacture (v)
make
produce

manufacturer (n)
boss
maker

**massacre
(nouns)**
butchery
carnage
genocide
killing
murder
slaughter
(verbs)
butcher
destroy
kill
murder
slay

maximum (adj)
biggest
ceiling
highest
top
most

**measure
(nouns)**
amount
size
(verbs)
assess
mark up
mete
rate
scale
size
weigh

mediator (n)
envoy
go-between
good offices

mediate (v)
fix
help
intervene
link

meeting (n)
caucus
forum
talk(s)

merchant (n)
dealer
trader

merchandise (n)
goods

message (n)
letter
news
word

messenger (n)
courier
envoy
runner

minimum (adj)
least
lowest

miscalculate (v)
err
fail
fall

mis-statement (n)
error
falsehood
fault
misreport

moderate (v)
allay
control
lessen
limit

modification (n)
alteration
change
switch

N

nationalisation (n)
conversion
take-over

nationalise (v)
acquire
grab
take over

nationalised (adj)
state
state-run

necessary (adj)
needed

negotiate (v)
bargain
confer
discuss
haggle
meet
talk

negotiation (n)
haggle
parley
talk(s)

neighbourhood (n)
area
district
locality
place
region
town
zone

nominate (v)
appoint
call
choose
invest
name
propose
term
return

nomination (n)
place
seat
ticket
vote

O

object to (v)
abuse
attack
censure
denounce
dispute
fight
knock
protest
rap
rebuke
slate

objection (n)
attack
outcry
protest

objectors (n)
anti-
critics
enemies
foes
rebels

observe (v)
check
eye
inspect
note
spy
watch

observation (n)
eye
note
look-out
watch

obstinate (adj)
firm
hard
solid
stubborn
tough

occupation (n)
job
role
tenure
work

occupant (n)
dweller
inmate
resident

operate (v)
act
control
run
work

operation (n)
action
act
deed
surgery
work

opportunity (n)
chance

oppose (v)
bar
battle
block
chide
censure
clash
combat
decry
deplore
differ
fight
hit
lash
rebuff
reject
repel
rule out
slap
slate
veto

opposition (n)
'antis'
critics
enemies
foes
opponents
rebels
rivals

organisation (n)
institution (n)
body
board
club
corps
firm
group
set-up
society
unit

organise (v)
call
develop
fix
form
knit
join
plan
pool
run
set up
tie
unite
weld

P

pacification (n)
compact
concord
cooling
healing
peace-making
settling/settlement

pacify (v)
allay
calm
cool
heal
settle

performance (n)
action
display
exploit
show

permanent (adj)
abiding
constant
durable
lasting

give permission (v)
agree
allow
approve
OK
pass
permit
say yes to

petition (n)
plea

plebiscite (n)
vote

population (n)
people
number

postpone (v)
block
delay
hold up

precedent (n)
custom
habit
model
practice
rule
standard
use

preclude (v)
hinder
forestall
prevent
stop

presentation (n)
gift
party
testimonial
tribute

procedure (n)
action
conduct
habit
practice
process

proclamation (n)
decree
edict

programme (n)
campaign
drive
effort
move
plan

prohibit (v)
ban
bar
block
check
curb
embargo
end
forbid
halt
kill
limit
peg
prevent
stop
veto

prohibition (n)
axe
ban
bar
curb
embargo
end
halt
veto

promising (adj)
bright
hopeful

proposition (n)
idea
plan
thesis

prosecute (v)
arraign
charge
cite
sue
summons

prosecution (n)
case
cause
charge
citation
suit
trial

pursue (v)
follow
harry
hunt
search
seek
trace
track
trail

pursuit (n)
chase
hunt
quest
search

Q

qualification (n)
ability
art
craft
gift
skill
talent

quantity (n)
amount
number

question (v)
ask
challenge
doubt
probe
query
quiz

quotation (n)
price
quote
tender

R

ratification (n)
approval
consent
signing

realignment (n)
change
move
revision
switch
shake-up

reapportion (v)
change
move
re-allot
switch

reapportionment (n)
part
share

reasonable (adj)
fair
right

rebellion (n)
mutiny
revolt
rift
riot
rising
sedition
strife

reception (n)
party
welcome

recession (n)
slump

recommend (v)
advise
back
boost
commend
counsel
laud
pass
praise
proposal
puff
push
suggest
urge

recommendation (n)
advice
backing
idea
plan
word

recompense (v)
benefit
make good
repay

reduction (n)
cut
fall

redundant (adj)
needless
sacked
spare
surplus

referendum (n)
vote

reflation (n)
boost
spurt
tonic

regulation (n)
code
rule

regulate (v)
control
run
vet

relinquish (v)
abandon
leave
quit
resign

renounce (v)
drop
forgo
give up
lay aside
quit
recant

renunciation (n)
about-face
desertion
disavowal
reversal

repudiate (v)
deny
disclaim
rebuff
reject
repel
snub
spurn
throw back
unload

requisition (v)
acquire
get
seize
take
take over

resignation (n)
abdication
departure

resign (v)
give up
lay down
leave
quit

resolution (n)
motion
vote

responsibility
(n)
duty
job
task

revenue (n)
cash
income
money
tax(es)

S

sanction (v)
approve
OK
pass

satisfactory (adj)
adequate
enough
good
right

scrutinise (v)
check
inspect
vet
watch

settlement (n)
bargain
bond
deal
pact
peace
treaty

significant (adj)
marked
notable
weighty

specification (n)
account
detail
plan

statement (n)
advice
news
notice
report
view

supplication (n)
entreaty
plea
prayer
request

support (v)
aid
back
brace
feed
foster
help
prop
push
stand by
uphold

T

temporary (adj)
brief
short (-term)

terminate (v)
end
stop

testimony (n)
evidence

tolerate (v)
abide
allow
endure
let
live with
permit
stand

toleration (n)
leniency
licence

transaction (n)
affair
deal
process
trade

transformation (n)
change
shake up

transgression (n)
offence
sin
trespass

treasure (n)
riches
spoils
wealth

U

unauthenticated (adj)
unproven
unsure

unblemished (adj)
clean
guiltless
spotless

uncompromising (adj)
unyielding (adj)
firm
fixed
game
solid
steady
tough
unmoved
unshaken

unconcerned (adj)
calm
quiet
unmoved

underestimate (v)
err
misjudge
misprize
underprize
undervalue

undermine (v)
belittle
burrow
damage
hurt
impair
sap
weaken

undertaking (n)
deal
mission
plan
plot
quest

V

vacillate (v)
demur
dodge
evade
hedge
wobble
wriggle

vanquish (v)
beat
defeat
rout
scatter

vindication (n)
acquittal
clearance
defence

vindicate (v)
acquit
bear out
clear
justify
set right
uphold

vulnerable (adj)
suspect
tender
weak

W

warranty (n)
bond
pledge
promise

withhold (v)
bar
ban
deny
keep back
refuse

wreckage (n)
damage
debris
rubble
ruins
waste

10 Glossary

This glossary of newspaper and printing terms in common use on both sides of the Atlantic is relevant to all five volumes in the series, but especially Books Two and Three which are more concerned with typography. European and American terms sometimes differ, just as much as Anglo-American measurement units differ from European; for instance, a caption to a European deskman is the wording underneath an illustration whereas to an American that is a cutline and a caption is the wording *over* a picture. Where specifically American terms are included here, the definitions are prefixed with (US).

I have been assisted by consulting the British Standard 2961: 1967; *Harper's Dictionary of the Graphic Arts*, by Edward Monington Allen (New York: Harper and Row, 1963); and, for American terms, *Modern Newspaper Editing*, by Gene Gilmore and Robert Root (Berkeley, Calif.: The Glendessary Press, 1971), and *Modern Newspaper Design* by Edmund C Arnold (New York: Harper and Row, 1969). Peter Hiley, of the Thomson evening paper group at Reading, helped with terms used in filmset, offset newspapers, and Oscar Turnill (assistant editor, *The Sunday Times*) with all the glossary.

Of course the responsibility for the entries is, I should add, mine. Where there is a distinction between normal definition and current usage I have taken usage as the basis of my selection.

A

abbreviations Or abbrev. Commonly used in copy (e.g. f = for, wh = which, whr = where, fgn = foreign, bec = because) but use only where printer can certainly follow copy; if in doubt, spell out.

ABC Audit Bureau of Circulations; source of authoritative figures for newspapers' net sale over specified periods, important as advertising rates are related to circulation figures.

accents Frequently omitted in newspaper practice, even on foreign words; may be part of matrix forming letter, or 'floating'; a good deskman should know which the printer can supply.

account executive Member of staff of ad agency dealing with clients and preparing ads.

ad Advertisement, *classified* or *display*.

ad alley (US) Section of composing room where advertisements are assembled.

add Written on copy to be added at end of story already set or subbed and sent to printer (see *insert*).

ad dummy Miniature set of pages marked with ad placings and sizes of advertisements. Sometimes called 'the scheme'.

ad rule Rule separating ads from editorial matter.

advance Story anticipating scheduled event, often as holding story to be overtaken by report for later edition.

advertisement manager Newspaper executive in charge of advertising in newspaper.

advertising agency Organisation preparing ads for clients and buying space in newspapers and magazines, and TV time.

AFP Agence France Presse, French news agency.

agate Old name for $5\frac{1}{2}$pt type; classified ads measured in agate lines (US). Fourteen agate lines are 1 in. deep.

agency Organisation supplying news but not publishing or printing newspaper; or advertising agency.

A insert Copy to be inserted (according to marked accompanying proof) into matter already set; separate inserts marked A, B, C, etc., for clarity, and long inserts numbered A1, A2, etc.; always mark the end of an insert.

all in Proof reader's term meaning all copy and proofs are in the reading room.

all in hand Printer has received and is setting all copy and headings for a particular story or page.

all out Printer has dispersed all copy for setting.

all rights reserved General copyright warning, usually to avoid lifting of exclusive material/information.

all up All copy has been set, but not necessarily read and corrected.

alterations Changes on proof that differ from original copy (i.e. not simply corrections).

A matter Paragraph to stand at the head of a story or feature, or insert into matter already set.

ampersand &; ligature representing 'and', formed from Latin 'et'.

angle Aspect or point of approach in a story; 'play up this angle' = give it emphasis.

ANPA American Newspaper Publishers Association.

AP Associated Press, US news agency.

arabic numerals Those we commonly use: 1, 2, 3, etc. (as distinct from roman numerals: i, ii, iii, iv and I, II, III, etc.).

arm Horizontal stroke on T, diagonal lines of Y and K.

art Frequently means pictures and other illustrations plus layout and design; use is changing with increasing role of designer–artist in newspapers.

art editor Picture editor, responsible for acquiring photographs and in charge of photographers; or (more recent) design editor.

art paper Coated paper with high finish. Process departments require proofs on art paper to make white-on-black headings, strip type into illustrations, etc.

ascender Part of letter rising above x-height; e.g. f, h, k, all have ascenders.

ASNE American Society of Newspaper Editors.

assignment Reporter's specified task; in UK office jargon, 'job'.

author's marks Corrections on proof made by author as distinct from those made by reader.

author's proof Proof altered, corrected or passed by author.

B

back numbers Previous issues of the paper kept for sale (see *circulation*).

back room, back shop (US) Mechanical department of a newspaper.

back set Section of a newspaper printed and folded separately at the end (back) of the first.

bad break Incorrect division of a word between the end of one line and start of the

next; turning (from one column to next, or to another page) on a divided word.

bad letter Broken type, not printing fully.

bad spacing Irregular or over-spacing of a line of type; space not distributed correctly for sense and appearance.

bank (i) Part of a multiple headline; (ii) place where matter in type is assembled (see also *random*).

banner (i) Title of newspaper on front page or above editorials on leader page; (ii) large headline across all or most of top of page.

bar Horizontal stroke on e and A.

barker (US) Headline variant in which one line, usually one word, is set in large type over deck of smaller headline.

bastard measure Type set to a width different from the basic column width or multiples of it.

beard Projecting part of type mount or shank producing white space below character when printed; varies between typefaces but needs to be taken into account in page design and measurement.

beat (i) Reporter's regular or special area (e.g. courts, politics, crime, etc.); (ii) exclusive story gained in competition with rivals (what used to be called a 'scoop' until Evelyn Waugh made that a joke term).

bed Part of printing press that carries type forme or plate to be printed.

Ben Day Mechanical tint for producing shadings on blocks.

bf Abbreviation for *boldface*.

bill Poster announcing newspaper contents; wording is supplied by editorial but bills are distributed by circulation department.

bind, binding A type forme that will not lock up squarely and evenly is 'binding'.

bite off (US) To remove complete paragraphs at the end of a story to fit the space. The noun 'bite-off' is what has been removed.

black (i) Carbon copy of reporter's story or feature; (ii) boldface type.

blackletter Old black, angular, spiky typefaces based on handwritten books; basis for modern types in this style.

blanket Newspaper page proof.

blanket head (US) Headline covering all columns occupied by a story or combination of related stories.

bleed Arrange picture so that it is at very edge of page when trimmed; not possible in newspaper letterpress work.

blind ad (US) In which the identity of the advertiser is not revealed.

blind interview (US) One in which the source is quoted but not named.

blobs Black circles (properly, fullface circles), useful for adding colour to a page by itemising or setting out a series of points in a story without numbering (any can be held out without ruining sequence).

block Illustration in metal form, either *half-tone* or *line*, or combination of both.

block heading Heading enlarged photographically from proof, useful for producing headlines in larger sizes than normally available.

blow up Enlarge(ment), applied to pictures and other artwork, including headings photographically enlarged from proofs.

blurb Commonly a publisher's eulogy on the jacket of a book, but in newspapers, outside the literary department, is more frequently used to mean a preliminary paragraph set up distinctively to introduce a feature or news story. See *precede*.

body Type has thick, thin, medium, etc., body according to thickness of vertical strokes.

body matter Text set in newspaper's body type, or the text as distinct from headings, cross-heads, etc.

body type Typeface in which the main text of a newspaper is set, usually in sizes 4¾, 5, 5½, 6, 7, 8, 9, 10, 12pt.

Bodoni Type series in common use for headings, etc., distinguished by its clean lines, fine serifs, and vertical stress.

boiler plate (US) Editorial term for timeless raw 'filler' material.

bold, boldface Typeface which varies from the standard (or regular) form by having thicker vertical strokes so that it prints blacker.

bowl Curved stroke of letter surrounding closed 'white' area or counter as in letters o, b, a.

box Type matter enclosed by rules on all four sides (see *panel*); also in some offices the stop-press column (see *fudge*).

brace Sign (}) linking two or more lines of type; rarely used in newspaper text, occasionally in diagrams or set-out material (e.g. knock-out sports tournament).

bracket (i) Curved parenthesis mark: xxxx (——) xxxx; (ii) square parenthesis mark: [ ] used for inserting explanatory phrase in a quotation, or for parenthesis within parenthesis.

bracketed Serifs are said to be bracketed to the stem when they are joined to it in a continuous curve rather than set at a sharp right-angle. Old face types have bracketed serifs.

break (i) Convenient or appropriate place in text to insert cross-head or make a turn (US jumps) to another page; (ii) tear in web of newsprint feeding the presses.

break up Disperse type material from a page, either for melting down and re-casting or to typecases.

break line Short line of type at end of paragraph (a single-word break line is called a widow). At the top of a turn, it is called a jackline.

brevier Old name for 8pt type.

bridge Proof reader's mark showing that words or characters are to be joined together.

brief Short news paragraph.

broadsheet A page the full size of a rotary press plate, approximately 22 in. deep by 15 in. wide.

broadside (i) Full-size newspaper page as printed on a rotary press; (ii) old announcement or newspaper page printed as a single sheet irrespective of how it is to be folded; (iii) fiercely polemical article.

broken matter Text, headings, etc., that have been taken out of a page and are probably disordered (pied).

broken word Word turned from one line to another, with a linking hyphen at the end of the first line: words should be split to respect sense and etymology; vertical ranks of hyphens should be avoided.

bromide Piece of positive film—of either type or illustration—used for sticking on to page in photoset newspapers; also a trite expression.

bucket Rules below and on both sides of type matter.

budget (US) Day's schedule of news stories and events; in national finance, Budget.

bug (US) Fancy typographical device to break up areas of type. See *dingbat*. Also telegrapher's key and union label of the International Typographical Union.

bulk Bench or stone where assembled type is kept ready for use.

bulldog (US) First edition of the day.

bulletin (US) Short message giving new development or latest situation on running story.

bullets See *blobs*.

bump Add extra spacing material to type matter to make it fill a given space.

BUP British United Press, news agency.

bureau (usually US) Editorial office separate from main publishing building, mostly in another city or country.

buster Headline with too many characters and spaces for the given measure.

by-line Line of type indicating authorship.

C

cabalese, cablese Set forms of words and abbreviations used in cabled copy to reduce expense of transmission.

cancelled matter Type material removed from stories by corrections, cuts, etc.

c & lc Caps and lower-case, i.e. the normal mixture of capital and small letters. Often written as u & lc (upper- and lower-case), which is the same thing.

c & sm c Caps and small caps, i.e. capital letters with the small capitals (the same height as lower-case letters) belonging to the same size and type. The abbreviation is sometimes rendered c & sc.

canned copy (US) Publicity material sent to newspaper. See *handout*.

caps Capital letters, i.e. A, B, C, etc.

caption (US) Headline appearing over a picture; (UK) line(s) of type below a picture or other illustration (US, cutline). Old name for caption was legend.

caret Proof reader's mark (⁁) indicating something is to be inserted.

carry-forward Instruction to comp to carry text matter to next page or to turn.

case Tray holding individual type characters or type matrices.

case rack Cabinet for holding cases.

case-room, case department Printers' workshop, composing room.

case work In newspapers, usually composition of headlines and display ads.

Caslon Solid, serifed typeface often used for feature display.

cast Printing plate, produced by molten metal from a cast (matrix) of a forme.

cast off Estimate space required for copy at a given type size and measure.

cast up Measure matter standing in type.

catch Notice an error, or make a last-minute correction to a page (rectifying a bad error is called a 'good catch').

catchline Identifying word on copy or proofs enabling related material to be identified quickly and brought or kept together.

centre spread Two facing pages at middle of newspaper. A *spread* is any two facing pages.

Century Maid-of-all-work type series for modern newspapers, serifed, with vertical stress but robust rather than elegant like Bodoni.

CGO (US) Short for 'can go over'. Indicates that the copy may be held over until the following day or days.

chapel Union organisation within a printing house (named from monastic origins of printing).

chapel father Elected senior officer of union chapel.

Chart-pak rules Trade name for rules, dotted borders and other designs supplied on transparent sticky tape for use in make-up of photoset newspaper.

chase Metal frame in which type is assembled to make up a newspaper page; when filled it is called a forme.

check Confusingly for the layman, printer's readers use a tick (✓—which elsewhere denotes that something is correct) to indicate the need for a check to determine accuracy.

chimney Grouping of pictures and/or headlines (or advertisements) so that they run in a narrow band from top to bottom of the page.

choked type Type filled with ink or dirt, producing blotchy printwork.

circled numbers Instruction to printer to spell out; applies also to abbreviations.

circulation Number of copies sold; not to be confused with readership, which is usually about three times as high.

circulation manager Newspaper executive in charge of paper's distribution to wholesale and retail trade; except for back numbers, newspapers (UK) do not sell copies directly to the public.

city desk (US) Newsdesk, in charge of home news reporters.

City editor (UK) Editorial executive in charge of business and financial pages; (US) deskman in charge of hometown reporters' copy.

City office Business and finance department of editorial, usually separate from main publishing office, often (UK) in City of London.

classified Small advertisements, set single-column, and charged and measured by the line.

classified display Advertisements in the classified columns given prominence by rules and use of boldface or larger type, at extra charge.

clean copy Copy that can be read easily and without ambiguity, both for setting and checking against proof.

clean proof Proof of type matter after all alterations and corrections have been made.

clip, clipping (US) Item clipped (cut) from previous issues or other publications and filed for reference.

close quote(s) Punctuation mark(s) indicating end of direct quotation.

close up Reduce space between words, letters or lines of type.

cockup (i) Initial letter rising above the line of smaller type on which it stands; (ii) incompetent confusion at any point of the newspaper-making process.

col Short for column.

cold type Filmset type.

collate Sort into series or related groups (e.g. four proofs of each of six galleys into four complete sets).

collect running Arranging the presses and folders so that each press unit prints only one of several sections.

colophon Printer's identifying endpiece; symbol placed on title-page and spine of a book identifying the publisher: not newspaper usage.

colour Pleasing or provocative effect of design on black-and-white printed page, from careful use of illustration, variations of typeface, weight and style, rules, etc.; avoidance of greyness, over-regularity; also descriptive writing.

column, column measure Basic division of newspaper page into seven, eight or nine vertical lengths of equal width (usually $10\frac{1}{2}$, 11 or $11\frac{1}{2}$ ems).

column-inch An area one column wide and one inch deep, used as a unit of measurement of newspaper space, and as a basis for advertising charges.

column rule Thin type rule used to divide adjoining columns.

columnist Regular writer, either on a particular subject or in a special place in the paper.

comp Compositor; craftsman who assembles type.

composing stick Small, hand-held tray on which type is composed.

composite Block combining several elements (drawing, photograph, text, etc.), and made as a single block to reduce time and risk of error in making up a page.

condensed type Narrower, thinner version of standard type, providing contrast with it (see *extended, expanded type*).

copy Written or typewritten material which the printer sets in type according to the instructions given. See also *MS*.

copydesk (i) Central desk in composing room at which copy arrives from sub-editors or advertising department, and from which it is distributed for setting; (ii) (US) table where copy editors (sub-editors) work and over which all editorial copy passes.

copy editor (US) Sub-editor, marks and prepares editorial copy for printer.

copyholder Proof reader's assistant.

copy paper Usually newsprint reel-ends cut into blocks or pads of a convenient size for typewriter and setting purposes.

copyright Ownership of original elements and form of words in written and printed material.

copytaker Typist to whom reporters out of the office can dictate copy; sometimes called 'telephone reporter'.

copy-taster Sub-editor (US deskman) who reads all incoming copy and estimates its worth for publication.

corr (i) correspondent; (ii) correction.

correct Mark proofs so as to make them conform with copy.

corrigenda Corrections to be made; not newspaper term, but occasionally found in hastily printed official reports, etc.

counter The interior 'white' of a letter, either fully enclosed as in o or partially as in E.

cover (i) Report an event or situation, have responsibility for a particular area of news-gathering (see *beat*); (ii) deputise for a colleague otherwise engaged.

coverage Extent of newspaper's attention to particular events or situations.

CQ (US) Correct. Marked on margin of copy to tell typesetter that what looks wrong is right.

credit Photographer's or artist's by-line, usually in small type below or next to block/cut.

Creed Teleprinter machine; usually applied to Press Association news service.

crop Reduce limits or frame of picture to concentrate on required area, and/or to fit required shape.

cross-head, cross-line Sub-heading placed in text, between paragraphs.

cross-ref(erence) Line of type directing attention to story or picture on another page.

cursive Flowing style of type, resembling handwriting but without joining-up of letters; see *italic*

cut (i) Make deletions from copy or text in type; (ii) illustration block (US).

cut in Make deletions from copy or type to reduce to a required length, or to get in add matter.

cutline (US) caption: line(s) of type below a picture or other illustration.

cut-off rule Rule separating one story or advertisement from another above or below.

cut-out Half-tone plate in which all background has been removed, leaving figure in silhouette.

cuttings Items cut from previous issues and other publications and filed for reference (US clippings).

cuttings job Story compiled from cuttings, with little or no additional research or information.

CX (US) Correct. This symbol is used on proofs corrected by editorial. Symbols 'Krect' and 'X-correct' also used as warning that error is only apparent.

D

daily Daily, usually morning, newspaper.

dak edition (India) Up-country edition containing matter that has already appeared in a previous final edition.

dateline Place and date of origin of newspaper story; sometimes attached to by-line, sometimes given separately.

dc Double-column.

dead Copy discarded (killed) and not used. Also text, headlines, etc., removed after being set or being run for an edition.

dead bank Storage area for dead type.

deadline Time by which copy must be delivered to appear in a particular edition; varies from page to page for each edition, and also according to whose deadline it is (on the same story there will be progressively different deadlines for copy to subs, copy to printer, set matter to page, and page to press).

deck One unit of a multiple headline, or one line of a two-or-more-line heading.

delete Take out; proof reader's mark (⌐).

descender Part of letter protruding below x-height (e.g. in g, j, y).

design (i) Selection of typefaces, illustrations, rules, determination of spacing and general visual style of a newspaper; (ii) layout of individual pages or articles.

desk (US) Sub-editors' table; (UK) news editor's desk.

diary Daily list of jobs to be covered by the newsroom.

Didone British Standards Institution classification of types uses this name for what are popularly called modern romans —such as Bodoni, Didot and Walbaum.

Didot point Unit of type measurement in Europe, except Britain and Belgium. It is larger than the American–English point, being 0·01483 in.

dingbat (US) Any typographic decoration; also *bug*.

dinky dash (US) Shortest horizontal line used to separate sub-divisions of a story.

dirty copy Copy so heavily marked and corrected that it cannot be read easily or is ambiguous.

dirty proof (i) Proof so marked that changes cannot be easily followed; (ii) proof containing so many literal and other errors that it cannot be worked on until matter is corrected.

dis Break up type from page for return to cases or melting for recasting; the word is short for 'distribute'.

display (i) Headline and illustrations for feature; (ii) display ads department.

display ads Larger ads, frequently designed in ad agencies and supplied to newspapers as stereo plates, to be mounted for use in page.

district man Reporter, usually on regional paper, responsible for coverage of town or area outside publishing centre.

divided word See *broken word*.

dog A non-story, one that fails to live up to its promise.

dot, dot, dot Properly, ellipsis (. . .); used to denote omission from quotation or, at the end of sentence, idea that does not need to be stated.

dot leaders Dotted lines (e.g. those relating one column of figures to another).

dotted rule Rule composed entirely of dots.

double (i) The same story, whether in identical or different form, appearing twice in the same edition; (ii) repetition of words in different headlines on the same page.

double-column Across two columns; measure is not simply twice single-column, but also includes the space between columns.

down Instruction on copy or proof: make capital a lower-case letter.

downstyle Style with minimum of capital letters.

DPR, NPR Telegraph symbols for day press rate and night press rate.

drop cap Initial capital covering more than one line, but hanging below the top line.

drop head (US) Headline in which each line is set further to the right; (UK) stepped head.

drop in (i) Put type metal into page; (ii) insert.

dummy (i) 'Miniature' of paper showing where ads have been booked; (ii) mock-up of newspaper for design experiments, rearrangements, launching and promotional use, etc.

dummy run Producing a new newspaper or section up to any stage short of actual publication.

dupe Duplicate (see *black*).

duplex Line-casting matrix which carries two characters; also (US) make of newspaper press.

Dutch wrap (US) Running text type from one column to another without covering column 2 (or 3, 4, etc.) with a headline.

E

earpieces Ads or ad spaces to left and right of page one banner.

ears Curved projections of letters such as r, g.

edit Prepare copy for printer.

edition One of several separate issues of a newspaper on the same day.

editor Chief journalistic executive of newspaper, responsible for all it contains, including advertisements.

editorial Leader, leading article: expression of the newspaper's opinion.

editorialise Insert opinion in what is meant to be informative copy.

egyptian Type family distinguished by thick slab serifs and heavy main strokes; also known as 'antique'.

ellipsis Omission of letters, words or sentences needed for complete sense. Normal practice to use dash (—) to denote omission of letters; line of dots (. . . . . . .) for omission of words; and line of stars (*******) when whole sentences or verse omitted.

Elrod Machine which casts rules, borders, spacing.

em Unit of linear measurement, the square of any type size, but usually the 12pt em (six to 1 in.) also called a 'mutton'.

embargo Request not to publish information supplied in advance until specified time or circumstances.

em dash Dash one em long.

em quad Spacing unit, below type height, one em wide.

en Half an em.

English Old name for 14pt type. Double English is old name for 28pt.

engraving Printing plate produced by engraver.

erratum Error discovered after printing: errata is plural of erratum.

etaoin shrdlu Letters on the first two vertical rows of line-casting machine. When deliberately set are sign by operator that this is a line he intends to discard.

excelsior Old name for 3pt type.

exclusive Overworked newspaper word for material or information that no other newspaper has.

Extel Extel Telegraph Company, news agency.

extended, expanded Typeface with width greater than normal.

extra Extra or special edition.

extra-condensed Exceptionally narrow typeface.

eyebrow (US) Short line in smaller type, often underlined, above main deck of headline—other US terms: teaser, highline, overline; (UK) strap.

F

face Engraved image which carries the ink to be impressed on the paper. See *typeface*.

facsimile Exact reproduction of the original. Also method of transmitting news pages by wire or radio waves for printing in second centre.

fake Falsified story.

faking Patching several photographs together for special effect.

family All the type of any one design, e.g. 12pt Bodoni Bold and 14pt Bodoni Bold Italic, and 72pt Bodoni Black are all members of the Bodoni family.

feature Editorial article distinct from hard-news reporting, e.g. a columnist or cartoon rather than a catastrophe. As verb, to display prominently or emphasise.

file To send a story by wire; one day's output by a news agency.

files Back issues; library clippings/cuttings are also 'on file'.

filler Short item used to fill out a column. Evening papers rushing to press need a good supply of fillers of varying lengths to suit the varying size of 'holes' in a page after the main stories and pictures have been placed.

fingernails (US) Slang for brackets.

first proof First pull of a setting after line-casting which is read from copy. It is then corrected and reproofed as 'clean'.

flag Title plate on the first page of a newspaper. Also a piece of paper or *slug* inserted in galley of type to remind printers that a correction, or insert, is required at that point.

flash Urgent, brief message on wire service announcing big story, e.g. FLASH, KING DEAD.

flat-bed press Press which prints from a level surface.

flimsy Thin-paper carbon copy of a story.

floating accents English term for separate accent marks which may be used with any letter; (US) piece accents.

flong Blank sheet of absorbent paperboard used to make mould, or matrix, in stereotyping.

flush To set type even with the column rule or margin, on either left or right. A 'flush left' head has all the lines ranging evenly on the left.

fold (*n.*) Point at which the newspaper is folded horizontally. Commonly, in newspaper display, 'below the fold' means, in a broadsheet 22 in. deep, any point below 11 in.

folio Page or page number.

folio line Technically, line at top of page carrying page number, but generally now means inside page line carrying page number, name of newspaper, and date.

folo Abbreviation for follow. Usual use is to mark related news story 'folos President' meaning it should be added to end of the President story.

fc Follow copy

follow copy Instruction to printer to set copy exactly as written despite apparent errors.

follow (US) Story that follows up a first day story.

follow up To seek new information on an earlier story; a story that takes an earlier story further.

format Strictly, the size and shape of a page, newspaper or book. More generally refers to the fixed elements in a newspaper design—shape and size of the page, plus the number and measure of columns to a page.

forme Combination of type, blocks, etc., locked up in a chase and ready to go to press or to the foundry for duplicating.

foul copy Copy so heavily corrected and marked it is difficult to follow.

foul proof Proof set aside by the compositor (usually spiked) after he has made the corrections marked on it; proof containing errors, so not to be used for sending corrections to printer.

fount All the characters of any one typeface in any one size needed for a piece of printing; pronounced 'font'.

Fourth Estate The public press; the three original Estates were the Lords Temporal, the Lord Spiritual, and the Commons.

freelance Self-employed writer, artist, editor or advertising man.

free line-fall (US) Ragged right setting of text type; also called unjustified setting.

fudge Small box-like device inserted into cylinder of newspaper to permit printing directly from slugs of type. The fudge *box* is used for printing late news 'on the run'. The fudge or box is also the name for the place on the page where the late news, so printed, appears.

fullface Old term for boldface. Contraction: ff.

full line Line set 'flush' both to left and right.

full measure Type composed to the full width of the column (or page).

full out Type composed the full normal measure of page or column. Full left is type full out to the *left*, but ranging freely on the right; full right is type full out to the *right*, but ranging freely on the left.

full point Printer's term for full stop.

furniture Wood or metal, less than type high, used to fill in blank spaces in the chase.

future Note in 'futures book' or 'futures file' of story to be followed up later.

FYI For your information, wire service abbreviation.

G

galley Shallow, three-sided metal tray in which type is assembled and proofed; also, about twenty column-inches of text matter.

galley boy Apprentice who pulls proof and stores galleys.

galley press Press which produces printed image on proofing paper of type in galley.

galley proof Impression taken on a strip of paper by inking a galley of type, and 'pulling' a proof so that the type can be checked with the original copy for errors.

galley slug Slug with catch word, phrase, or number placed on galley of type to identify it, e.g. News 20.

Garalde British Standards Institution term for classifying what is popularly called old face roman type, such as Bembo, Garamond, Caslon.

gate-fold Wider or deeper page in magazine or book which has to be folded to fit the format. To be read properly it has to be swung open like a gate. Usually sold to advertisers in a magazine.

get in Instruction to printer to make adjustments to spacing, etc., to accommodate extra letters, or words.

ghost (i) Ghost writer is the author of stories that bear someone else's name. Sports pages used especially to be haunted; (ii) to soften or lighten obtrusive background in a photograph, without removing entirely.

gimcrack (US) Printing ornament.

give it some air Instruction to printer to add white space.

glossy A shiny-finished photograph usually preferred for making half-tone engravings; a magazine printed on glossy paper.

gone to bed, gone to press Page or edition forme has left the composing room and is being, or about to be, printed.

good catch Detection of a bad error in proof or copy.

good matter Matter in type which can be used again.

goodnight Signal from wire agency or news department that it is closing down.

gothic Type family of monotone letter forms without serifs and with vertical emphasis. Gothics is U.S. term; Europeans prefer to call these types grots (grotesques).

go up Instruction to printer to increase a type to the next larger size. Also (US) 'Use one more column of horizontal space than type fills': produces wide space between columns.

graf (US) Abbreviation for paragraph.

grafhead (US) Heading to a paragraph.

great primer Old name for 18pt type.

green proof Uncorrected proof.

grid Basic divisions and sub-divisions of a page which the designer uses as a skeleton for his layout. Also clear sheet of plastic used in making up photoset papers. It is a bit larger than page size and is graduated in lines: a blank sheet of paper is attached to the grid and bromides are assembled on it in the same way that type is put into a chase.

grot Abbreviation for grotesque, type family of monotone letter forms without serifs. Modern types based on early nineteenth century forms and, despite name, have subtle appeal which makes them best of sans serifs for newspaper display. US term for grots is gothics.

gutter Blank margins between two printed pages. Also a river of white caused by wide spacing or spacing occurring in awkward pattern.

H

hairline Thinnest stroke in letter form; thinnest rule used in newspapers. Also unwanted wisps of metal which sometimes adhere between letters on a slug and so impair printing.

hair space Thinnest spaces in linecasting, six to an em or thinner.

half-tone Engraved plate reproducing, by pattern of dots, gradations of tone of photograph or drawing.

hammer (US) One- or two-word heading set flush left over main heading of about half the size.

handout Copy supplied by speaker or publicity agent.

hand-set Type set by hand; newspapers try to avoid much hand-setting, though Ludlow headline matrices are assembled by hand before casting.

hanging indent Style for text and headline composition in which first line is set full measure and all succeeding lines are indented an equal amount at the left. This entry is set with a hanging indent.

hanging par One paragraph set with a hanging indent.

hdg, head Abbreviation for headline.

head to come Notice to composing room that headline will be sent after the story.

head up Headline has been written for casting.

headline schedule Sheet or booklet displaying all headline types used by a newspaper. Displays are grouped in column widths, or scored with pica rulings: unit count per column may be given.

heavies British term for papers 'heavy' in content rather than in volume, because they concentrate on serious reporting of government, law, and foreign affairs.

hed sked (US) Headline schedule.

hold News copy which is to be set but not published without a release notice. Speeches are often supplied by *handout* ahead of delivery; obituaries are also commonly 'set and hold' material.

holding Delaying sending a page or edition to press while waiting for a late story.

hold over Instruction to keep, rather than discard, the type of all or part of a story which has not been published. A held-over story is one it is intended to publish at the next opportunity. See *overmatter*.

hole Gap in page chase or dummy where type and illustrations insufficient to fill; see also *news hole*.

hood Rules arranged around three sides of a headline, top, left and right.

horizontal make-up Style in which multi-column headlines are arranged across the page with text type running underneath in short legs.

hot metal All metal printing materials; composition by metal rather than by filmset type which is pasted-up.

house rules Style notes and precedures laid down by individual offices.

HTC, HTK Head to come.

human interest Stories about people rather than deficit financing.

Humanist British Standards Institution classification of types uses this name for what are popularly called venetian faces—Verona, Centaur, Kennerley.

I

imposing stone Full title of the composing room 'stone'.

imprint Name and address of the publisher.

indent To set narrower than normal measure by having blank white space at either beginning or end. Pronounced INdent.

indention, indentation White space at the beginning or end when a line is set short of full measure. The usual paragraph indention is one em quad of the body size.

inferior letters/figs Small letters or figures cast on the lower part of typeface as in H_2O.

in hand Copy is being set or a block is being made.

initial letter Large letters used at the start of a story, rapidly becoming archaic in newspapers; see *drop cap*.

in metal Copy has been set into type.

insert Copy or type to be inserted in the body of a story to interrupt the sequence already set or being set. Inserts are marked A, B, C, etc., and their placing is indicated on galley proof.

inside columns Columns on any page which are not either at extreme left or extreme right.

inside page Any page except the front or back.

intaglio Printing process from sunken images; see *offset gravure*.

interrogation marks Question marks, or queries.

Intertype Trade name of keyboarded line-casting machine.

in the page Type already transferred from galley to chase.

intro Introduction or opening paragraph of a story; (US) *lead*, pronounced leed.

in type Warning to printer to indicate that what appears as copy to be set is already available in type from earlier setting.

IOJ (UK) Institute of Journalists.

ITN (UK) Independent Television News.

inverted pyramid Headline style of centred lines in which each successive line is shorter than the one above: also story structure which arranges facts in descending order of importance.

island (US) Style of planning newspaper advertising so that it is completely surrounded by editorial.

issue All copies of one day's newspaper. An issue may consist of several *editions*.

italic Type with letters and characters that lean to the right.

ital(s) Abbreviation for italic.

ITU International Typographical Union.

J

jim dash Small rule, usually three ems long, to separate decks of headline or headline from text.

journalese Offensive term for shoddier styles of newspaper writing.

jump (US) To continue a story from one page to another.

jump head (US) Headline on continued part of story.

jump line (US) 'Continued from page I....'

jump story (US) Story continued from a previous page.

Justape Trade name of computer which converts raw tape into justified form.

justifier Compositor who corrects metal in the chase.

justify To space out a line of type so that it fills the column measure; to space out a column of type so that it fills the page measure.

Justowriter Trade name of typewriter which sets cold type from perforated tape.

K

keep down Instruction to printer to set in lower-case.

keep in Instruction to compositor to use thinnest spacing possible to keep all words in a line or section.

keep standing Instruction to hold type available for use.

keep up Instruction to printer to set in capitals.

kern Any part of the face of a letter which extends over the edge of the body, as in italic or script type. A kern is supported on the shoulder of an adjacent letter.

kicker (US) Small headline, usually underscored, placed above and to left of main headline. Also eyebrow, teaser, overline.

kill Do not publish. The instruction may refer to part or all of a story. Copy marked 'kill' is spiked; type is killed by discarding in the hellbox.

Klischograph Trade name for electronic engraving machine.

knifing corrections Corrections made in photo-composed newspapers by chopping up printed images and superimposing on photoset material in the page grid.

L

label News headline with no force or life; or standing features headline such as Women, Sport, etc.

late man Deskman who stays behind to fudge or replate for late news when last edition has gone to press.

lawyer's alts Alterations made according to lawyer's advice (usually to avoid libel).

layout Plan showing how type matter is to be fitted into space available.

lead (US) Pronounced leed. First paragraph of a news story. See also *intro*.

lead Pronounced led. Strip of metal less than type high, used for increasing the space between lines of type.

lead all A lead (leed) or intro containing a general summary of a long news story. Also called a *news lead*.

leader (UK) Leading article or editorial carrying newspaper's opinion. Leader page carries the leader and other opinion.

leaders Dots to lead the eye across the page.

lead story Story supporting the main display headlines on a page.

lead to come Signal to printer that the opening paragraphs—lead or intro—will come later.

leg Vertical sub-division of text type arranged in several columns. Thus in horizontal layout there are three legs of type under a three-column headline.

leg art (US) Any sexy illustration.

legend Obsolete word for caption or cutline.

legman Reporter who collects facts but does not write the story.

letterpress Printing from a relief, or raised, surface. The raised type and blocks are inked and come in direct contact with the paper.

letterspacing Thin spacing inserted between letters of a word, as in this e x a m p l e, usually to justify a line.

library Collection of clippings, newspaper files, reference books and photographs.

lift To carry type forward from one edition to another, either all or part of a story or illustration. Also to steal a story from another publication.

ligature Two or more letters joined together and forming one character or type, as in ae, ffi.

light box Back-lighted work surface for viewing transparencies, negatives, and for marking on back of photo prints.

lightface Type with lighter appearance, compared with bold.

light table Back-lighted work surface used in photo-composed newspapers. The compositor places the page on it to assemble the elements of the page.

line Single line of headline or text type.

lineage, linage Measure of printed material based on the number of lines printed. Freelance copy is lineage copy because it is normally paid so much a line. In US, term more commonly used for amount of advertising printed in specific period.

line-and-tone Process-engraved printing block combining both screen and line-etching techniques.

line block An engraving which prints only black and white without the shades of a *half-tone*.

line-casters Typesetting machines such as Linotype and Intertype which cast text type in lines. Also operator who uses keyboard of a line-casting machine.

line cut (US) *Line block.*

line drawing Brush or pen drawing consisting of black-and-white elements.

line up To arrange evenly flush left or right.

lining Type in which the faces of the characters align along a base line. Lining figures, in contrast to old-style figures, are of uniform size and height.

Lino Abbreviation for Linotype.

Linofilm Trade name of photosetting machine.

Linotron Trade name for photosetting machine using cathode ray tube.

Linotype Trade name for keyboarded line-casting machine.

literals Typographical errors in composition.

lithography Planographic method of printing from ink impressed on a sheet.

live Type that will be used in the edition going to press.

live copy Copy yet to be set into type.

lobster trick, shift (US) Early-morning news workers or printers on a daily; night-shift of an afternoon paper.

localise To stress local appeal or angle in story.

lock up (a page) The process of placing the type and illustrations in a chase, and adjusting the *furniture* and *quoins* so that the type is firmly held and the forme can be sent to foundry or presses.

logo Abbreviation for logotype.

logotype Nameplate for a newspaper or identification of a section, Business, Family, etc., cast on one block of type.

long measure Width of line longer than usual for the size of type. An 8pt line of 24 picas, say, would be long measure.

long primer Old name for 10pt type.

long run When a printing press is not interrupted for a long time by a new edition, or when a page similarly remains unchanged; or greater-than-usual space given to a single story or feature.

long stop Late man, q.v.

loose Too much letter- or word-spacing in composition.

lower-case Letters which are not capitals, thus c, d, e. Also the name given to the composing case which holds these letters.

Ludlow Trade name for machine which casts larger sizes of headline on a slug from hand-assembled matrices.

M

machine border Border cast on such machines as Elrod, Linotype, Intertype, Monotype.

machine-set Type which can be set mechanically on a keyboarded line-casting machine, as distinct from hand-assembled type or matrices. Newspapers prefer machine-set text, captions and small headlines for speed.

magazine Container which holds matrices on a line-casting machine.

mailers (US) Staff who count and pack papers for delivery: equivalent to UK publishers or packers. Also a folding wrapper for protecting posted material.

majuscules The capital letters of the alphabet.

make 'How much will it make?' means 'How much space will the copy occupy?'

make even Instruction to typesetter to make a section of type matter even with the end of the line, so that another typesetter, working on the next take, can start even.

make over Process of rearranging a page of type or series of pages to accommodate later news, improve appearance or make corrections.

make-ready The process of preparing a page forme or stereo plate for the presses. Sheets of paper are trimmed and laid beneath areas, especially blocks, to assure an even impression on every part of the printing area.

make-up To take type from a galley and arrange in pages with illustrations; the physical appearance of the paper; and, sometimes, the dummy page plan for the disposition of stories and pictures.

make-up editor (US) Journalist who supervises the make-up of the paper in the composing room. See *stone sub*.

managing editor Senior editorial executive. In US frequently man in charge of news department while 'editor' controls the editorial page. In UK usually subordinate to the editor and with administrative as well as editorial duties.

mangle Stereotyper's moulding machine which takes a papier-mâché impression of the type.

margins The unprinted surround of the area occupied by reading matter.

marker (US) Story from one edition clipped from the paper and pasted on copy paper to be marked for changes for the next edition—adds, inserts, corrections, cuts. Or a page proof or page from one edition marked with cuts and new stories. Also called a mark or markup.

marketing Division of newspaper which deals with sales strategy, including sales promotion and circulation.

markets Section of newspaper devoted to stock, commodities or livestock news.

masking Technique of obscuring part of a photograph (e.g. by paper overlay) to indicate the section to be printed.

master proofs Set of proofs, galley or page, incorporating all writer's and editor's corrections.

masthead Strictly, heading on editorial or leader page which gives paper's name and (in US especially) the paper's ownership and management. Often confused with nameplate or flag.

mat Abbreviation of matrix.

matrix, matrices (pl.) A die or mould from which type is cast. Also: the papier-mâché mould from which a stereo plate is made.

matter Any type or blocks. It may be body matter (the text setting); standing matter (not intended for immediate use); straight matter (simple setting); solid matter (without leads); open matter (leaded); live matter; dead matter; and so on.

matt finish Dull finish to photograph or printing paper; contrast *glossy*.

mean-line The line indicated by the top of the lower-case x.

measure The width of a line, column, or page of type, usually expressed in pica ems. Also: a graduated ruler showing the point size of type.

medium The weight of type the maker puts forward, under the name of the family, as representing the design in normal weight from which variants have been derived.

mf Abbreviation for 'more follows'.

Mickey Mouse A Linotype line-casting machine stripped down to its casting mechanism so that headlines can be cast from hand-assembled Linotype matrices.

middle leads 2pt leads (leds): called middle because they come between thin and thick leads.

middle space A space of four ems.

milline rate, millinch rate Unit for measuring the advertising cost of a newspaper in terms of its circulation. The 'line' rate is the cost of reaching the readers of one thousand copies of the paper with one line of classified advertising. The millinch rate is the cost of reaching one thousand with one inch of space.

minion Old name for 7pt type.

minionette Old name for 6½pt type.

minuscules Lower-case letters of the alphabet.

misprint Inaccurate setting, a typographical error, a literal.

mitre Corner-piece of rule or border cut at angle of 45 degrees to form a perfect joint; to bevel a rule or border so that there is a neat fit at the right-angle.

mitred rule Angle-corner rule used to make perfect joints.

modern Term for typefaces having abrupt contrast between thin and thick strokes; the axis of the curves is vertical; and there are often no brackets on the serifs. Classified Didone in the British Standard 2961:1967.

mofussil Indian newspaper term for local or regional news; also mofussil desk, etc.

Monotype Composing machine which casts each character on a separate type body.

montage Arrangement or mounting in one composition of pictorial elements from several sources.

more Written at foot of copy or proof to show that more is to follow.

more later Written at foot of copy or proof to show that more copy will follow but not immediately; printer can use the interval to correct this matter and go on to other setting.

morgue Old name for library; or file of prepared obituaries.

mortise To cut an opening, usually rectangular, in an engraving so that type or another picture can be slotted in. An external mortise or notch is such an opening cut out of the corner of an engraving. An internal mortise is a hole surrounded by engraving; a bay is an opening with engraving on three sides.

MS, MSS (pl.) Manuscript: typed or (properly) handwritten copy of book or article; displaced in newspapers by *copy*, but survives in book production.

mtc Abbreviation for 'more to come'.

multiple rules Three or more type rules of the same or differing point sizes cast on a single body and running parallel.

must An instruction, from a senior newspaper executive, that the copy or proof on which it is written must be followed and published without fail.

mutton Printers' slang for the em.

mutton quad An em quad—a metal body one em square and less than type high which is used for spacing.

N

NANA North American Newspaper Alliance, an editorial syndication service.

national advertising Advertisements placed in media with a national circulation; an advertising campaign on a national scale.

nationals Newspapers available for sale at the same time in all parts of a country.

NEA (US) National Editorial Association, a group of editors of weekly and small daily papers. Also Newspaper Enterprise Association, a syndicated feature service.

Nebitype Trade name for Italian machine which casts metal slugs from hand-assembled matrices—its own or Ludlow/Intertype/Linotype.

neck Link connecting the two bowls of g; sometimes loosely used to specify the *beard*, q.v.

negative-working Process used in production of photoset web offset newspapers. Most pictures are inserted as negatives. On the paste-up an opaque patch is placed where a picture is to go. When the page is photographed, the patch, being reversed, becomes a window and shows clear on the page negative. The screen negative of the illustration is then placed in the window.

new lead Pronounced new *leed*. A new intro paragraph or several paragraphs making a new *news lead* to replace the existing intro or news lead when this is poorly written or overtaken by later developments.

news editor (UK) Editorial executive who assigns reporters their tasks; (US) executive who lays out the stories in the paper and is sometimes called make-up editor.

news hole (US) Total editorial space in a newspaper after the ads have been placed.

news lead First few paragraphs summarising key points of long or complex story.

newsprint Generic term to describe the pulp paper widely used for newspaper production.

NF (UK) Printers' abbreviation for 'no fly'—slang term meaning that an instruction is cancelled.

NGA (UK) National Graphical Association, trade union of line-casting operators, comps, etc.

NIBS News in brief section.

nick Groove running across the front of the body of all pieces of type; it helps the compositor to ensure he has the type the right way round.

night editor (UK) Senior executive in charge of a morning paper, especially presentation, though sometimes subordinate to a deputy editor (night). (US) *news editor*, q.v., of a morning paper.

night side Night shift on a newspaper.

nonp Abbreviation for nonpareil. Commonly used to indicate spacing—'add a nonp' means add half a pica (12pt) em of spacing, or about one-twelfth of an inch.

nonpareil Pronounced nonprul. Old name for 6pt.

notch Opening cut out of corner of engraving to accommodate type: an external *mortise*, q.v.

NPA (UK) Newspaper Proprietors' Association, association of owners of national newspapers.

NPR Telegraph symbol for night press rate.

nrm 'Next to reading matter'; request by advertisers for the placing of their ad, and written in newspaper dummy.

NS (UK) Newspaper Society, association of provincial newspaper proprietors.

NUJ (UK) National Union of Journalists, trade union.

nut Printer's term for an *en*, the unit of measurement half as wide as an *em* of the same type.

nut and nut Type indented one en at each end of line.

nut quad An en quad—a metal body one en square and less than type high, used for spacing.

nutted Type indented one en.

O

obit Obituary, biography of person who has died.

oblique A form of *italic*, q.v. It slopes to the right but has the same form as its roman counterpart and has not the handwritten appearance of italic.

oblique stroke One sloping to left or right, diverging from vertical or horizontal.

odd folio First, third, and all unevenly numbered pages. The odd folio is always a right-hand page.

office style House style: standard system of spellings and punctuation laid down for a newspaper so that continuity is recognisable or recognizable, depending on style.

off its feet Type which is not standing straight, causing the characters to register inexactly.

offprint Reprint of an article or illustration specially run off after publication in a newspaper or magazine.

offset Strong candidate for most misused term in history of newspaper production. It is not a description of setting, but of printing. Papers set by photographic methods are often printed offset, but papers set in metal can also be printed offset, which means printed by the planographic printing process in which the image is transferred from a lithographic plate to a rubber roller, then set off this on to paper. Offset has become a synonym for lithography.

offset blanket Blanket made of rubber which takes designs from the lithographic plate and impresses them on the paper.

offset gravure Fine printing process giving wide range of tonal expression. Printing is by plates and impression rollers as in offset, but here the image is in intaglio or beneath the surface of the plates.

offset paper Absorptive, non-curling paper suitable for offset printing process; or the newspaper produced by offset printing.

offset press Press which prints by the indirect method of lithography.

OK Proof-reader's sign to indicate that there is no error on the proof.

Old English A style of black, script type.

old face, (US) old style Style of typeface in which the axis of the curves is to the left; there is a gradual transition from thick to thin; and the serifs are bracketed, e.g. Garamond, Caslon. British Standards preferred term is Garalde.

old-style figures Numerals that follow the old forms with ascending and descending strokes; e.g. 3, 4, 9.

on the hook Edited copy awaiting setting in the composing room.

op-ed Usefully laconic American expression to describe page facing the editorial or leader page.

open format Style of newspaper page with white space dividing columns.

open matter   Type which is either well leaded or has lots of short lines.

open quotes   Begin with quotation marks ("); the beginning of a quotation set off by quotation marks.

open spacing   Wide spacing of type, whether by white between letters, words, or lines.

optimum format   (US) Page format where the optimum line length for easy reading—around 15 picas in 9pt—determines the column width.

outline   A type which, on the British Standard definition, has a continuous line of more or less consistent width outlining the shape of the character.

out of sorts   Shortage of some characters in a fount of type.

over   Too much type for the space; or printing placed over a first impression, a superimposition.

overbanner   Banner headline running higher than the nameplate of the newspaper. Also called sky-line(r) and over-the-roof in US, where it is depressingly common.

overlay   To place a transparent covering over an illustration, or a filmset page over a filmset page, to indicate colour separation or alterations or corrections.

overline   Display type over a picture, also sometimes called a title. Also a line of smaller type over the main headline, which, in turn, may be called (UK) a strap or (US) an eyebrow.

overmatter, over-set   Type set for an edition but squeezed out by shortage of space.

over measure   Type set too wide for space allocated.

overnight pages   Pages scheduled to go to press early, late p.m. or early a.m., before work begins on the pages of the day's newspaper.

overrun(ning)   To reset type to insert matter omitted, or have better word-breaks, or to run round a block more neatly.

Oxford rule   Heavy and light rules running close together in parallel, not to be confused with simple parallel or double rules; also (UK) house rules of the Oxford University Press, as published.

P

p   Abbreviation for page, hence p 1: p 2, etc. Its plural is pp.

PA   (UK) Press Association, national news agency.

padding   Portions of copy not necessary for the narrative; to pad out is to make a story or headline longer than the message or sense strictly demands.

pagination   The numbering of pages; the pagination budget for a newspaper is the number of pages it is budgeted to achieve.

panel   Shortish editorial item indented either side and with a strong rule top and bottom. Some offices still call it a panel when it has rules on four sides, but *box* is the preferred term; (US) a cartoon consisting of a single rectangle.

paragraph indent   Beginning the first line of a paragraph with a white space, usually one pica em quad.

paragraph mark   Signal to a line-caster to begin the line with an indention.

parallel rule   Rule with two lines in parallel and of equal weight.

parentheses   (Brackets).

paste-on   Cold type pasted on to page plan for the platemaker.

paste-up   To arrange cold type on a page plan (or 'mechanical', as it is sometimes called) for the platemaker.

pearl   Old name for 5pt type.

perforator   Machine which punches holes in tape to a pattern which, when fed into a line-casting machine, produces lines of type. Also the operator of a perforator or tape-punching machine.

period   Another name for full point, full stop.

personal column   Once very much 'Meet me at 10, all forgiven' classified advertising paragraphs, but more often today a ragbag of classified under a masquerade.

photo-chase   Film bromides pasted on to thin strips of polstyrene for easier movement. Often used to collate columns of classified advertising.

photo-engraving   See *process engraving*.

photogravure   Fine printing method. The paper sheet passes between a rubber-covered impression cylinder and an intaglio plate, photographically prepared, and in so doing takes the ink from the finely etched recesses in the plate.

Photo-Lathe   Trade name for mechanical engraving machine.

Photon   Trade name for phototype-setting machine.

photoset   Abbreviation for photo-composition—the reproduction photographically on film or paper of lines of type characters. Photoset newspapers are called cold type papers in contrast to hot metal papers composed from lines of metal type.

Photostat   Misused as general term for photo-copy. It is a trade name for the machine and the photo-copies it produces.

pica   Printer's unit of measurement, there being 12 points in a pica. Also old name for 12pt type.

pica em   Standard unit of square measurement, a pica em being 12 × 12 points.

pick up   Proof instruction from editorial to pick up type already set, and incorporate with new material.

pics, pix Abbreviation for pictures, usually half-tone illustrations.

pie, pie line Disarranged type, freak line cast when a Linotype operator has made a mistake and fills out a line at random.

plain rule Rule with plain, straight lines, in variety of sizes, but without decoration.

planer Flat wooden block which comps place over the type in the chase and hammer to ensure type surface is even.

plate Semi-cylindrical metal printing sheet cast from a *flong* for attachment to rotary press; or photographically engraved metal.

platen Surface which holds paper and presses it against an inked relief surface; roll holding paper in typewriter.

play Editorial term indicating emphasis to be given to a story. Points in a story can be played up or down or played lightly; if the story itself is played up it is given a big display.

plug To push the popularity of a show, book, or song by publicity. Also a wedge of wood used in some printing and engraving.

PM (US) An afternoon paper.

point Unit of measurement in type. It is about one seventy-second of an inch, actually 0·01383 in. The European Didot point (q.v.) is slightly larger.

point size The measurement of a type from the front of the base to the back. Also called the body size.

point system System of casting type and measuring areas in multiples of the point (q.v.).

points Punctuation marks. A full point is what follows the last letter of this sentence.

police blotter (US) Register of day's events kept in a police station and hopefully open to the press.

policy story (US) News item or feature which supports an editorial opinion of the newspaper.

pony service (US) Abbreviated teleprinter news service delivered by commercial telegraph or telephone.

popular papers Abbreviated to 'pops' and meaning, in Britain, papers of high circulation and mass appeal, i.e. the *Daily Mirror* rather than *The Times*, which is categorised as a 'quality' or 'heavy' paper.

pork-chop (US) Tiny half-column engraving of someone's face; also called thumbnail.

poster make-up Format which uses the front page as a poster—headlines and pictures, with little or no text, designed to attract the reader inside.

poster type Big sizes of type, upwards of 72pt, commonly made of wood.

pot Holds the molten type metal in a line-caster.

pp Pages.

PR Public or press relations.

precede Pronounced preecede. A new lead or story which takes precedence over an earlier story. Or a preliminary paragraph or two set up in different type to introduce, summarise or explain a succeeding story.

pre-date (US) Newspaper printed before the date of publication on the front page. In the US, a number of city newspapers put out a late night edition with the next day's date on it. Similarly, and famously, the now-defunct *Sunday Empire News* in Britain sold rapidly on Saturday night with football results.

preferred position Advertiser's request for position on a page.

prelim Introductory material.

preprint Most recently the advertising manager's delight and the production manager's worry: advertising, usually colour, printed on reels, rewound, and fed into newspaper presses to be folded in with the other pages of the newspaper. Also any material printed before normal production and fed or stuffed into the newspaper.

press(es) The printing machine(s) house in the pressroom and tended by pressmen. Derivation of 'press' to identify newspapers and reporters.

primary letters Lower-case letters without either ascender or descender, i.e. x, o, a, etc.

primer Old name for 18pt type; long primer (LP) is old name for 10pt.

print Total number of newspapers printed; or the positive picture taken from a photographic negative.

printer Sometimes means *the* printer, the man in charge of the composing room. Strictly, a craftsman who makes up formes or operates the presses, but loosely used to describe comps, line-casters, proof readers, and all those engaged in the making of print. Also abbreviation for teleprinter.

printer's devil Apprentice in the printing trade.

process engraving General term for producing an image on a sensitised metal plate.

promotion Publicity material to increase sales or improve public image.

proof Inked impression of type, or engraving, or page for study of accuracy or appearance before sending to press.

proofhook Assembly point of galley or page proofs.

proof press Machine for printing a galley or page proof. Proofs are said to be 'pulled' rather than printed.

proof reader Person who reads the proof to make sure it follows copy accurately.

proof reader's marks Standardised system of marks for correcting errors on proof. *See* the revised British Standard 1219.

proof-slip A long *galley proof* (q.v.). Also called slip proof.

ProType Trade name for phototype-setting machine, mainly for headlines.

PTI Press Trust of India, a national news agency.

publisher Entrepreneur in bringing together ideas, print, and readers; but also in some countries the employee who sees that newspapers are parcelled correctly and put on to delivery vans and trains.

 puff An editorial item designed to *plug* (q.v.) some product or personality.

pull Synonymous with proof. A proof is said to be pulled, so a pull of a galley or page is a proof of galley or page.

pull-out Section of a newspaper or magazine that can be extracted easily and read separately.

punch-tape head The signal from the keyboard or computer drives the punch-head to produce punch-tape for feeding into phototypesetting machine or line-caster for hot metal.

put to bed To put the forme or stereo plate on the press. When a page has 'gone to bed', it is too late to make corrections.

put up Instruction to printer to set letters indicated in capitals.

pyramid Headline form resembling a pyramid with lines succeedingly short, longer, longest. Also (US) pattern of arranging advertising on a page.

Q

Q and A Question-and-answer copy, as in formal interview or court badinage.

quad, quadrat A space. A piece of blank type of equal body size but less than type high used to fill spaces in a line of type. Quads are made six to a fount so that their widths are multiples of the em of the size of type used. Thus the em quad is the square of the body type; the en quad is half the body, and the smallest, the hair space, is about one-twelfth the body.

quality press Patronising European, mainly British, term for serious daily and Sunday newspapers which report Parliament, foreign affairs and court stories in addition to scandal and other frivolities. Reporters on *popular papers*, q.v., call the quality press 'the heavies'.

query Question raised on copy or on proof, or in a message to a news agency. Also a freelance's inquiry whether a newspaper is interested in such-and-such a story; also a question-mark (?).

quire Unit of newspaper circulation, normally 26 copies.

quoin Wedge-shaped metal device for locking type and plates in chases.

quoin key Iron key to tighten quoins in locking up chase.

quotation marks, quotes Punctuation marks to indicate that words are those actually used by a speaker or report. Can be double (" ") or single (' '). "If double quotes begin, single quotes are used for 'quotes within quotes' and vice-versa." Headlines should have single quotes; books usually have single quotes in text, newspapers double quotes.

quote Quotation; in newspapers, often means a sentence or paragraph of a speaker's words.

R

railroad (US) To rush copy for setting.

random Composing-room table, divided into galley-widths, where galleys are assembled before make-up.

rate card Schedule of advertising spaces available and the cost of each.

readability A story is said to be readable and have readability if it has a compelling narrative easy to grasp. Readability in typography means the ease with which the eye skims the type.

reader Man who checks proofs for consistency with copy and corrects errors in setting, punctuation, etc. The 'readers' is the department where proof readers and their assistants, copyholders, do their work as correctors of the press.

readership Not the same as circulation of a newspaper. Something like three people read a single copy and market research to count readership is an aid in selling advertising.

reader traffic How the readers move through the paper; surveys show how long they spend on each succeeding page or part of it.

readout (US) Subsidiary headline that 'reads out'—follows and substantiates—a main deck.

recast To cast a new plate for a page whose content, usually editorial but sometimes advertising, has been changed; re-plate.

reefer (US) Taken in its legal and desirable sense slang for cross-reference line or two of type which directs reader to associated story in another part of the paper.

reel Roll of newsprint fed into the presses; the revolving drum or core which receives and winds the paper.

reel-end Part of the paper machine where the web is reeled up; the last few yards of a reel of newsprint.

register To coincide or fit together when two or more formes are printed on the same sheet, especially important in colour printing.

reglet Narrow strip of wood, 12 or 6 points wide, for spacing type in the forme.

regular type Standard width of a typeface, as distinct from extended or condensed versions. The preferred term, specified in the British Standard 2961, is medium type.

rejig Editorial alterations to a story in type, usually involving a change in the sequence of paragraphs in type, deletions, and the insertion of new matter. When a story is rejigged, the type standing in the page will be taken out and the new arrangement assembled on the random.

release Glorified name for a handout; to 'okay' for publication.

removes The difference between one size of type and another.

replate Recast a page of type for later news or corrections. The forme for the existing page on the presses is 'brought back', opened, and the type changed in large or small degree.

reporter Man who gets the facts; a journalist, said H L Mencken, is someone who bums a drink off a reporter.

repro proofs Proofs of high quality, on art paper usually, to be made into engravings.

re-punch Repetition of a telegraphed message by the sending station, usually for the correction of an error in transmission.

retouching Improving a photograph by painting in certain tones; most useful in painting out any streaks on photographs received by wire, before engraving; most questionable when photographic content is altered or inserted.

Reuters Famous independent international news agency not, repeat not, owned by the British Government.

revamp (US) Altering a story by changing the sequence of paragraphs, but not by rewriting.

reverse indent The first line of type is full measure and the remainder of the paragraph lines are indented one or more ems at the beginning. This is the reverse of normal indentation where it is the first line only which is indented. Also called a *hanging indent*.

reverse kicker (US) Same as *hammer*, q.v.

revise Second or subsequent proof incorporating corrections made from previous proof.

rewrite To write a story again, rather than simply edit the copy. Deskmen do it when the reporter seems to have hold of the wrong end of the stick. American newspapers have a rewrite man to put telephoned facts into prose.

ribbon (US) Grotesque editorial space of two or three inches deep running horizontally above ad that much less than full-page depth. Also sometimes used to specify a banner headline across the top of a page.

rim (US) Outer edge of copy desk where copy editors sit; the copy editors who sit there.

ring To circle a correction in copy.

rising initial First letter of word in large size and sometimes ornamental design which stands on same baseline as succeeding letters but projects above height of ascenders.

rivers Ugly streaks of white space in a page caused by over-spacing between letters and words.

RO 'Run on': instruction on copy to set two written paragraphs as one, or treat set-out matter as a single paragraph.

rotary press Conventional newspaper printing press in which both printing surface and impression cylinder rotate at high speed.

rough Undetailed sketch of page or advertisement layout or illustration. Or rough proof obtained by impressing paper by hard roller with type in forme; or uncorrected galley/page proof.

round-up Collation of separate items into one story or under one headline; a common one is a weather round-up.

ruby Old name for 5½pt. English equivalent of US agate.

rule Type-high metal strip that prints as line or lines.

run Duration of printing an edition; or number of copies printed.

run in full Senior editorial instruction that copy must not be cut.

running story A story which changes rapidly between editions, as in a plane crash (*see* Book Two). Or a story which develops over several days.

run of paper Advertising which may be placed anywhere in the paper. Contrast 'preferred position'.

run on See *run*. Also additional copies printed immediately after the original run. Newspapers with rising sales sometimes worry about the run-on costs.

run out and indent Another term for reverse indent or hanging indent.

run round Setting type round irregular edges of an illustration.

roman Group of alphabets in the printers' fount which is distinguished from italic by verticality and the shape of certain lower-case letters (British Standard definition).

roman numerals I, II, III, IV, V or i, ii, iii, iv or iiii, v, instead of 1, 2, 3, 4, 5.

routing Cutting away unwanted metal from any part of an engraving plate.

RP Reprint.

rush Urgent news agency summary of news break. Or a direction on copy asking the composing room to give it priority.

S

sacred cow (US) Copy or subject given favourable treatment; copy which is not to be cut or changed.

sandwich (US) Panel inset in text type cross-referring to associated material elsewhere; or, as Americans would say, a reefer in a sideless box.

sans, sans serif Type without serifs on the ends of the strokes, classified Lineale in the British Standard BS 2961: 1967.

SAP Soon as possible. When a correspondent or agency is asked to file sappest they do their bestest.

Scan-A-Graver Trade name for mechanical engraver producing plastic half-tone relief plates.

schedule Confusingly popular term. There is the time schedule, or sheet, listing deadlines for pages, the chief sub's or (US) city editor's schedule recording stories processed; and the headline schedule which categorises all headlines used in the paper, often to a code.

schlock (US) Slang for heavy, ugly advertising, of which there is a lot.

scoop Nowadays a rather jokey term for a story or picture of some importance nobody else has; an exclusive, or beat.

screamer Crude, sensational headline; exclamation mark.

screen Given number of dots to a square inch (of a process engraving) which make up the light and shade of the picture. Fine screen engraving is suitable only for the finer quality paper.

script Typefaces that imitate cursive writing, such as Palace, Script, Legend, Mistral.

seal Wording or symbol at the top of the front page indicating the edition, i.e. City edition, late edition, etc.

second-day Story developing one previously published; a follow-up.

second-strike Pages printed after reverse side is printed. These second-impression pages are often better for reproducing half-tone engravings.

section(s) Part(s) of the newspaper separately folded to be detached and read apart. American newspapers are multi-sectioned; European newspapers, which are not, use the term less properly for separate editorial or advertising areas

identified in the paper with their own logo (Sport, Business, etc.).

see copy Direction to readers or composing room to check proof against the copy; 'out see copy' means that something has been omitted.

see other proof Indication that two or more proofs need to be combined to make all the necessary changes.

see scheme Direction to composing room to check page proof against the page scheme or layout; or to set a piece of copy according to a scheme sent to the composing room.

self-contained Any item which stands by itself—a self-contained caption or picture is one without an accompanying story; a self-contained story is one without any *cross-references* or *sidebars* or *shirt-tails*.

send (a page) Dispatch a page forme to the stereo department.

send (copy) Usually the instruction is to 'send it out' or 'send it down' or 'send it up' and they all mean the same thing: send the copy to be set.

separation Use of colour filters so that single-colour negatives can be made of multi-coloured illustration.

sequence Picture strip showing consecutive action in a number of pictures taken shortly after one another.

serial Of, in, forming, a series; article published in instalments. Generally used for fictional or biographical feature material and not for news series.

series Size range of any design of typeface. Also number of articles pursuing same theme but in different issues of the paper.

serif Line or stroke projecting from the end of a main stroke. Serifs are of different forms and join the strokes in different ways, and some types have no serifs (sans serifs).

set To compose in type, also the width of a piece of type from side to side.

set and hold Set in type but do not publish without a *release*.

set close Instruction to printer that minimum spacing should be used.

set flush To set matter 'full out' or without indenting.

set off Desirable and deliberate in offset printing, being the transfer of image from rubber blanket to newsprint; but accidental and undesirable in letterpress printing, being the transfer of ink from one printed page to the facing page.

set open Instruction to printer that type is to be well spaced.

set out Instruction to printer to tabulate the matter, setting up letters from a case of type so that wrong founts and pie can be picked out.

set solid Instruction to printer to dispense with leads (leds) and to set type on body of same size—8 on 8pt, rather than, say, 8 on 9.

set up To compose in type; or instruction to set in capital letters.

sexn Section.

SG Signal, teletype message of service nature between two offices.

Shadow Typeface in which a three-dimensional effect is created, such as Cameo, Graphique, Gill Shadow.

shank Rectangular main body of a piece of type; also called the stem.

sheet Slang for newspaper.

shirt-tail (US) Brief addition to a long story.

shooting a page Term in photoset newspapers. When the bromides of type are assembled in position on the page, the page goes to the camera room for 'shooting'—it goes into negative form ready for platemaking.

short measure Type set narrower than the standard width of a column in a newspaper.

shorts Stories of a few paragraphs with smallish headlines (up to, say, two lines of 24pt) intended for use down the page.

short takes Sheets of copy of only a paragraph or two; to 'send in short takes' means to send copy urgently to the composing room a sheet or two at a time.

shotgun head (US) Multi-deck headline—two or more decks of heading on the same story, each deck consisting of one or more lines.

shoulder That part of the upper surface of a type which carries no relief image itself and on which the relief image stands.

showthrough When the inked impression of type and illustrations on a backing page can be seen through the front sheet of the page.

shrdlu See *etaoin*.

shrinkage Narrowing of the stereotype flong during moulding process, producing page fractionally smaller than original typeset page.

side (US) Any department, thus feature side, city side, Sunday side.

sidebar Story related to main story and run next to it. Sidebar story often slugged 'with'—i.e. 'with Kennedy', 'with bank raid', etc.

side-head Small subsidiary heading in the body of a story, set left instead of centred (crosshead).

sidelight (US) Similar to sidebar but with emphasis on personalities.

side sticks, foot sticks Pieces of wedge-shaped metal or wood used to tighten type in a galley.

signature (US) Name of advertiser displayed in ad.

silhouette See *cut-out*.

single leaded Lines of body type separated by the insertion of a thin lead between each line.

single quotes 'These' rather than "these" are better for headlines.

single rule Rule printing one light line.

situationer News feature usually giving background information, as distinct from urgent, 'spot' news, and so will probably hold until space is available or events make it topical.

size down Instruction to printer to decrease the size of type—to the next size down unless specified.

size up Instruction to printer to increase the type to the next size unless specified.

sked (US) Slang for schedule.

sky-lin(r) (US) Headline running above the nameplate across the top of the page; also called over-the-roof. See also *overbanner*.

slab serif Typefaces with heavy, square-ended serifs with or without brackets (i.e. gentle curve) at the junction. Faces such as Rockwell, Clarendon, Playbill.

slip proof See *galley proof*.

slop Over-set matter.

slot (US) The centre of the inner side of the copy desk, traditionally horseshoe-shaped, the slot man or slot is the copy editor who sits here and instructs copy editors who sit on the *rim*.

slug Line of type cast on a line-casting machine; spacing material six points thick; the identifying word or phrase given to each story which is set in one line at the top of the story and discarded when the story is complete and 'clean'.

small caps Capital letters smaller than regular capitals of a particular typeface; they are much the same size as the lower-case letters of the same fount.

soc, sox (US) Abbreviation for society or women's sections or copy.

solid Type lines without any space between them.

SOP 'See other proof'.

sort Letter, figure, punctuation mark, sign or other character cast as type.

spaceband Metal wedge which automatically provides spaces of varying width to justify lines set by line-caster.

spaces Graded units, less than type high, used to separate words or letters.

s page Splash or front page.

Spectacolor (US) Form of preprinted colour advertising.

spike Basic tool of sub-editor (US, copyreader) and especially copy-taster, being a metal spindle on which unwanted copy is impaled. 'Spike it' means 'kill it, but keep the body available'.

splash The main story on the front page; the front page itself.

split fractions Type cast for setting fractions in two parts, one bearing the top figure, and the other the bottom figure with the horizontal line over it.

split page First page of the second section of a paper printed in two sections.

split run Division of a printing run into two or more versions of the same newspaper. The difference may be in one or more pages; an advertiser may ask for a split run to try the effectiveness of two presentations of the same ad.

spot colour Non-process colour. No special plate is prepared but colour is applied during the run to selective parts of the page, usually one place and one small amount of colour, as in a coloured seal or coloured fudge.

spot news Unexpected news such as accidents or fires, as distinct from scheduled news (court cases, speeches).

spread Two facing pages, or a major display which covers part of two facing pages; (US) also an advertisement that covers full page or almost.

squib (US) Filler or short, q.v.

S/S Same size: instruction to process to make engraving the same size as the original.

staggered head Headline in which each line is set with an indention on the previous line; opposite effect of a centred headline.

standfirst Brief few sentences to introduce a news or feature, set in distinctive type at the top. See also *blurb, precede.*

standing type Type composed and stored awaiting use.

stars Common symbol for editions—one star, two star, etc.—often apparent only to the trained eye.

state editor (US) Deskman who supervises coverage of state or that part nearest the publishing area.

stereotype Plate cast in metal from a papier-mâché mould of type and/or blocks. Stereotyping is the process.

stem See *shank.*

stepped head See *staggered head.*

stet Let it stand: a sign on copy that a correction or deletion has been made in error and should be ignored. The words affected are underlined with dots and the word 'stet' written in the margin.

stick Metal tray used to hold type being set by hand. Its size provides a rough common measurement: a stick of type is about twenty lines of 8pt type, two inches or so.

stone The imposing surface on which pages are made up; it is now steel, not stone.

stonehand Print worker who arranges type in page forme often called comp (compositor).

stone sub Editorial man who works at the stone in the composing room, seeing that the make-up is followed, cutting stories which run too long in type, and ensuring that deadlines are kept.

story Any news item, any editorial item in a newspaper other than leading articles (US, editorials), features, letters and illustrations. Fairy stories are fiction, newspaper stories are fact, we hope.

straight matter Ordinary editorial setting in regular column width without illustrations.

straight news Story without colour or interpretation of any kind.

strap Subsidiary headline in smaller type over main headline. See *overline* and (US) *eyebrow, kicker.*

streamer Headline running across top of all or most of the columns.

strikeon Material for photographic reproduction produced by typewriter or similar setting machine such as *Varityper,* q.v.

stringer Non-staff reporter who is paid on the basis of what is published, plus, perhaps, a small retaining fee. Term most generally used for overseas reporters, freelance being the commonest term for domestic non-staff contributor. The term comes from the old accountancy habit of saving the outside man's newspaper clippings on a string, or pasting them together as a continuous ribbon. The verb, to string, means to work as a stringer.

string-tyers (-tiers) Machinery which ties string round bundles of newspapers coming from the presses.

strip in To combine line and half-tone negatives before making offset plates; to arrange for a headline to be superimposed on a half-tone block.

strip the forme Take type and furniture out of the chase.

style System of spellings, punctuation, capitalisation, etc., followed in an office. See *house rules.*

style sheet Pages listing office or house style.

sub (UK) Sub-editor; to edit a story and write the headline. Also, substitute

story (subst is preferred); instruction to printer to replace story already in type with one so marked.

sub-editor British term for the editorial craftsman who edits copy for sense and length and legal safety and writes the headlines. (US) copyreader.

sub-head Small subsidiary heading in the body of a story, usually centred. See *cross-head, cross-line.*

subst Substitute, meaning story so marked is to run in place of another.

summary Brief précis of a story. See *news lead.*

Supercaster Trade name of Monotype machine which casts large sizes of type for headlines, borders, rules and leads.

superior letters or figures Small letters and figures cast on the shoulder of the type so that they print above the level of primary letters, as in p^1.

swash letters Those embellished with tails and flourishes in the manner of sixteenth-century capitals.

swelled rule A rule that is thicker in the centre and tapers to each end.

swindle sheet Slang for expense account.

symmetrical make-up Attempting to balance display elements in a page on either side of a given central axis.

syndicate Organisation selling and buying feature or news material; group of newspapers; to sell editorial material or circulate widely.

T

tab, tabloid Newspaper half the size of broadsheet, approximately 11 in. wide by 16 in. deep. The term is also used, allusively but inappropriately, for sensational journalism.

tag line Smaller line attached to a head-line to attribute source of statement there: 'I'll love him till I die'.
——Countess.

tail Curved part of **g** below baseline, tiny flourish on Q. The thickening at the end of the stems of the lower-case j, y, f is known as the tail-dot.

tailgate Printing trial pages at the end of normal press run.

tailpiece Short addition to a story, separately displayed, usually of only a paragraph or two and of a light nature.

take Each sheet of copy for a story, or each line-caster's portion of it when a single sheet is cut up in the composing room to speed setting.

take copy Typing copy dictated over the telephone.

take in Instruction to typesetter to thin-space a line or lines to get in an extra syllable or words; direction on proof to incorporate insert matter at that point.

take up To pick up type and move it to the page chase or random.

tape Strictly, ribbon of paper with per-forations which actuate a teleprinter to type copy or a line-caster to set copy in metal. Also loosely used to refer to news agency or wire copy.

Tass Telegraphic agency of the Soviet Union.

taste To skim a story or stories in copy and assess their editorial value.

taster Abbreviation for *copy-taster*, q.v.

tear sheet Single newspaper page to show article or advertisement to contri-butor or reader or advertiser; pronounced tare sheet.

teaser Headline or caption to picture which rather than informing the reader intrigues him to read further: e.g. 'Why the soprano blushed'.

telegraph editor (US) Editorial desk-man who deals with wire-service news.

On a smaller paper he may edit it all him-self; on larger papers the duties will be shared.

Telephoto United Press agency photo-graph transmitted telegraphically. Also, loosely, to send a picture by wire, or a photograph taken with a telescopic lens.

Teletype Machine that types out news coming from a news agency—too often in capital letters that hinder readability. Also called a teleprinter or ticker, or just 'the wire'.

teletypesetting System in which line-casting machines are operated from code in perforated tape. Tape may be punched at the local plant but in US is commonly supplied to newspapers all over the country by central news agency.

ten-add (US) Method of sending story to be set before the intro or news lead is ready. The initial take is marked 10-add, plus the catchline, hence 10-add Church. The next is 11-add Church and so on.

text Body matter, as distinct from illus-trations, headlines and white space.

text-size Broadsheet newspaper—which term is preferred.

text type Type in which the body of the paper is set, as distinct from headline or display type.

Text type Old English or blackletter type style with bold thick bodystrokes and sharp thin serifs.

thick lead 3pt lead (led).

thick space Space of 3 points.

thinkpiece Article of opinion or inter-pretation rather than straight news report.

thin lead 1 or 1½pt lead (led).

thirty, 30, 30-dash Sign at the end of a story, either in type or copy. It is written '30'; in metal it is a dash of about six picas.

three-line cap See *two-line cap*.

thumbnail (US) Half-column portrait block, also called pork-chop; or rough

small dummy for advertisement; also single quotation mark or apostrophe.

ticker See *Teletype*.

tie-back (US) Background information in a story to help reader.

tight line Line with inadequate space between words or, in headlines, between that line and the next.

tight paper One with too little space for the news.

tight story One written so concisely it cannot be cut without damage.

tight sub (UK) Sub-editor expert at slicing the fat from a story.

time copy 'Anytime' copy, meaning copy—or type matter—which is timeless and can be run at any time.

tint Engravers can offer a variety of plain or decorative tints, shading from palest grey to near-black, to superimpose on a picture, type, or background.

tint block Block or surface used for printing flat background colour.

tinted headline One in which the black of the type has been softened to a grey.

tip Hint or information worth checking for a story.

titling Fount of type manufactured specially without lower-case letters and usually having minimal beard.

toby man (UK) He travels round retail outlets on day of publication to check that they have enough copies after initial deliveries and sales.

toenails (US) Slang for parentheses.

tombstoning Old-fashioned news-paper display in which a page was made up of single-column headlines in identical type side by side.

tone The amount of reflected light; the difference of the areas of light and dark on a printed page.

top deck The first deck or bank of a headline of several decks.

tops Originally stories intended for the top of a page, and hence carrying a certain minimum size headline. Now, with the development of horizontal layout and also the use of below-the-fold display, any stories having a headline over a set minimum size wherever they appear.

tramlines Unsightly effect of two rules running close and parallel.

Transitional Typeface mid-way between old style and modern, or Garalde and Didone in the British Standard, and there defined as typefaces in which the axis of the curves is vertical or inclined slightly to the left; the serifs are bracketed, and those of the ascenders in the lower-case are oblique.

transpose Mark on proof (trs) instructing the printer to change the order of the lines, words, or letters as indicated.

trim To shorten copy by small amounts —nibbling at it rather than cutting severely.

trs Abbreviation for *transpose*.

TTS Teletypesetter, the trade name for machine which does *teletypesetting* (q.v.).

tube Suction tube, common method of delivering copy around a newspaper.

turn Part of a story continued on another page; (US) *jump*.

turn head Headline on inside page identifying resumption of story continued from another page. US term is *jump head*.

turn line Line of type, in bold or italic usually, directing reader to continuation of story on another page ('continued page'); also the line on the inside page identifying the beginning of the continuation ('continued from page one').

turn up Direction to printer to turn over a slug in the galley or page as an indication that an insert or correction must be made at that place. The turned slug shows up as a rough black line on any subsequent proof.

turtle Steel trolley with a flat surface used to move a single page forme from the stone; just large enough to hold a single page, the turtle is also used sometimes as a make-up stone.

two-decker, three-decker Headline composed of two or three decks, i.e. self-contained units which may each have several lines.

two-line cap Capital letter, usually at the beginning of text as a *rising initial* (q.v.), having the depth of two lines of the accompanying text.

two-line double pica Old name for 44pt type.

two-line English Old name for 28pt type.

two-line pica Old name for 24pt type.

2pt lead Lead (led) which is two points thick, the commonest.

type A piece of metal or wood bearing a relief image of a letter or character for printing.

type area The amount of space on a page to be filled with type.

typeface Any individual type; its appearance when printed. Usually defined by name of type family (e.g. Bodoni, Century, etc.), style (roman, italic, etc.) and point size.

type high Of the same height as type: English type is 0·918 of an inch high.

typo (US) Name given to compositor. Elsewhere abbreviation for typographical error.

typographer Student of the use and design of type.

typographical error Mistake in setting the copy (as distinct from editorial error).

Typosetter Trade name for photographic machine producing cold display type.

U

uc *Upper-case*, or capitals.

undated story (US) A pull-together or round-up in which material from several sources is presented in one story; (UK) copy to be used when convenient.

under-dash matter (US) Prepared, set-and-held background material which is released when the foreground makes news. When something makes the material topical, it is published underneath the main story but separated by a *dinky* or *jim dash*.

underline Wording, call it *legend* or *caption* or underline, beneath an illustration.

under measure Setting which falls short of the standard column measure.

underscore To underline a word or letters in copy or in type.

uneven folios Page numbers of the right-hand pages, 3, 5, 7, 9, 11, etc; also called *odd folios*.

unit matrices A product of teletypesetting, matrices in which each letter image is designed to a constant ratio of width so that the lines produced by centrally punched tape fed into local line-casters justify equally well in Maine and New Mexico.

units Standards of measurement, the *point* being the unit of measurement for type size, the *pica* (12 points) for area of type lines, white spaces, pages, etc.

universal desk (US) A copydesk which receives and examines all copy: telegraph copy, city copy, state copy and so on. Most British newspapers operate, without knowing it, a 'universal desk'.

UPI United Press International, news agency.

upper-case The capital letters of a fount of type.

V

Varityper Trade name for electric automatic-justifying machine producing strikeon material and with great facility for changing typefaces.

Venetian Typefaces classified as Humanist in the British Standard in which the cross stroke of the lower-case e is oblique; the axis of the curves is inclined to the left; there is no great contrast between thin and thick strokes; and the serifs are bracketed, e.g., Verona, Centaur, Kennerley.

vertex Junction of two diagonal strokes at bottom of letter such as w, v, y.

vertical make-up Once the standard, now the rarity: page make-up in which no display element is allowed to cross a column rule, i.e. all single-column headlines or pictures, or an emphasis in that direction.

vignette Small illustration or decoration not squared up or enclosed by a border.

W

wash drawing A sketch made with a brush in washes with more tonal scale than simple black and white, and hence suitable for half-tone reproduction.

waste copies Copies of a newspaper run off at the beginning of a run when ink and registration are being adjusted.

wavy rule Rule that prints undulating line.

waxing Process in photoset newspapers. Each bromide of type is fed into a heated roller machine which coats the reverse side of the bromide with an adhesive wax so that the film can be stuck down on paper.

wayzgoose Old printers' festival or outing, hence *Wayzgoose Gazette*, *Wayzgoose News*, and so on, as names for printers' journals or house magazines.

web Roll of paper which is threaded through the printing presses.

web offset Web-fed lithography, in which printing is done not directly from the plate but from a rubber blanket that has picked up the images from the inked plate. See *offset*. 'Webb', who does not exist, is often credited with this invention through an error in spelling.

web press Printing press in which a continuously running web of paper is fed in between an impression cylinder and another cylinder carrying the printing plate. See *rotary press*.

weight The degree of blackness of a typeface.

wf Abbreviation for *wrong fount*.

when room Indication that story will hold for a few days and can wait to be published when space is available.

white Any part of the page which does not carry ink—spaces around headlines, in and around words and letters, margins, etc.

white out To put more spacing material in the page where indicated.

wide leaded Lines of type separated by more than one thickness of lead.

wide meas Wide measure, lines of type longer than normal for the newspaper or for the size of type used. For instance, setting across 24 pica ems would be wide measure for a type as small as 7pt.

wide open A term that editors believe is becoming obsolete: when there is more than enough space in the newspaper for the news available.

widow A solitary word (or two short words) making up a line at the end of a paragraph.

width Typefaces vary in width between ultra-condensed and ultra-expanded.

wild ad, wild copy Run of paper ad or copy which can go anywhere.

windy line Line with excessive white space.

wire editor See *telegraph editor*.

wirephoto Telephonic photo transmission system operated by Associated Press. See also *Telephoto*.

wireroom Department which receives teleprinted copy and photographs from the news agencies and correspondents on distant assignments.

wraparound Occasional publishing device in which the normal newspaper is enclosed within four extra pages. The London *Times* did a vivid wraparound, in colour, for the first moon landing pictures.

wrapped up All the copy has been sent to the composing room, all the blocks to process, and the make-up, too, has been completed.

wrong fount A mistake in composition by using a letter of the wrong size or not of the same design as the rest.

X

x-height The height of all the primary lower-case letters which, size for size, are almost identical, and omitting those letters of the alphabet with ascenders or descenders.

x-ref *Cross-reference.*

Y

yellow journalism The motto is 'never let the facts stand in the way of a good story'. It is sensational, scare journalism and especially that exploiting chauvinism.

Z

zinco Strictly, half-tone plate engraved on zinc, but commonly used for all photo-engravings, whatever the metal.

Zip-A-Tone Trade name for tinted sheet added to line drawings or headlines.

zombie Body-type setting which, near the end of the line, splits words for the convenience of the line-caster rather than the ease of the reader.

References

Chapter 1

1 *Headlines and Deadlines*, Third edition (New York and London: Columbia University Press, 1961).
2 *The English Newspaper 1622–1932* (Cambridge University Press, 1932).
3 *Newspaper Design*, Second edition (London: Oxford University Press, 1967). *See* Chapter 3, The English Newspaper 1932–1967.
4 The two books of pages are *America's Front Page News 1960–1970*, edited by Michael C Emery, R Smith Schuneman, and Edwin Emery, published by Vis-Com Inc, Minneapolis, and distributed by Doubleday and Co, New York, 1970; and *Newspapers of the First World War*, edited by Ian Williams, published by Times Newspapers Ltd, London, and David and Charles, Newton Abbot, 1970.
5 *Newspaper Design*, Second edition, p. 129.
6 *Modern Newspaper Design* (New York: Harper and Row, 1969), p. 67; and *Functional Newspaper Design* (New York; Harper and Bros, 1956), p. 55.
7 In a letter to the author, October 6, 1970.

Chapter 5

1 *See: An Atlas of Typeforms*, by James Sutton and Alan Bartram (London: Lund Humphries, 1968).
2 James Mosley, 'New Approaches to the Classification of Typefaces', *British Printer*, March 1960. *See also: Types of Typefaces*, by J Ben Lieberman (London: Ward Lock, 1968).

3 British Standard 2961: 1967.
4 *Newspaper Design*, Second edition (London: Oxford University Press, 1967), p. 100.
5 *An Atlas of Typeforms*, p. 110.
6 *Film-Setting*, by Westerham Press Ltd, a valuably clear little guide.
7 *Dot Zero*, No. 3, Spring 1967, p. 16 (New York, 1967).
8 *The Encyclopaedia of Typefaces*, by W Turner Berry, A F Johnson, and W P Jaspert (London: Blandford, third edition, 1962).
9 *Newspaper Design*, Second edition, p. 16.

Chapter 7

1 *Watch your Language*, by Theodore M Bernstein (New York: Channel Press, 1958), p. 223.
2 *Watch your Language*, p. 227.

Chapter 8

1 *Pitman's Book of Synonyms and Antonyms*, Fifth edition (London: Pitman, 1965).
Everyman's Thesaurus of English Words and Phrases, revised from Peter Roget by D C Browning (London: Dent, 1955).
2 *Roget's Thesaurus of English Words and Phrases*. This celebrated work, first published by Peter Mark Roget in 1852, has undergone much revision since. The latest edition, 'completely revised and modernized by Robert A Dutch', appeared from Longmans, London, in 1962. Its extensive prelims should be studied in a quiet moment.

Index

Journals cited